PENSION FUND INVESTMENT MANAGEMENT

A HANDBOOK FOR

SPONSORS AND THEIR ADVISORS

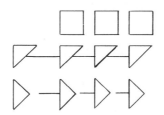

FRANK J. FABOZZI

EDITOR

NICK MENCHER
ASSOCIATE EDITOR

PROBUS PUBLISHING COMPANY
Chicago, Illinois
Cambridge, England

ISBN 1-55738-107-0

Printed in the United States of America

BB

3 4 5 6 7 8 9 0

Available from Probus Publishing
Additional Titles by Frank J. Fabozzi

Active Total Return Management of Fixed Income Portfolios, Ravi E. Dattatreya and Frank J. Fabozzi

Advances and Innovations in the Bond and Mortgage Markets, Frank J. Fabozzi, Editor

Advances in Bond Analysis and Portfolio Strategies, Frank J. Fabozzi and Dessa Garlicki-Fabozzi, Editors

Asset Allocation, Robert Arnott and Frank J. Fabozzi, Editors

Asset Liability Management for Banks and Thrifts, Frank J. Fabozzi and Atsuo Konishi, Editors

Fixed Income Mathematics, Frank J. Fabozzi

Fixed-Income Portfolio Strategies, Frank J. Fabozzi, Editor

Floating Rate Instruments, Frank J. Fabozzi, Editor

Handbook of Fixed-Income Options, Frank J. Fabozzi, Editor

Handbook of Mortgage-Backed Securities, Revised Edition, Frank J. Fabozzi, Editor

The Handbook of U.S. Treasury & Government Agency Securities, Revised Edition, Frank J. Fabozzi, Editor

Interest Rate Futures and Options, Mark Pitts and Frank J. Fabozzi

The Japanese Bond Markets, Frank J. Fabozzi, Editor

Mortgage-Backed Securities, Frank J. Fabozzi, Editor

The New Corporate Bond Market, Richard S. Wilson and Frank J. Fabozzi

The New Stock Market, Diana R. Harrington, Frank J. Fabozzi and H. Russell Fogler

Portfolio and Investment Management, Frank J. Fabozzi, Editor

Winning the Interest Rate Game, Frank J. Fabozzi, Editor

Also Available from Probus Publishing
Fabozzi's Fixed-Income Calculator

Contents

Contributors   vii

1   Introduction
Frank J. Fabozzi, Massachusetts Institute of Technology
Nick Mencher, BARRA

    1

2   Investment Policy: The Missing Link
Jeffery V. Bailey, Richards & Tierney, Inc.   9

Appendix
Michael J. Menssen, Minnesota State Board of Investment   27

3   Defining and Managing Pension Fund Risk
Robert D. Arnott, First Quadrant Corporation
Peter L. Bernstein, Peter L. Bernstein, Inc.   31

4   Managing the Asset Mix: Decisions and Consequences
Robert D. Arnott, First Quadrant Corporation   55

5   Organizing Internal Asset Management for the 1990s
Garry M. Allen, Virginia Retirement System
Mark T. Finn, Delta Financial, Inc. *and* Virginia
    Retirement System
T. Daniel Coggin, Virginia Retirement System   87

6   Benchmark Portfolios: The Sponsor's View
Daralyn B. Peifer, General Mills, Inc.   103

 7   How Sponsors Can Use Normal Portfolios
     Arjun Divecha, BARRA
     Richard C. Grinold, BARRA   **121**

 8   The Sponsor's View of Risk
     Richard C. Grinold, BARRA   **143**

     Appendix   **161**

 9   Manager Fees from the Performance Viewpoint
     Arjun Divecha, BARRA
     Nick Mencher, BARRA   **165**

10   Structuring Managers Using Fundamentals
     Ronald J. Surz, Becker, Burke Associates Incorporated   **181**

11   Money Manager Selection: A Top-Down Approach
     Veena A. Kutler, T. Rowe Price Associates, Inc.   **199**

12   Attributing Performance to Sponsors and Managers
     Ronald J. Surz, Becker, Burke Associates Incorporated   **217**

13   Selecting an International Investment Manager
     Margarett H. Gorodess, Becker, Burke Associates
     Incorporated   **243**

14   Fixing the Accounting Standards for Pension and
     Health Care Benefits: Advice for FASB
     Keith P. Ambachtsheer, The Ambachtsheer Letter   **259**

15   Blurring Lines Between Public and Private Pension Funds
     Nick Mencher, BARRA   **277**

     Index   **297**

Contributors

Garry M. Allen, *Virginia Retirement System*

Keith P. Ambachtsheer, *The Ambachtsheer Letter*

Robert D. Arnott, *First Quadrant Corporation*

Jeffery V. Bailey, *Richards & Tierney, Inc.*

Peter L. Bernstein, *Peter L. Bernstein, Inc.* and *The Journal of Portfolio Management*

T. Daniel Coggin, *Virginia Retirement System*

Arjun Divecha, *BARRA*

Frank J. Fabozzi, *Massachusetts Institute of Technology* and *The Journal of Portfolio Management*

Mark T. Finn, *Delta Financial, Inc.* and *Virginia Retirement System*

Margarett H. Gorodess, *Becker, Burke Associates Incorporated*

Richard C. Grinold, *BARRA*

Veena A. Kutler, *T. Rowe Price Associates, Inc.*

Nick Mencher, *BARRA*

Michael J. Menssen, *Minnesota State Board of Investment*

Daralyn B. Peifer, *General Mills, Inc.*

Ronald J. Surz, *Becker, Burke Associates Incorporated*

CHAPTER 1

Introduction

FRANK J. FABOZZI, Ph.D., CFA
VISITING PROFESSOR OF FINANCE
SLOAN SCHOOL OF MANAGEMENT
MASSACHUSETTS INSTITUTE OF TECHNOLOGY

NICK MENCHER
CONSULTANT
BARRA

In the old days, pension fund sponsors inhabited a quiet, comfortable world in which they turned over everything to the local bank trust officer and took a two-hour lunch.

Anyone who doubts those days are gone forever has been asleep for the last few decades. Today, fund sponsors are legally responsible for the investment of millions, often billions, of dollars in a dazzling array of investment classes and assets. Often, he or she is also responsible for the in-house management of assets invested in a wide range of instruments while, at the same time, finding, hiring and overseeing a collection of diverse outside managers whose contributions must be molded into a coherent whole.

As if the hats of economist, personnel director and investment manager were not enough, sponsors often add another role to their already overstuffed vitaes—that of public figures. The pension fund community has recently been thrust, not always willingly, into the center of public attention. Recent articles in national newspapers and magazines have focused on the new visibility and size of U.S. pension funds and their success in investing for the benefit of their members.

Other articles have emphasized the new shareholder activist role of some officers. Public attention has also focused on legislative efforts to influence fund management by taxation, as some officials see pension portfolio turnover as behind the decline of the U.S. economy and seek to address the problem by taxing so-called short-term profits. Some have even targeted indexing as a villain, and others have gone so far as to brand indexing as "un-American" and the source of market volatility. (This argument involves a curious logical leap, as index funds traditionally hold stocks far longer than their active "fundamental" portfolio cousins.)

A new ingredient has been added to the stew: a perception by the public and plan beneficiaries that fund suppliers, including brokers, managers, and bankers, have no interest at heart but their own. A raft of recent books has savaged Wall Street—portraying it as greedy and blind to the effects of its actions on mainstream America.

These books reflect the growing conflict between the values, goals, and motivations of plan members and their perceptions of the values of plan service providers. Reducing commissions and instituting manager performance fees have done little to persuade plan members that they are getting value for their money. If Wall Street continues to project an image of unalloyed greed, sponsors may find themselves in the unenviable position of defending their suppliers to plan members. Beneficiaries themselves are finding new authority—aided by the government. One recent U.S. Department of Labor proposal would pay a 10% bounty of any fines collected to informers reporting ERISA violations.

While these issues bubble, and pundits and politicians take turns stirring up the pot, sponsors have the task of actually doing the work: there is money to invest, liabilities to be matched, and a population whose retirement happiness in the next century depends in large part on the decisions sponsors make today.

This book was written as a guide for those in the trenches. It is intended as a reference work to which sponsors and their advisors can turn to find ways to better handle the increasingly complex responsibilities of running a pension fund.

The growth of pension assets in absolute terms and their role in the bond and equity markets has been breathtaking. Inextricably bound up with this rise has been the increase in sponsor sophistication and skill in handling pension assets.

How has the increase in sponsor success come about, and how will it expand in the 1990s? In the relatively brief period since legislative actions forced a reexamination of pension fund policy, plan sponsors and their advisors have risen to the challenge of investing for the retirements of their members. They have also risen to the challenge of mastering increasingly complex management techniques and assets.

Some of the skills required to implement these techniques were formerly the province of consultants or outside managers, and the industry is beginning to experience the financial equivalent of the empty nest syndrome as some sponsors move away from the protective arms of their former consultant relationships. Pressure by large funds on their consultants to unbundle services is increasing, and some funds are beginning to take back pieces of the consultant's work to be handled in-house.

This book attempts to describe some of the ways sponsors are meeting their new challenges. By soliciting the thoughts and experiences of practitioners representing both the funds themselves and their advisors, we believe we have developed both a guidebook to the present and a rough map to the future. While no book can completely cover all facets of the sponsor's profession, we are confident we have come close. Sponsor tasks, from creating the overall policy of the fund to finding and evaluating managers, are discussed in detail.

The overall message, the common thread running through these 15 chapters, is that running a pension fund successfully requires an ability to set long-term goals, policies and strategies and to ignore temptations to "tinker" with the plan in response to market shifts. The approach of hiring and firing managers based on short-term performance has given way to a philosophy which views asset allocation and targets in terms of decades rather than quarters, which values the aggregate of the plan over its parts, and which strives to create a well-molded unity. As one author points out, in managing a pension fund the whole is far more than the sum of its parts.

The importance of this view, along with a step-by-step description of ways to create an overall vision which includes the specific needs of pension funds, is contained in Chapter 2, "Investment Policy: The Missing Link." Jeffery V. Bailey proposes a world-view where sponsors are objective risk controllers and long-term planners as opposed to short-term return maximizers. He describes a process which helps sponsors define the mission of their fund and its investment objectives. He discusses sponsor tolerance to risk and how to develop a policy asset mix, structure a team of outside managers, and evaluate the performance of both the managers and the fund. The greatest benefits to setting an investment policy, the author claims, come during periods of adverse market performance, when having a long term view can stabilize and balance sponsor reaction to adversity. As an appendix to the chapter, the investment policy of the Minnesota State Board of Investment is included so sponsors can see how this approach works when implemented.

The role in asset allocation that pension fund risk plays is further discussed in Chapter 3, "Defining and Managing Pension Fund Risk." Here Robert D. Arnott and Peter L. Bernstein argue that the nature of liability risk is not as simple as it appears at first blush. FASB 87, they also point out, has suggested an unduly simplistic view of pension fund risk—one which, if not examined carefully and individually for each fund, can lead to inappropriate allocation to long-term bonds. The authors argue that pension fund decisions need to be examined in light of their impact on corporate risk, and that a careful study of all aspects of the plan should precede asset allocation.

The importance of not allowing the market to determine asset allocation policy is stressed in Chapter 4, "Managing The Asset Mix: Decisions and Consequences." Here, Arnott discusses both creating the asset mix policy and rebalancing the asset mix to suit the needs of the individual fund, taking into account its attitude to various sources of risk. The importance of sticking with the long-term policy and resisting the "temptation to tinker" is again stressed. In addition, active allocation techniques such as tactical asset allocation and dynamic strategies are discussed in detail. Like many of the authors, he argues that sponsors must resist the urge to hire and fire managers based on the popularity of their strategies.

Many sponsors have decided to resolve manager issues by doing some of the work themselves, and perhaps the greatest indication of the increasing role sponsors play is seen with in-house, or internal, management of complex financial instruments—from equities to bonds to derivatives. The increase of in-house asset management has been accompanied by the increasing need for sponsors to redesign the structure of their funds.

In Chapter 5, "Organizing Internal Asset Management For The 1990s," Garry M. Allen, Mark T. Finn and T. Daniel Coggin propose a way to manage internal managers that is a dramatic departure from the traditional pyramid management method. The authors argue that internal management, if it is to achieve high returns, needs to operate on a level plane of organizational teams where creativity and flexibility replace the hierarchical function of the pyramid. Plan sponsors concerned with the performance of their internal managers will find this approach an exciting possibility for maximizing internal performance.

Many sponsors, in their management of assets in-house and in their management of outside managers, use several types of performance benchmarks. These tools can clarify and help form a coordinated plan for pension funds. We have included two chapters on the use of benchmark portfolios. In Chapter 6, "Benchmark Portfolios: The Sponsor's View," Daralyn B. Peifer describes how benchmarks can be used to define and fill manager assignments, communicate sponsor expectations of portfolio risk and return to managers, and set overall asset policy. Building fixed income portfolios is examined in this chapter, and the author looks ahead to the future of benchmarks for other asset classes such as real estate.

Equity benchmarks are examined in detail in Chapter 7, "How Sponsors Can Use Normal Portfolios" by Arjun Divecha and Richard C. Grinold. This chapter also looks at some of the areas where customized benchmarks have raised the ire of investment managers. Both chapters agree on the role benchmarks can play in helping sponsors determine the desired risk/return profile of their funds.

The importance of viewing portfolio risk arising from the fund's managers in the overall sense is stressed in Chapter 8, "The Sponsor's View of Risk." Grinold argues that failure to assess managers as part of an aggregate leads to the inefficient allocation of assets. The author proposes using information ratios to assess each manager's ability to add value, and combining these estimates with the sponsor's aversion to risk and manager aggressiveness to determine manager allocation. Such an approach leads the author to conclude that compensation plans based on assets under management are not consistent with the sponsor's goal of maximizing the value-added capability of aggressive managers. These fee schemes can also lead managers to adopt low-risk strategies to gain more assets, thus jeopardizing the aggressiveness the sponsor seeks.

The limits of fees based on assets under management are further discussed in Chapter 9, "Manager Fees from the Performance Viewpoint." Here, Divecha and Nick Mencher describe a proposed performance-based fee plan which may help mitigate some of the drawbacks of both conventional fee schemes and proposed performance schemes. The authors make the point that performance fees require sponsors to exercise greater care and vigilance in their management of managers.

The changing relationship between sponsors and their managers is the focus of five chapters in this book. In Chapter 10, "Structuring Managers Using Fundamentals," Ronald J. Surz urges sponsors to link asset allocation policy to manager allocation to enhance the fund's diversification and capitalize effectively on manager skill. This procedure takes into consideration differences in manager skill and style and structures the manager team to maximize the managers' collective skills without jeopardizing fund diversification. By using an optimized allocation process to incorporate the skills and styles of managers, sponsors can better link their managers to the fund's overall policy guidelines.

The idea of viewing fund management as an organic whole is continued in the discussion of selecting managers in Chapter 11, "Money Manager Selection: A Top-Down Approach." Veena A. Kutler argues that the fund's total plan plays the key role in the manager search and hiring process. The contrasting style—bottom-up selection—is found to place sponsors in the undesired position of creating an undiversified plan where risk is not necessarily compensated by expected excess return. A top-down approach helps sponsors avoid hiring and firing managers based on their current popularity, and the unintended sponsor bets that arise from selecting managers without reference to the plan's overall sector targets. The author takes sponsors through the top-down process from asset liability analysis to manager monitoring, and suggests that sponsors compare the performance of their plans to that of their peers as part of the increasing professionalism, recognition and compensation of pension plans and their sponsors.

A proposed mechanism to measure the role sponsors play in the performance of their funds, along with the managers working for the fund, is contained in Chapter 12, "Attributing Performance to Sponsors and Managers." Surz argues that the effects on performance of manager and sponsor decisions can be difficult to untangle, but must be understood if the fund is to succeed. Performance attribution, following the author's scheme, involves estimating the contribution to fund performance of the sponsor's policy, timing and selectivity, and the manager's timing and selectivity. Using this approach, sponsors can determine which parts of overall performance are due to the work of the manager and which are due to the work of the sponsor. Such analysis clearly indicates the critical role sponsor decisions on manager allocation play in fund performance.

The theme of the sponsor's role in overall fund performance continues in Chapter 13, "Selecting an International Investment Manager" with an investigation of how sponsors' allocation of assets to regional international specialists also constitutes active regional bets. Margarett H. Gorodess discusses the key issues of selecting an international benchmark, deciding whether or not to hedge currencies, selecting between active and passive management and selecting investment style. The author also discusses the overweighting of Japan in capitalization weighted indices, and how some managers are using gross domestic product weighted indices as a remedy. In addition, a matrix is provided which allows sponsors to organize the sometimes baffling array of international manager styles into groupings similar to domestic equity managers.

A different type of challenge is described in Chapter 14, "Fixing the Accounting Standards for Pension and Health Care Benefits: Advice for FASB" by Keith P. Ambachtsheer. Here the problems inherent in one of the most controversial sets of standards for corporate pension plans are presented. The author argues that the rules should be reconsidered and revised to better accomplish their initial goals. In addition, the proposed standards for postretirement health care benefits are discussed.

The increasing similarity between the methods used by corporate and public funds is discussed in Chapter 15, "Blurring Lines Between Public and Private Pension Funds" by Mencher. This chapter also argues that an ethical dimension to fund management might help to attract and keep capable personnel in the public sphere.

The field of pension fund management continues to increase in challenge, reward and importance. It is our hope that *Pension Fund Investment Management: A Handbook for Sponsors and Their Advisors* will serve as a useful guide and information handbook for pension fund sponsors and officers whose stewardship of assets plays such a critical role in so many people's lives.

CHAPTER 2

Investment Policy:
The Missing Link

JEFFERY V. BAILEY, CFA
VICE PRESIDENT
RICHARDS & TIERNEY, INC.

Over the last two decades, U.S. pension plan sponsors have succeeded in bringing professional management and advanced technology to the investment of plan assets. From elaborate valuation models to program trading systems, plan sponsors now have access to an almost overwhelming array of investment management tools through which to compete in the increasingly complex capital markets. Yet, despite this apparent sophistication, a glaring deficiency remains in the investment programs of many pension plans—a failure to adequately relate the needs of the plan sponsor to the management of plan assets through a comprehensive and consistently applied investment policy.

Single employer-defined benefit U.S. pension plans control over $700 billion in assets. Among corporations, pension assets typically constitute one of the largest investments. State and local governments face similar situations. Yet, despite both the importance of a successful pension plan to the financial health of the sponsoring organizations, and the inherent uncertainty of that success, managements often treat long-term strategic planning for pension assets as an afterthought. As Charles Ellis has noted, "It is hardly conceivable that senior corporate management would routinely delegate full operating responsibility for comparable millions of dollars . . . with only such broad guidelines or instructions as 'Try to do better than average,' or 'You're the experts, see what you can do for us.'"[1] Nevertheless, this description aptly fits many plan sponsors of all types and sizes.

Regrettably, little information has been systematically gathered concerning the investment policies of plan sponsors. However, our experience with a large number of pension plans indicates that few plan sponsors have adopted and diligently implemented well-conceived investment policies.

11

Instead, we find that plan sponsors usually rely on ad hoc approaches to pension management.[2] We can only speculate why plan sponsors so often follow this path: perhaps an insufficient understanding of the investment policy's importance, or an unwillingness to tackle difficult issues, or a tendency to view themselves as return maximizers rather than as risk controllers. In any event, the manifestations of these inadequate pension management practices are more evident—a short-term focus on issues of only minor consequence to the ultimate success of the pension plan, while consideration of more important matters goes relatively unattended. For example, the hiring and firing of individual money managers frequently receives an inordinate amount of attention from investment committees, while the subject of the committees' risk tolerances rarely, if ever, comes up for discussion.

These myopic attitudes generate a hodgepodge of constantly changing and ultimately inefficient investment strategies. They prevent plan sponsors from conducting realistic appraisals of their objectives and from implementing stable, productive investment programs designed to achieve those objectives.

Investment policy offers plan sponsors a means of overcoming this shortsightedness by assisting them in identifying and prioritizing those issues that are of direct importance to the success of their pension funds. Investment policy forges the link between the application of investment techniques and the fulfillment of a pension fund's fundamental goals.

INVESTMENT POLICY DEFINED

What do we mean when we speak of investment policy? Investment policy is a combination of philosophy and planning. On the one hand, it expresses the plan sponsor's attitudes toward a number of important pension management issues: What is the purpose of our pension fund? How do we define success? To what extent should we expose ourselves to the possibility of failure? To what extent do we believe that active management can be productive? How do we evaluate the performance of our investment program? The varying financial circumstances of the sponsoring organizations, as well as the diverse temperaments of their pension fund decision-makers, will (and should) cause plan sponsors to differ in their answers to these questions, despite being faced with essentially the same investment opportunities. By formulating their individual responses to these questions through explicit investment policies, plan sponsors construct their own unique investment philosophies.

Investment policy is also a form of long-term strategic planning. It delineates the specific goals that the plan sponsor expects the pension fund to accomplish and it describes how the plan sponsor foresees the fund realizing those goals. In this sense, investment policy comprises the set of guidelines and procedures that direct the long-term management of a plan's assets.

Investment policy is an equilibrium concept, established independent of current relative values among asset classes, economic sectors, or individual securities. Transitory market movements have no bearing on its validity. In setting investment policy, the plan sponsor accepts, as given, the long-run investment opportunities afforded by the capital markets as well as the plan's obligations to its beneficiaries. A consistently applied investment policy produces successful results not because of any unique investment insights, but because of its concentration on the pension fund's primary goals and the continuity of its investment strategies.

COMPONENTS OF INVESTMENT POLICY

Plan sponsors' interpretations of what constitutes investment policy will vary. Essentially, any relatively permanent set of procedures that guides the management of a plan's assets falls under the rubric of investment policy. Nevertheless, we believe that a comprehensive investment policy should address a group of issues that includes (but is not restricted to):

- The fund's mission
- Investment objectives
- Plan sponsor risk tolerance
- Policy asset mix
- Investment manager structure
- Performance evaluation

The Fund's Mission

The intricate nature of pension management demands that the plan sponsor isolate those issues of true consequence to its investment program. A statement of the pension fund's mission serves this function by highlighting the plan sponsor's fundamental goals. What is the fund expected to accomplish? At the most basic level, the plan sponsor seeks to secure the benefits

promised to the plan's participants. However, the issue is far more complicated than this simple directive would imply. How does the plan sponsor
define its obligations to the plan participants? A plan sponsor might view
the fund's obligations very narrowly; that is, with benefits calculated exactly as stated in the participants' employment contract, with no consideration of future adjustments. Or the plan sponsor might define its pension
promise broadly; that is, with benefits adjusted for inflation and gains in
productivity in order to maintain the relative living standards of the participants during their retirement years. The plan sponsor's working definition
of its pension obligations (which may differ from that stated in plan documents) will depend on both the sponsoring organization's competitive situation versus those of other employers and its attitude regarding its
responsibilities to plan participants.

The fund's mission will also reflect the plan sponsor's funding target.
By what margin should the plan's assets be expected to exceed the value of
the plan's liabilities? Within the lower and upper limits set by the IRS,
numerous targets are plausible. A large surplus will provide greater security to plan participants and reduce the likelihood of unanticipated contributions being required. However, a large surplus may also generate employee
demands for benefit enhancements, or increase the sponsoring
organization's vulnerability to corporate raiders.

In defining the fund's mission, the plan sponsor must also consider
how the fund fits into the sponsoring organization's total finances. A plan
sponsor, such as a governmental organization, might view its pension fund
as a separate financial entity and seek only to secure promised benefits
while holding expected funding costs to acceptable levels. Alternatively, a
corporation might see its pension fund as an integrated element of the
firm's total financial operation. It will treat the fund as it does any other
capital project, evaluating its investment in the fund relative to other uses
of cash. The plan sponsor might employ the fund to minimize the
organization's total tax liability. Alternatively, it might view the fund as a
source of "financial slack," enabling the corporation to avoid external financing at disadvantageous times. Or, in light of the recent FASB 87 ruling, it might wish to insulate the organization's earnings from fluctuations
in the plan's pension expense.[3]

The fund's mission establishes the framework around which the plan
sponsor designs the rest of its investment policy. By requiring that each of
the other components of investment policy contribute to the attainment of
the fund's mission, the plan sponsor creates a focal point for the remainder
of its investment program.

Risk Tolerance

By definition, the act of investing entails risk. An investor defers current consumption in the anticipation of increased, but uncertain, future consumption. Despite its ubiquitousness, risk is a nebulous concept, highly dependent on the context in which one evaluates it.

In terms of setting investment policy, we find it useful to think of risk as the probability of failing to achieve the fund's mission. Investment textbooks treat risk as a one-dimensional concept, interpreted equivalently by all investors. However, the investment policy perspective on risk provides us with a valuable insight: a given policy-asset mix and investment-manager structure could vary dramatically in their risk implications for plan sponsors with different missions. A plan sponsor whose mission calls for minimizing fluctuations in the plan's pension expense will view a large policy allocation to equity assets as very risky, but will see a sizable commitment to interest-sensitive assets as low risk. Conversely, a plan sponsor whose mission requires it to provide benefits adjusted to maintain plan participants' relative living standards will find the high equity exposure policy to be of relatively low risk, but will view the interest-sensitive asset allocation as high risk.[4]

A plan sponsor's risk tolerance expresses its willingness to bear adverse outcomes in the pursuit of the fund's mission. Risk tolerance indicates the trade-off that the plan sponsor will accept between the probability of failing to achieve the fund's mission and the reward derived from achieving the mission in excess of expectations. For any given policy-asset mix and investment-manager structure exhibiting a particular level of risk (that is, a distribution of outcomes relative to a fund's mission), a plan sponsor with a low risk tolerance will require a greater expected payoff than will a plan sponsor with a higher risk tolerance.

In practice, specifying a plan sponsor's risk tolerance generally proves difficult, in part, because usually more than one person makes decisions for the plan sponsor. These persons, who have their own individual attitudes toward risk, must reach a consensus regarding their joint risk-sensitivity. In addition, investors typically have trouble quantifying their willingness to trade off increased rewards for increased risk. As a result, investment policy designers must usually settle for indirect indicators of the plan sponsor's risk tolerance. For example, the plan sponsor decision-makers could be shown a series of simulated results (relative to the plan's mission) of various policy-asset mixes and investment-manager structures.

Their responses to the various distributions of outcomes provides a qualitative sense of their aversion to risk.[5]

Investment Objectives

The fund's investment objectives identify the set of portfolio management results that the plan sponsor believes would signal a successful investment program. As opposed to the broad statements of purpose described in the fund's mission, the fund's investment objectives comprise a specific list of quantifiable investment results expected to be achieved over specified time intervals. The plan sponsor may set investment objectives at various levels of decision-making within its investment program: the total fund, asset classes, and individual managers. At each level, to facilitate the implementation of the plan's investment policy, the investment objectives should meet several criteria:

- *Unambiguous and measurable.* Because the effectiveness of the plan's decision-making will be judged relative to these objectives, there should be no confusion as to their definition.

- *Accordant with the fund's mission.* The plan sponsor should expect that if the investment program consistently fulfills the investment objectives, then the fund will be capable of carrying out its mission.

- *Reflect the plan sponsor's risk tolerance.* A plan sponsor with a high risk-tolerance will set more aggressive investment objectives (within the context of the fund's mission) than will a plan sponsor with a lower risk-tolerance.

The fund's investment objectives serve both prospective and retrospective functions in the plan sponsor's investment policy. In the former role, they help define the fund's policy-asset mix and investment-manager structure. For example, an investment objective of earning a positive real rate of return implies a policy-asset mix with a significant exposure to equity assets. Similarly, an investment objective of outperforming various market indices requires an investment-manager structure that includes an allocation of funds to active managers. In their retrospective role, the fund's investment objectives facilitate the performance evaluation process. The plan sponsor selects investment objectives that presumably, if achieved, would indicate a successful investment program. Therefore, the plan sponsor should judge the efficacy of its investment program in light of the fund's actual performance relative to those objectives.

Policy Asset Mix

In terms of direct impact on a fund's investment performance, the fund's policy-asset mix choice outweighs all other decisions. As a practical matter, active management strategies involving stock selection, sector weighting, or market timing have been shown to contribute relatively little compared to the impact of the long-term allocation to various asset classes set by investment policy.[6] Thus, how successfully the fund fulfills its mission rests largely on the choice of, and adherence to, an appropriate asset mix.

Plan sponsors use a number of different approaches to determine their policy asset mixes. Some employ very simple methods, such as picking the average asset mix of "similar" plan sponsors or taking the recommendations of professional market strategists. While these methods are easy to apply, they fail to account for the fund's particular mission, investment objectives, and plan sponsor risk tolerance.

In recent years, various quantitative asset allocation techniques have become popular. These methods identify a desirable policy asset mix by simultaneously processing expected asset class returns, the volatility of those returns, and the correlations of returns among asset classes, along with a formal specification of the fund's investment objectives. For example, portfolio optimization techniques create an efficient frontier of asset class combinations. Using a mathematical expression of the plan sponsor's risk tolerance, the optimization procedure selects the asset mix that supplies the greatest expected utility.

Users of quantitative asset allocation methods generally rely on historical capital markets data in forming asset class risk-reward expectations. As a result, the unavailability of reliable performance data for such asset classes as real estate and venture capital hinders these methods. In response, some plan sponsors have taken a heuristic approach to the policy asset mix issue. They develop a logical case for a particular policy asset mix based not only on the conclusions of the quantitative methods, but also on their own interpretations of the plan's needs and expected long-term capital markets opportunities.

In the rush to select an appropriate policy asset mix, plan sponsors may overlook an important element of that decision: the choice of asset class targets. An asset class target is a diversified collection of securities representing the set of feasible investment opportunities for which the asset class is included in the policy asset mix.

Typically, the most appropriate asset class targets are broad market indices (for example, the Wilshire 5000 for domestic common stocks and the Salomon Broad Investment Grade Bond Index for domestic fixed income). These market indices represent the full capitalization-weighted range of investment opportunities available to the plan sponsor within the respective asset classes.

However, situations may arise in which the plan sponsor will wish to restrict the composition of an asset class target. For example, statutory or regulatory requirements may prohibit ownership of certain securities within an asset class, such as the securities of companies doing business in South Africa. These securities should be removed from the asset class target. Similarly, a corporate plan sponsor may wish to limit the risk associated with owning its own stock (or even the stocks of other companies in its industry) by eliminating the stock (or stocks) from the domestic equity asset class target. Or the plan sponsor may perceive certain significant long-run investment opportunities within a segment of the asset class. The asset class target should be adjusted to emphasize that segment. For example, a plan sponsor might believe that small capitalization stocks offer attractive long-run risk-adjusted returns. In that case, the plan sponsor should adjust its domestic equity asset class target to give greater weight to the small capitalization segment of the market.

Investment Manager Structure

One of the most remarkable, but seldom discussed, pension management developments in the last twenty years has been the virtually complete transition by plan sponsors to multiple manager investment programs. Prior to the 1970s, plan sponsors generally entrusted their pension assets to a single balanced manager, often a bank trust department. These balanced managers made both asset mix and security selection decisions for their clients. With few exceptions, plan sponsors now assume the asset mix decision and allocate their funds within asset classes among a number of managers, each pursuing a distinct investment "style," or area of expertise.

We will not discuss the merits (and problems) of these multiple manager arrangements here. However, the decision to retain multiple managers has a significant policy implication for plan sponsors—they must develop coherent investment manager structures.

The investment manager structure describes the long-term allocation within each asset class to passive and active managers. Traditionally, these allocation decisions have involved two separate steps: first, the division of funds within the asset class between passive and active management, and second, the allocation of funds among various managers within the actively managed component.

The plan sponsor's views on the effectiveness of active management will largely determine its passive/active allocation. The debate between proponents of active and passive management has raged for years. For a number of reasons, most plan sponsors appear to hedge their bets on the issue, allocating at least some of their domestic equity investment (and often part of their domestic fixed-income and international investments) to passive management.

Within the active component, plan sponsors face two investment policy tasks. First, they must select skillful managers who they expect can each add value to their respective investment styles. Second, they must combine the managers in a way that their investment styles, in aggregate, are consistent with the asset class target. Plan sponsors have traditionally focused on the first task, with their difficulties in selecting skillful managers being well-documented. The second task has only recently begun to receive attention. Plan sponsors have discovered that their active managers, in aggregate, maintain persistent biases relative to the asset class targets (for example, within the domestic equity asset class, a concentration in small capitalization growth stocks). These biases introduce the unintentional (and uncompensated) risk that the plan sponsors' investments within an asset class will perform quite differently than the asset class target. The investment policy solutions to this problem, which lie in the concepts of benchmark portfolios and completeness funds, extend beyond the scope of this discussion.[7]

Performance Evaluation

Performance evaluation refers to the process of measuring and interpreting the performance of a plan sponsor's investment program. Performance evaluation delivers an informed look at past performance that relates investment results to the fund's investment objectives. Properly conducted, performance evaluation provides the plan sponsor with valuable information concerning the investment program's strengths and weaknesses and identifies areas of potentially profitable enhancements.

We distinguish performance evaluation from performance measurement. The latter is a technical accounting function that computes the return on the fund's total portfolio and constituent segments. Performance evaluation, alternatively, uses the information generated by performance measurement to attribute investment performance to the important decision points in the plan sponsor's investment program. What did the policy allocations to asset classes and individual managers contribute to investment results?

How effective were the managers' active investment judgments? How did the plan sponsor's choice to deviate from investment policy allocations affect results? This last issue is of particular interest because plan sponsors so often concern themselves solely with the performance of their money managers. They fail to consider how their own implementation of investment policy allocations to asset classes and managers affects their funds' investment performance.

Performance evaluation operates as a feedback and control mechanism carried out within the context of investment policy. Therefore, it cannot be used to judge the appropriateness of investment policy. Performance evaluation is designed to keep the plan sponsor's investment program on track toward achieving the plan's mission, however defined. Thus, we can reasonably expect performance evaluation to answer a question such as, "Was Manager XYZ's return last year acceptable?" Conversely, we should not expect performance evaluation to answer, "Is our policy asset mix too aggressive?"

INVESTMENT POLICY AS A STABILIZER

Investment policy would be of little interest if it were merely a perfunctory description of the plan sponsor's investment program. Investment policy derives its importance from the complex and dynamic environment faced by plan sponsors. They must make allocations across a number of asset classes and choose among a proliferation of money managers who offer an array of investment approaches. To coordinate the management of these far-reaching investment programs in a logical and consistent framework requires a formal, long-term strategic plan: an investment policy.

During periods of financial market prosperity, such as the 1980s, the advantages of a comprehensive investment policy may appear marginal. After all, under favorable market conditions, almost any investment program, no matter how inconsistent its design and how short its time horizon, will generate impressive absolute performance. Many plan sponsors fail to appreciate that investment policy will produce its greatest benefits during periods of adverse market performance. At these times, plan sponsors are most tempted to alter an otherwise sound investment program as the irrational fear of even worse future calamities builds. Decisions to change course in these situations inevitably prove to be very costly.

In adverse environments, investment policy acts as a stabilizer. Its existence forces plan sponsor decision-makers to pause and consider why the existing policy was established in the first place and whether the current bad market conditions were actually predictable—not in their timing, but in their intensity and unexpectedness. This type of review increases the likelihood that cooler heads and a longer-term outlook will prevail.[8]

The discipline provided by investment policy protects against more than just unwise asset allocation shifts. Plan sponsors have shown a propensity to mistime their selection of investment managers, emphasizing investment styles that have recently been in favor, only to see those styles subsequently underperform the broad market. Investment policy establishes a clear rationale for the existing manager allocation, thereby placing the burden of proof on those advocating a shift in allocations.

THE PLAN SPONSOR AS THE RISK CONTROLLER

Plan sponsors all too often operate under a serious misconception that hampers their development of investment policy; they fail to recognize that the primary function of a plan sponsor should be that of a risk controller as opposed to a return maximizer.

By specifying the fund's mission, and the risk it is willing to bear in pursuit of that mission, the risk controller controls the tone of the plan's investment program. Furthermore, the risk controller devises the strategic plan that channels the investment of the plan's assets in certain broad directions, consonant with the fund's mission and plan sponsor risk tolerance. In contrast, the return maximizer attempts to generate the highest returns within the constraints imposed by the risk controller. Those constraints could be very tight, as in the case of an index fund manager, or very liberal, as in the case of an aggressive common stock manager.

Pension plans typically create a nominal division between these two roles. Money managers, either external or internal, are hired to carry out the return maximizer's functions, while the board of trustees and the pension staff (effectively, the plan sponsor) act as risk controllers. Unfortunately, plan sponsors tend to view the return maximizer's role as more glamorous and more consistent with action-oriented management than the risk controller's role, which seems mundane by comparison. As a result, plan sponsors have been drawn to the return maximizer's functions, while neglecting their risk control responsibilities. For confirmation, one need only survey the investment industry publications that herald the frequent manager hirings and firings by certain plan sponsors or the dabbling in tactical asset allocation by others.

Part of this problem may stem from a failure to clearly distinguish between setting investment policy and engaging in active management. Investment policy uses consensus long-term forecasts regarding the plan's obligations and investment opportunities. It implies no attempt to "beat the market" in any sense of the term. Active management, on the other hand, involves an effort to achieve success at the expense of other investors. It requires access to information either not available to, or improperly used by, other market participants.

A plan's investment policy may include an allocation of part, or all, of the plan's assets to active management. However, the allocation of funds to active management and the actual active management of those funds should remain two separate processes. Those plan sponsors who overlay active management responsibilities on top of their policy setting duties face potentially troubling problems. As the distinction between policy setting and active management blurs, the discipline of the long-term strategic plan, which controls the direction and the aggressiveness of the plan's active management, breaks down as does the objectivity of performance evaluation.

Plan sponsors can be most productive when they focus their efforts on the risk controller's functions and implement those functions by developing and consistently applying sound investment policies. By creating a clear division of labor between the roles of risk controller and return maximizer, the plan sponsor can more objectively establish, monitor, and when necessary, modify investment programs.

POLICY REVIEWS

Investment policy rarely requires alteration, simply because the factors that determine a plan's policy do not often change. For example, the plan's pension obligations or the risk tolerances of the plan sponsor's decision-makers are not dynamic variables. The fundamental nature of the capital markets changes even less frequently. Importantly, bear markets are not indicators of significant change, but merely represent normal market fluctuations that should be built into the plan sponsor's risk expectations when designing investment policy.

We can approach the issue of regular policy reviews from two perspectives. On the one hand, periodic policy reviews aimed at educating plan sponsor decision-makers serve a productive purpose. Particularly to the extent that decision-makers do not routinely deal with investment issues, policy reviews reinforce the logic of current policy and, thereby, reduce the chances of unnecessary alterations. Conversely, policy reviews directed toward constantly reassessing existing policy are counter-productive. Frequent policy changes take on the tone of active management, blurring the distinction between policy and operations, to the detriment of the investment program. As discussed, particularly at market extremes, this tendency to tinker with policy can lead to ill-advised short-run decisions.

Despite the infrequent need for policy modifications, a plan sponsor may determine that sufficiently significant events have occurred to warrant an alteration in existing investment policy. For example, the company's financial condition might change radically due to a bankruptcy, or its pension obligations might be altered because of a merger with another company. In these situations, the plan sponsor should recognize that policy modifications are never time-sensitive and should avoid hurried, and possibly haphazard, responses. In fact, the greater the seeming urgency of policy changes, the more likely those changes are really active management decisions posing as policy issues.

THE INVESTMENT POLICY STATEMENT

A plan sponsor's investment policy finds its most effective articulation through a written document, which we refer to as an Investment Policy Statement (IPS). Even the best conceived investment policy will be of little use if it cannot be succinctly conveyed to interested parties.

Investment policy statements can take many forms. However, an appropriate IPS should contain several basic elements:

- An overview of the plan's delegation of authority and responsibility among its various decision-making groups, including the board of trustees, pension staff, the actuary, and investment managers.
- The plan sponsor's definition of the primary investment policy components.
- A specification of the plan sponsor's strategy with respect to each investment policy component.
- An explanation of the plan sponsor's rationale underlying the choice of investment policy strategies.

Consider, for example, the investment manager structure of a plan sponsor's investment policy. The IPS should briefly discuss how the plan sponsor defines the concept and its importance to the investment program. The IPS should also explain who is responsible for selecting (and terminating) managers and for allocating funds among the managers. The IPS should present the details of the plan sponsor's current investment manager structure policy within each asset class; specifically, the allocation between active and passive management and the specific active and passive managers retained and their respective allocations. Finally, the IPS should discuss the reasons behind the particular active/passive mixes selected and how the allocations to the managers are consistent with the plan sponsor's selected asset class targets.

THE ROLE OF THE IPS

An investment policy statement serves three primary functions:

- Facilitates internal and external communication of investment policy.
- Ensures continuity of policy during periods of turnover within a plan sponsor's organization.
- Provides a clear baseline against which to review proposed policy changes.

With respect to the first function, the IPS communicates the plan's investment policy to insiders, such as the board of trustees or plan sponsor staff, and to interested outsiders, such as the fund's money managers. By formally describing the plan's investment policy, the IPS helps prevent confusion over interpretation of that policy. In addition, a regular presentation of the IPS keeps the plan sponsor's investment policy fresh in the minds of decision-makers. For example, the IPS could be included at the front of all meeting documents distributed to board members.

Regarding the second function, the IPS serves as a permanent record that enhances continuity in the plan's investment program, particularly during periods of board or staff changes. Turnover among plan sponsor decision-makers is inevitable. For newcomers, the IPS provides a concise and accessible reference describing the fund's long-term goals and strategies. Its existence also reduces the urge on the part of these new decision-makers to revise the plan's investment policy when they observe that the existing policy is the product of a thorough and deliberate process.

Finally, the IPS serves as a standard against which to consider proposed changes to the plan's current investment policy. Policy changes presented for consideration should be described in terms of alterations to the existing IPS. In that way, the proposed changes and the current policy can be directly compared, and the merits of the changes will be easier to evaluate. This process limits the likelihood that emotional appeals for change will sway decision-makers. Proponents of modifications will be forced to submit their proposals to the same disciplined analysis that brought about the current policy.

CONCLUSION

The long-run success of a pension fund depends far more on the design and consistent implementation of sound investment policy than it does on such ephemeral activities as manager selection or tactical asset allocation. Investment policy reflects the plan sponsor's investment philosophy and long-term strategic plan for managing pension assets. As a result, it serves as the foundation upon which a plan sponsor should build an investment program.

Regardless of whether a plan sponsor chooses to formally enunciate the investment policy, the pension fund will operate under a policy. No decision is still a decision. The plan sponsor's real choice involves whether to devise and consistently apply an investment policy consonant with targeted needs or to proceed with an ad hoc approach.

No simple investment policy recipe exists. To design an effective investment policy requires that the plan sponsor be thoroughly familiar not only with the risks and returns offered by the capital markets, but with the financial circumstances of the pension plan and the attitudes of the plan sponsor's decision-makers as well. This latter requirement dictates that setting investment policy cannot be delegated to outside parties such as money managers. Only the plan sponsor can make the appropriate choices necessary to align investment policy with the preferences of its decision-makers and the needs of the plan.

Development of sound investment policy requires the plan sponsor to assume the role of risk controller and delegate the return maximizer function to other parties. A clear separation of these responsibilities permits the plan sponsor to take an objective, long-term perspective toward the management of the plan's assets. Only from this perspective can the plan sponsor make the requisite decisions to produce long-term investment results consistent with realistic expectations.

NOTES

[1]   Ellis presents a clear, concise discussion of investment policy in Charles D. Ellis, *Investment Policy*, (Homewood, IL: Dow Jones-Irwin, 1985). Keith P. Ambachtsheer, *Pension Funds and the Bottom Line: Managing the Corporate Pension Fund as a Financial Business* (Homewood, IL: Dow Jones-Irwin, 1986) also provides a thorough analysis of investment policy fundamentals.

[2]   An interesting exception to this general observation is given in James A. O'Connell, "The Policy Level Management Gap in Corporate Pen-

sion Administration (And How One Corporation Bridged It)," *Financial Analysts Journal* (March/April, 1987), pp. 76-79.

3   Thoughtful perspectives on the nature of the plan sponsor's mission are found in Wayne H. Wagner, "The Many Dimensions of Risk," *Journal of Portfolio Management* (Winter 1988), pp. 35-39, and Keith P. Ambachtsheer, "Pension Fund Asset Allocation: In Defense of a 60/40 Equity/Debt Asset Mix," *Financial Analysts Journal* (September/October, 1987), pp. 14-24.

4   This point is addressed in Robert D. Arnott and Peter L. Bernstein, "The Right Way to Manage Your Pension Fund," *Harvard Business Review* (January/February, 1988), pp. 95-102.

5   In Dean LeBaron, Gail Farrelly, and Susan Gala, "Facilitating a Dialogue on Risk: A Questionnaire Approach," *Financial Analysts Journal* (May/June, 1989), pp. 19-24, the authors develop a survey designed to indicate the respondents' risk-taking preferences.

6   For substantiation, see Gary P. Brinson, L. Randolph Hood, and Gilbert L. Beebower, "Determinants of Portfolio Performance," *Financial Analysts Journal* (July/August, 1986), pp. 39-44.

7   The completeness fund approach reverses the traditional procedure of setting an investment manager structure. The plan sponsor first selects its active manager alignment and then devises a passive portfolio to complement the aggregate investment styles of these active managers. The concept of completeness funds is described in David E. Tierney and Kenneth Winston, "Dynamic Completeness Funds," *Financial Analysts Journal,* forthcoming.

8   Investment policy also operates as a stabilizer in periods of strong positive market performance. Here again plan sponsors are tempted to change their investment programs, making those programs more aggressive, as they extrapolate the current market trends into the future.

APPENDIX

Michael J. Menssen
Investment Analyst
Minnesota State Board of Investment

Drafting an investment policy requires more than a cookie-cutter approach. The previous chapter laid out the basic components of a pension fund's investment policy. However, given the differences that exist among plan sponsors in terms of their organizations, legal restrictions, objectives, and risk tolerances, these basic components require customization to match a plan's particular characteristics and needs. This appendix describes the investment policy adopted by the Minnesota State Board of Investment for its largest pension plan, the $7 billion Basic Retirement Funds (BRF).

Fund's Mission

The BRF's mission statement reflects the broad pension goals pursued by the Minnesota State Board of Investment in the management of this fund. Specifically, the BRF's primary mission calls for the investment of employer/employee contributions to secure sufficient funds to finance promised benefits to participating public employees upon their retirement. Secondarily, the BRF's investments should generate additional funds that permit either the reduction of contributions or the enhancement of benefits.

Risk Tolerance

The Board views its tolerance for risk in managing the BRF's assets to be relatively high. Given the BRF's adequate funding and its middle-aged participant demographics, the Board takes a long-term view in establishing the BRF's risk-return posture. As a consequence, the Board has adopted an aggressive, high expected return investment program consistent with the BRF's mission statement. The Board is willing to accept volatile short-term investment results with the expectation that the volatility will be more than compensated by superior long-term performance.

Investment Objectives

Based on its mission statement and risk tolerance, the Board has established the following investment objectives for the BRF:

1. To generate a total annualized rate of return 3-5% greater than the rate of inflation over a rolling 10-year period.
2. To exceed a composite of asset class target returns, weighted in accordance with the policy asset mix, over a rolling five-year period.

The investment objectives indicate the Board's high risk tolerance and long-term investment horizon with respect to managing the BRF. These objectives provide direction in developing the BRF's policy asset mix and investment management structure. They also provide the basis for evaluating the performance of the BRF's investment program.

Policy Asset Mix

To achieve the investment objective of a 3-5% real rate of return necessitates that the BRF maintain a significant exposure to equity assets. The current BRF policy asset mix set by the Board is shown below:

Equities	
Domestic Common Stocks	60.0%
Real Estate	10.0
Venture Capital	2.5
Resource Funds	2.5
Total Equities	75.0%
Fixed Income	
Domestic Bonds	24.0%
Cash Equivalents	1.0
Total Fixed Income	25.0%

In conjunction with setting the BRF policy asset mix, the Board has selected appropriate targets, where available, for the asset classes that make up the BRF total portfolio.

Asset Class	*Asset Class Target*
Domestic Common Stocks	Wilshire 5000
Real Estate	Wilshire Real Estate Index
Domestic Bonds	Salomon Brothers Broad Bond Index
Cash Equivalents	90-Day Treasury Bills
Venture Capital	None selected
Resource Funds	None selected

These asset class targets represent the broad market investment opportunities available to the Board. In addition, the Board can readily access information on these indices when conducting performance evaluation.

At this time the Board has not identified appropriate asset class targets for the venture capital and resource funds. For performance evaluation purposes, the actual performance of the BRF's venture capital and resource fund investments serve as the benchmarks for those asset classes.

Investment Management Structure

The BRF investment objective of exceeding the performance of a composite of the asset class target requires that the BRF investment management structure include active management. The Board has established that a minimum of 50% of the BRF common stock and bond investments be passively managed. The Board restricts active management to a range of 10-50% of the BRF's common stock and bond investments. The exact allocation to active management varies over time depending on the Board's confidence in the BRF's active managers.

While they have not been listed here due to lack of space, the Board also assigns policy allocations to each of the BRF investment managers. The Board bases its allocations on its perceptions of a manager's investment skills and the extent to which the manager's investment style serves to diversify the BRF's investments within an asset class.

Performance Evaluation

The Board conducts performance evaluation for the BRF at the total fund, asset class, and individual manager levels. At the total fund level, the

Board analyzes results relative to the BRF real rate of return and composite indices objectives. Further, the Board breaks down investment results into the effects of policy decisions and the impact of deviations from policy allocations.

On the asset class and individual manager levels, the Board assigns benchmark portfolios to all BRF investment managers. These benchmarks are a vital element in the evaluation of individual and aggregate manager performance within each asset class. The Board uses these benchmarks not only to review the value added by the managers individually and in aggregate, but also to examine the extent of manager structure biases relative to the asset class targets.

CHAPTER 3

Defining and Managing Pension Fund Risk*

ROBERT D. ARNOTT
PRESIDENT & CHIEF INVESTMENT OFFICER
FIRST QUADRANT CORPORATION

PETER L. BERNSTEIN
PRESIDENT
PETER L. BERNSTEIN, INC.
AND CONSULTING EDITOR
THE JOURNAL OF PORTFOLIO MANAGEMENT

The way we manage risks is ultimately going to depend on how we define those risks. This is often a more complicated task than it appears to be at first glance. Risk is such a many-headed monster that selecting the right head to focus on can be a major challenge.

Although the analysis that we offer here relates specifically to pension fund risk, the development of our argument and the issues that we raise lend themselves to broad generalizations. The precise definition of the risks we face is critically important, and risk management must be exquisitely sensitive to that definition.

Corporate executives have traditionally defined pension fund risk in terms of the trade-off between risk and return on the *assets* accumulated to fund pension obligations. Although there has been a slowly growing recog-

* This chapter is an adaptation and expansion of Robert D. Arnott and Peter L. Bernstein, "The Right Way to Manage Your Pension Fund," *Harvard Business Review*, January/February 1988. Copyright 1988 by the President and Fellows of Harvard University.

nition that this focus on asset risk was much too narrowly defined, there has also been strong resistance to breaking deep-seated habits.

Assets do not exist in a vacuum, seeking return and avoiding risk for their own sakes. This may seem obvious when stated in so many words, but it has taken the arrival of Financial Accounting Standards Board Statement 87 (FASB 87) to bring the variability of pension fund *liabilities* to front and center. FASB 87 focuses on the pension fund *surplus*—the difference between the assets and the liabilities. This focus has been reinforced by the Omnibus Budget Reconciliation Act (OBRA) of 1987. OBRA adds legal weight to the FASB accounting guidelines by mandating pension contribution rates and Pension Benefit Guaranty Corporation (PBGC) insurance premiums which are sensitive to the pension funding ratio. The result is a belated awakening to the simple idea that the assets need to have some systematic relationship to the character of the liabilities that they fund.

Nevertheless, the implications of new notions are frequently subtle, and the response of pension fund strategies to FASB 87 and to OBRA is no exception. At most corporations, the definition of pension fund risk has shifted, but remains flawed because it remains oversimplified. This means that the restructuring of those funds may still be inappropriate in terms of the "true" risks of the pension plan. The oversimplification arises from paying too much attention to the interest sensitivity of the pension surplus, a result of FASB 87's emphasis on defining the surplus in terms of the interest sensitivity of the fund's actuarial liabilities.

These considerations are highly significant in their impact on corporate profitability and financial health. Pension fund assets have accumulated to a point where they tend to loom large relative to the total pool of assets in the corporation. Their variability and their rate of return have a meaningful influence on the company's bottom line; under FASB 87, their relationship to the liabilities of the pension fund may become visible on the published balance sheet as well.

Senior management should seek to achieve two objectives. First, the pension fund deserves as much attention as any significant operating division. Second, senior management must begin to analyze pension fund decisions in the context of potential long-term returns *measured against the true impact on corporate risk.*

THE CONVENTIONAL VIEW OF PENSION FUND RISK

As pension funds began to assume importance among corporate assets— say, over the past quarter century—pension fund management focused on the trade-off between the expected returns on their investments and the volatility of those returns. The idea was to maximize return consistent with some control over the magnitude of year-to-year, and sometimes even quarter-to-quarter, variations in the rate of return.

Volatility was of concern for three reasons:

1. First, all other things being equal, volatility tends to reduce returns over the long run. To put it simply, if you lose 50%, you have to gain 100% to break even.

2. Second, even if you believe that the assets you select can return enough to overcome the drag imposed by variability, the variability by its very nature creates uncertainty as to what the assets will be worth when liabilities come due.

3. Finally, corporate managements tend to like smooth numbers. Irregular numbers raise questions that most people would be just as happy to avoid.

The traditional approach, therefore, was to seek the highest possible return at an acceptable level of volatility or, alternatively, to minimize volatility at any given level of expected return. This view of risk and reward was described in an array such as that shown in Exhibit 1, which plots expected asset returns on the vertical axis and variability of asset returns on the horizontal axis. The array runs from cash at the low end to stocks at the high end.

Putting all your eggs in one basket is never optimal. By employing the magic of diversification to reduce variability, you can obtain more expected return per unit to risk or reduce the risk per unit of expected return by combining assets instead of selecting just one. That process results in the curve known in investment parlance as the "efficient frontier." This curve shows the best return that can be achieved through diversification at any given level of risk.

The popularity of this approach to pension fund management rested on its simplicity, its familiarity and its convenience. It became a total expression of the culture of the pension fund world in the 1970s. The evaluation of assets based on market levels fits the intuitive idea of what investing in a pension fund is all about. As Exhibit 2 suggests, other important variables—future contributions to the fund, estimated future wage growth and the discount rate used to calculate net present values were all determined by the actuary, were independent of movements in the capital markets and were changed infrequently.

EXHIBIT 1:   RISK AND REWARD—THE TRADITIONAL PERSPECTIVE

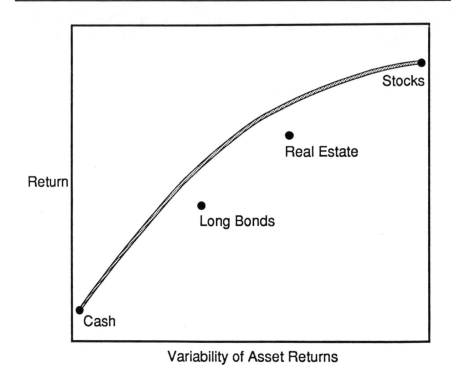

Variability of Asset Returns

This traditional view of pension risk suggests that pension plans with low tolerance for risk will tend to locate themselves toward the left-hand side of the frontier, with more in bonds and cash and less in stocks. Those with a greater willingness to bear risk in the search for higher returns will locate themselves toward the right, with heavier concentrations in the riskier assets like stocks and real estate.

As is evident in Exhibit 3, the slope of the efficient frontier is relatively flat in the zones where most funds position themselves. This feature of the frontier would lead us to conclude that most funds are highly tolerant of risk, because a curve with only a slight upward slope means that these funds will accept a large increase in risk for a modest increment in expected return.

This view of pension risk and reward is unrealistic for three reasons:

1. First, corporate pension fund sponsors tend to be prudent, careful investors, with risk tolerances that cover a wide range from conservative to moderately aggressive. They take their fiduciary re-

EXHIBIT 2:   RISK AND REWARD—TRANSITION TO FASB-87

	Traditional	*FASB–87*
Assets	Variable: Market-Driven	Variable: Market-Driven
Asset Growth	Fixed*	Fixed*
NPV Liability Components		
Wage Growth	Fixed*	Fixed*
Discount Rate	Fixed*	Variable: Market-Driven

* Set by actuary.

EXHIBIT 3:   RISK AND REWARD: THE TRADITIONAL PERSPECTIVE—
OBSERVED RISK TOLERANCE

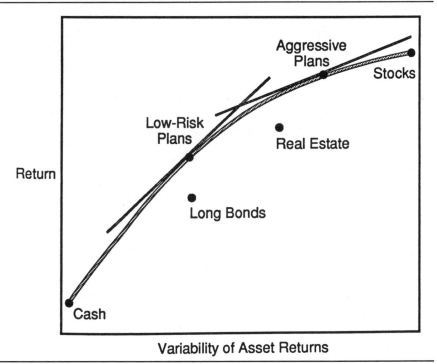

sponsibility seriously. Relatively few have risk tolerances as high as Exhibit 3 suggests.

2. Furthermore, this traditional perspective is silent on the subject of liabilities—it tells management nothing about where they should position themselves on the frontier. It provides information only on what the shape of the frontier is like. Corporations with a mature workforce or with unique business risks should hardly want to be on the same point of the frontier or at the same level of risk tolerance as corporations with a young workforce or with stable earnings power.

3. Finally, the definition of risk here is limited to variability of expected returns on assets, with no attention given to the variability patterns of the liabilities the assets are to fund. Pension liabilities are highly sensitive to many factors, including changes in interest rates, which suggests rather a different definition of pension risk from what we see here.

THE IMPACT OF FASB 87

FASB 87 brings the liabilities into the picture by putting the focus on the *surplus* of the pension fund—the difference between the assets and the liabilities. This introduces an extra level of complexity. The value of the assets is easy enough to measure, but the liabilities are something else again. As shown in Exhibit 2, the major change induced by the accounting standard has been to mandate the use of market interest rates on long-term bonds for the calculation of the net present value of those liabilities. Projections of asset growth and wage growth remain in the domain of the actuary. (See Exhibit 4.)

The rationale for the insistence on market-determined discount rates is simple enough. Actuarial valuations tend to lag reality and aim, like many other features of corporate bookkeeping, at smooth changes. The capital markets are anything but smooth, but their view of the appropriate discount rate is immediate and inescapable. In addition, the markets are undoubtedly more accurate than the view, no matter how judicious, of a single individual or organization aiming to be conservative, avoiding frequent changes and shunning disruptive numbers.

The consequence of this redefinition of risk is profound. If the objective is to maximize the excess of assets over liabilities, while seeking to minimize the *variability* of that excess, then we have to ask which assets best match the variability pattern of the liabilities. As FASB 87 treats the liabilities as fixed obligations, discounted at a market interest rate, this is

EXHIBIT 4:   WHAT ARE FASB 87 AND THE OBRA?

FASB 87 is the recent ruling by the Financial Accounting Standards Board relating to pension accounting. For many corporations, FASB ruling #87 will have more impact on corporate earnings than any other ruling to date. FASB 87 mandates that:

- For both reported earnings and balance sheet calculations, pension accounting for defined benefit plans must estimate liability by applying a *market* interest rate to the expected obligations served by the pension plan, in order to determine the net present value of those obligations. This means that as market interest rates move, so too does the liability. If market rates rise, the net present value of future obligations declines, and vice versa.

- For those defined benefit plans with an underfunded pension plan (i.e., the net present value of the liability exceeds the assets in the plan), the liability side of the balance sheet must include this unfunded pension liability.

- *Changes* in the surplus for the pension plan, if larger than 10% of plan assets or liabilities, must be reflected in the *earnings* statement in the form of operating earnings. This takes the form of an allowance for changes in pension contributions, amortized to compensate for the change in pension surplus. Whether or not the corporation chooses to actually change their pension contribution rate, FASB 87 requires the corporation to treat reported earnings as if contributions are adjusted to reflect a change in the pension surplus.

The Omnibus Budget Reconciliation Act of 1987 (OBRA) is a recent legislative initiative which reinforces the FASB 87 interpretation of liabilities. OBRA mandates that:

- Pension contributions for an underfunded pension plan (with an ABO funding ratio below 100%) must accelerate contributions to the pension plan. The underfunded liability must be amortized over a period of just five years.

- A pension sponsor with an ABO funding ratio in excess of 150% must cease pension contributions.

- Underfunded pension plans must pay a significantly increased insurance premium to the Pension Benefit Guarantee Corporation (PBGC). Because of a conservative definition of the discount rate used to calculate liabilities, this applies to pension plans with a funding ratio below approximately 125%.

EXHIBIT 4: WHAT ARE FASB 87 AND THE OBRA? (Continued)

These two sets of rulings may have a profound effect in shortening the investment horizon of the corporate pension sponsor. For the pension fund that slides from marginal funding into underfunded territory, many ills are visited upon the corporation: pension expense rises, thereby reducing reported corporate earnings; contributions to the pension plan must sharply accelerate; PBGC insurance premiums rise rapidly; and, last but not least, a new liability appears on the balance sheet. The stipulation that contributions must cease for well-funded plans will also have a potentially serious effect. Without contributions, the well-funded pension plans will gradually be forced down to ABO funding ratios which will result in some vulnerability to the adverse consequences detailed above. The net result may be a gradual but long-term shift in the direction of more conservative pension management policies in order to prevent the pension plan from adversely affecting corporate management or earnings. If this shift to conservatism takes place, it would be at the cost of reducing long-term rates of return for pension management and increasing the long-term cost of pension plans.

DEFINED BENEFITS VS. DEFINED CONTRIBUTION

Clearly, neither ruling applies to defined *contribution* plans which make up some 30% of all pension assets. If a corporation offers a defined contribution plan to their employees, there is no pension surplus or unfunded liability. A defined contribution plan involves a contractual commitment to contribute a certain amount of money to a pension plan, with no guarantee as to how much money will be in the plan at retirement and no guarantee as to the annual retirement benefit that the employee will receive. A defined *benefit* plan does the opposite. While it makes no guarantee as to the amount of contribution which the corporation will make, it does guarantee a defined annual retirement benefit to the employee.

In a defined contribution plan, the employee bears all market risk and captures all of the reward in the event of strong markets. In a defined benefit plan, the corporation bears the market risk: if the performance is disappointing, the corporation must suffer the penalty of increased pension contribution costs, hence increased labor costs. If results are strong, the corporation reaps the benefit in the form of reduced pension contributions, hence reduced labor costs. These new regulations have an important impact on the balance sheet and earnings statement for any company which has a defined benefit pension plan.

equivalent to asking, "Which assets act most like long-term bonds?" The answer is obvious. As we shall see shortly, the answer is perhaps too obvious.

The immediate implication of FASB 87 is that long-term bonds are the lowest risk asset, replacing cash in that enviable spot. Therefore, we have to redraw our chart showing the trade-off between risk and expected return. The result appears in Exhibit 5. The expected rates of return are the same, but the riskiness of the assets has changed.

In the context of the FASB 87 definition of surplus valuation, the chart tells us that any asset with variable income or whose principal value does not move closely with the bond market will be a risky asset. At the extreme, cash becomes anathema, with its low expected return and high variability of income; its much-vaunted stability of principal does no good in hedging liabilities whose principal value can vary widely over time.

The clear implication of this shift in viewpoint is that bonds provide the risk-minimizing choice for pension funds, at an attractive long-term rate of return. Other assets can still make good sense, but at a considerable increase in risk. In fact, the simplicity of the analysis presented here is so attractive that one may be sorely tempted to pronounce the problem of pension fund investment solved and to turn one's attention to more pressing matters.

This is precisely the wrong conclusion to reach. FASB 87 suggests an unduly simplistic view of pension risk, which is only one step in the right direction. Compelling reasons to favor other assets exist for many funds, although not for all.

The search, and the justification for, an appropriate framework for pension management depend upon the manner in which we define pension fund risk. If pension fund risk is related solely to the variability in the discount rate used to calculate net present values, then bonds are the asset of choice. Any alternative *must* be justified only on the basis of a substantial return enhancement. When we widen the definition of risk, on the other hand, assets with variable rather than fixed-income streams can become the low-risk assets.

The critical question then becomes how to determine whether discount rate variability should be the dominant consideration in the definition of pension fund risk.

ANALYZING THE CHARACTERISTICS OF THE LIABILITIES

The attraction of bonds is greatest where the interest sensitivity of the liabilities is highest. Or, put a little differently, the attraction of bonds is

**EXHIBIT 5: RISK AND REWARD: THE FASB-87 PERSPECTIVE—
OBSERVED RISK TOLERANCE**

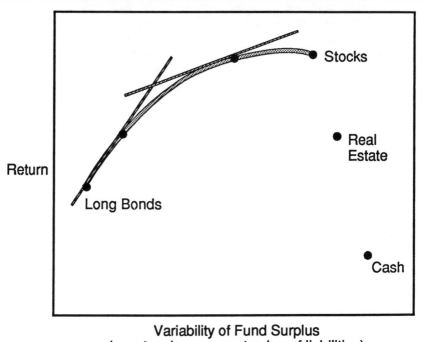

**Variability of Fund Surplus
(assets minus present value of liabilities)**

greatest where the dollar amount of the liabilities, like the dollar amount of the bond coupon payments, is fixed. Under those circumstances, the only factor influencing the present value—and the ultimate obligation—of the liabilities is the relevant rate of interest.

The obligation to cover pensions for retirees meets this criterion most precisely. This is an amount that the actuaries can estimate with great accuracy. Unless the corporation assumes an obligation to protect its retirees from inflation, the retiree liability is as close to a fixed and predetermined sum as can be found in the universe of pension liabilities.

This is why the dedicated bond portfolio has attracted such a large following in recent years. Here was an opportunity to create an exact match between assets and liabilities. The primary attraction was the elimination of risk, made possible by the use of immunizations and other forms of cash-matching techniques to make a perfect asset/liability match.

By "elimination of risk," we do not refer to return variability as such, but rather to the risk of having insufficient assets to meet the obligation as it comes due. This is, indeed, the only rational definition of risk; everything else is a variation on that theme. With interest rates so high in the late 1970s and the early 1980s, the dedication of income-matched bond portfolios to meet the obligations for retired lives (and the use of annuities to permit plan termination), enabled corporate management to free up pension assets for other uses.

As it happens, the definition of the Accumulated Benefit Obligation (ABO)[1] is remarkably similar to this retiree liability. FASB 87 defines this ABO liability as the amount to be paid to retirees and present employees assuming immediate termination of the pension plan. Essentially, this is the same as defining the size of an annuity to be purchased for these employees at retirement, with the size of the annuity to be determined on the basis of today's wages and today's "years of service."

This definition of the liability, as with the liability for retirees alone, creates a fixed nominal total pension liability. The present value of the liability so defined is the Accumulated Benefit Obligation. This present value of liabilities is deducted from the value of the pension assets to determine the ABO pension surplus.

Although an important improvement over the simplistic actuarial discount rate structures of the past, this model is also unrealistic once we look beyond the Accumulated Benefit Obligation. Indeed, to some extent, it is even unrealistic within the confines of that obligation as defined under FASB 87. Three problems intervene:

1. The duration of the bond portfolio may not be as long as the duration of the liabilities. That is, the flow of coupon payments and ultimately the return of principal may arrive sooner than the time needed to fully pay off the liabilities of the ABO, which may stretch far into the future. If that incoming cash cannot be reinvested at the same or a higher rate of interest than the rate paid on the original investment, the bond portfolio will fail to cover these obligations as they come due. This risk is known as reinvestment risk.

2. Many corporations assume the responsibility of providing their retirees with at least partial protection against inflationary inroads into the purchasing power of their pensions. A pension fund invested totally in long-term bonds will clearly not address this *implicit* component of the liability.

3. Finally, and most important, the ABO contains the unrealistic assumption of immediate pension plan termination. Growth in wages and assets between the present date and retirement are ignored, and only the current years of service, rather than the years of service at retirement, are reflected in the ABO. To make

matters even more unrealistic, the ABO also assumes that no new workers enter the workforce between now and the retirement of the present workforce. Implicitly, FASB 87 assumes that all of these additional obligations are addressed through future expense provisions.

THE IMPLICATIONS OF THE PROJECTED BENEFIT OBLIGATION

Corporate managements obviously realize that their pension liability goes well beyond the ABO. Active employees are going to earn higher wages in the future, which may grow faster or slower than the actuarial assumption, and will typically receive their pensions based on final pay. Asset growth also may be greater or less than the rate assumed by the actuary. Estimates of these uncertain but critical magnitudes must be added to the ABO to derive the true total pension liability, which is known as the Projected Benefit Obligation (PBO).

Many different factors will influence the actual size of the PBO. The dominant factors on wage growth will be inflation, productivity change and the fortunes of the company in question.

Over the long run, wages tend to keep pace with changes in the cost of living, even if the match is inexact. Much of the benefit of productivity improvement has been shared between workers and stockholders, with customers receiving an additional portion in the form of lower or less rapidly increasing prices. Even with high inflation and high productivity growth, an unprofitable company will be unable to keep compensation in pace with these forces; but a highly profitable company may treat its employees even better than inflation and productivity alone would warrant.

From this viewpoint, a 100% long-term bond portfolio may not be the risk-minimizing asset for hedging against the possibility of ending up with insufficient money to fund the true pension obligations. We now must seek assets, some with fixed-income returns, but many with variable-income returns, with the variability approximating as closely as possible the variability of inflation and productivity change. In addition, we should seek assets that diversify the inherent risks of the company in question, so that the company can pay its pensioners even if it falls on ill-fortune before or during their retirement.

Exhibit 6 provides some insight into how the income flows of stocks, bonds and cash have moved in relation to wage rates over the past thirty-odd years. The individual sections of the figure trace the path of hourly nominal compensation in the nonfarm business sector and the income flow from dividends, bond interest and Treasury bills.

The section on dividend income assumes simply that the fund bought the Standard & Poor's 500 Stock Composite Index at the beginning of 1954 and held it through to the end of 1986. We can see that dividends failed to keep pace with the growth in hourly compensation, primarily because of the steady shortfall from 1967 to 1976. Nevertheless, dividends have just about tracked the rise in hourly wage rates during the period since 1976, which includes the most virulent of the inflation years.

Our plot for long-term bond interest gives bonds the benefit of the doubt, but even so the mismatch between changes in bond income and wages after 1975 is painfully clear. Here we dropped the assumption of just one initial investment in 1954 and assumed that new money came into the pension fund each year and was invested in bonds at the rate of interest prevailing at the time of purchase.[2] The larger the inflow of new corporate contributions relative to the pool of monies already invested in the pension fund, the more closely the flow of interest income will keep up with inflation. But even so, it is evident that bonds are a miserable hedge against the inflation and productivity growth that drive wage increases.

A pension fund with a higher cash flow than we have assumed, or a younger fund started, say, in the early 1970s instead of the early 1950s, would have shown more favorable results. Note, however, that our equity graph assumed that no additional money came in after the fund was started in 1954, but dividends still provided an excellent hedge against wage growth.

The third section of Exhibit 6 also assumes just one investment in 1954, which was continuously rolled over into new Treasury bills every quarter. Here the variability of the income stream is the most visible feature. Nevertheless, the total flow of income from this hypothetical Treasury bill portfolio was the highest of the three shown here, comfortably above the cumulative total of the nominal compensation curve.

Note that Treasury bills represent a much better fit for the incremental PBO than for the ABO. Even though cash equivalents do not fluctuate in value with the net present value of the liabilities, they do provide a very good immunization against inflation. If cash is held for retirement benefits, with income reinvested, it can be expected to grow with inflation and hence with the magnitude of retirement benefits. If the corpus of that investment, rather than the income generated by the Treasury bills, is then distributed to pay retirement benefits, then Treasury bills actually represent a good fit with the incremental PBO. However, this good fit is only from the vantage point of risk. The long-term rates of return for cash equivalents

**EXHIBIT 6: HOW HOURLY COMPENSATION FARED AGAINST
DIVIDEND AND INTEREST INCOME AND TREASURY
BILLS: 1954-1986**

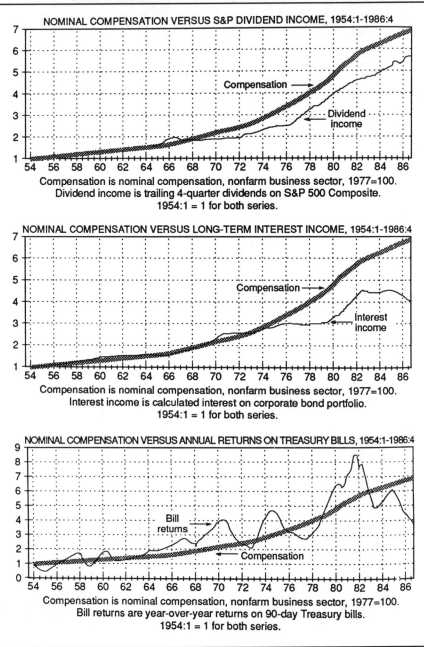

NOMINAL COMPENSATION VERSUS S&P DIVIDEND INCOME, 1954:1-1986:4

Compensation is nominal compensation, nonfarm business sector, 1977=100.
Dividend income is trailing 4-quarter dividends on S&P 500 Composite.
1954:1 = 1 for both series.

NOMINAL COMPENSATION VERSUS LONG-TERM INTEREST INCOME, 1954:1-1986:4

Compensation is nominal compensation, nonfarm business sector, 1977=100.
Interest income is calculated interest on corporate bond portfolio.
1954:1 = 1 for both series.

NOMINAL COMPENSATION VERSUS ANNUAL RETURNS ON TREASURY BILLS, 1954:1-1986:4

Compensation is nominal compensation, nonfarm business sector, 1977=100.
Bill returns are year-over-year returns on 90-day Treasury bills.
1954:1 = 1 for both series.

remain low. Thus, for the incremental PBO, cash remains an unattractive asset.

Although these graphs are meant only to be suggestive, their suggestions are significant. The emphasis on covariance with bond interest, as stipulated in FASB 87, becomes a dangerous oversimplification when the incremental liabilities of the Projected Benefit Obligation, above and beyond the ABO liabilities, are taken into consideration. Protection against the risk that the earnings of the pension fund will fail to cover the Projected Benefit Obligation requires a combination of assets—like equities—whose income flow is somehow related to the pressures of inflation and is also related to productivity change.

HOW TO BALANCE THE ABO AND THE INCREMENTAL PBO IN PENSION FUND RISK

Treasury bills, common stock, and other variable return assets may do a better job than bonds in hedging the long-term risks inherent in wage growth assumptions, but they have two important disadvantages. First, their income flows are too variable to fund the retirees or the Accumulated Benefit Obligation. Second, they are only partially interest sensitive, and sometimes correlate negatively with changes in long-term interest rates, which means that they add unwanted variability to the pension fund surplus, as defined under FASB 87—a central component of that surplus is the net present value of the liabilities, which are highly sensitive to interest rates.

The task of senior management in determining how best to hedge pension fund risk, therefore, is to weigh as accurately as possible the relative importance of the advantages and disadvantages of each type of asset. In essence, this involves employing fixed-income assets to fund fixed-dollar obligations, where the estimate of the liability has a high degree of certainty, and employing variable-income assets to fund variable-dollar obligations, where the estimate of liability has a high degree of uncertainty.

The best way to look at this problem is to make separate estimates of the ABO and the PBO and examine the size of the spread between the two, the incremental PBO. The more mature the plan, or the more mature the workforce, the smaller that spread is likely to be. In other words, the pension liability for a mature workforce, being by definition closer to maturity than a young workforce, lends itself more readily to certainty in the estimation process. In many such cases, the ABO can exceed 90% of the total PBO, leading to a relatively well-defined nominal liability. Mature plans, therefore, will have an incentive to favor long-term bonds at the expense of stocks or cash equivalents. Long-term bonds can provide certainty of return to cover the certainty of the liability. In addition, long-term bonds will provide maximum stability to the pension fund surplus within the definitions and reporting requirements of FASB 87.

Conversely, emerging plans, associated with younger or faster growing companies, will have a higher PBO liability relative to the ABO and therefore will have an incentive to hold a more aggressive asset mix, with a stronger relationship with future wage growth. In such a case, equities will tend to dominate.

This preference for equities is likely to hold true for reasons beyond the ability of dividends to keep pace with inflation and to reflect productivity improvements as well. Pension plans that cover young workers will start paying significant sums in pensions only in the far distant future. Reinvestment risk is minimized by matching the horizon of the liabilities. Equities can represent a good fit, because the principal is never repaid and because the cash return is expected to grow larger with the passage of time.

So far so good. Life is not quite this simple, however. We have yet to consider the conflict between the short run and the long run in pension planning, as well as the difference between variability in rates of return— essentially asset price variability—and variability in flows of income in each asset. Return variability and the short-run/long-run conflicts are interrelated.

In the short run, stability in the pension fund surplus is important because of its impact on current profitability and the balance sheet. The framers of FASB 87 knew what they were about in trying to arrive at a better definition of the influence of the pension fund on earnings and financial well-being. In the long run, on the other hand, stability of the surplus is not nearly as important as its size. The corporation would like to have something left over to accommodate reduced contributions during periods of earnings weakness. In essence, the pension plan acts as a tax-deferred savings plan, or an "IRA" for the corporation, right down to the penalty for early withdrawal.

The assets that best assure a surplus over the Projected Benefit Obligation in the long run are the riskiest in the short run, in that they add variability to the pension fund surplus. Stocks, for example, have the clear lead for matching the attributes of the longest-term liabilities, but their short-run returns are highly variable and only weakly correlated with interest rates. At the other end of the spectrum, cash equivalents tend to have low returns that are frequently correlated negatively with returns on bonds.

A graphic display of these dilemmas appears in Exhibit 7. Here the chart relates to the Accumulated Benefit Obligation and repeats the array shown in Exhibit 5. This is essentially the short-run view of the matter. The expected rates of return are the same as in the original array in Exhibit

1. The risks, however, relate primarily to the sensitivity of asset returns to interest rates, because it is interest rates that determine the net present values of the liabilities, and we want to stabilize the relationship between the assets and the net present values of the liabilities—that is, the surplus--in the short run.

Exhibit 8 shows what happens when we introduce the incremental Projected Benefit Obligation into our deliberations and begin to take a longer-run view. The variable-income assets now become less risky; the fixed-income assets become riskier. In plain English, this means that the variable-income assets increase management's confidence in their ability to fund the PBO, while bonds would not be the almost "risk-free" assets that they are for the ABO.

The shift in viewpoint is critical. Now we direct our attention to the ultimate future size of the liabilities, not just to their sensitivity to interest rates, which determine only their actuarial net present values. In other words, minimizing the long-run variability of the pension fund surplus de-

EXHIBIT 7:   RISK AND REWARD—THE ABO

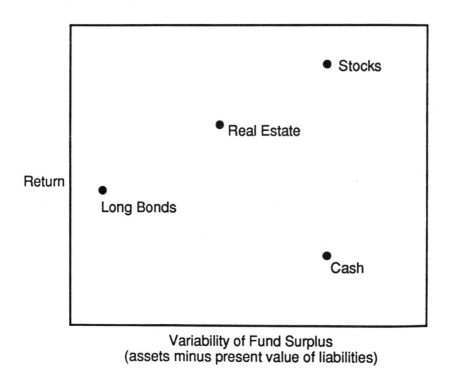

Variability of Fund Surplus
(assets minus present value of liabilities)

pends upon our ability to fund the PBO rather than merely minimizing the short-run variability of the ABO surplus.

Finally, Exhibits 9a and 9b demonstrate the differing choices available to mature and early growth funds. We show the location of the assets for the mature pension plan in Exhibit 9a and for the young plan in Exhibit 9B. Once again, we construct an efficient frontier composed of combinations of assets rather than portfolios of single assets.

The mature fund would take dangerously larger risks for each increment of return by moving very far from a bond portfolio. The fixed nature of the obligations makes anything other than fixed-income assets highly risky. The slope of the risk/return relationship is steep at the left-hand side, in the low-risk tolerance zone where this fund belongs.

In Exhibit 9b, the riskiness of variable-income assets declines as we lengthen the time horizon that is appropriate to a younger fund, while the riskiness of bonds increases. This fund has a greater appetite for riskier securities as we conventionally classify them. It will locate itself further

EXHIBIT 8: RISK AND REWARD—PBO - ABO

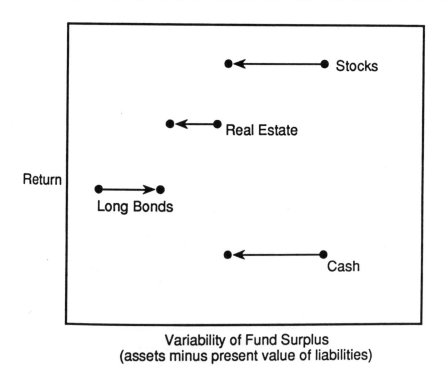

Variability of Fund Surplus
(assets minus present value of liabilities)

out to the right on the efficient frontier where the slope is flatter, as befits a fund with a higher risk tolerance. Indeed, even with the same risk tolerance (measured by the slope of the risk tolerance line) as the mature plan, the younger plan would use more stocks and real estate to match the greater sensitivity of liabilities to inflation or productivity growth.

SUMMARY

We began this analysis with the assertion that the management of risk depends critically on the manner in which we define risk. This discussion has attempted to demonstrate how inadequate or oversimplified definitions of risk have led to inappropriate asset allocation decisions for many pension funds. These inappropriate decisions have been the result of inadequate attention to the *true* nature of pension fund risk and the many forces that play upon it.

EXHIBIT 9a: "TRUE" RISK AND REWARD—THE MATURE PLAN (ABO DOMINATES)

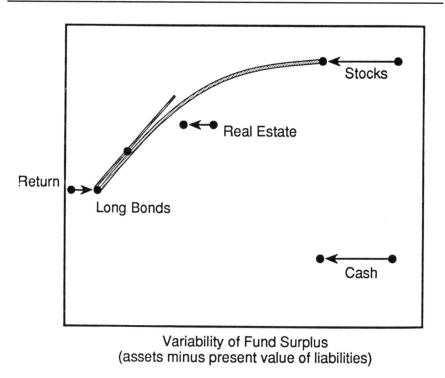

Variability of Fund Surplus
(assets minus present value of liabilities)

The simplest approach to pension risk analysis concentrates only on the riskiness of the assets themselves, without regard to their correlations with the riskiness of the liabilities. This has been by far the most popular approach, but it remains a most inappropriate way to approach pension fund management. We can be grateful to the Financial Accounting Standards Board for forcing the pension sponsor to weigh the assets *and* liabilities in assessing the merits of pension management strategies.

The current tendency is to put too much emphasis on the strictures of FASB 87 and to look to long-term bonds to save the day. Long-term bonds are appropriate for stabilizing the surplus in the short run, where the net present value of the liabilities is the crucial consideration. In view of the definition of the Accumulated Benefit Obligation, bonds are also appropriate where the liability is estimated with a high degree of certainty, as in the case of retired lives or a pension fund for a mature workforce.

EXHIBIT 9b: RISK AND REWARD—THE EARLY GROWTH PLAN (PBO > ABO)

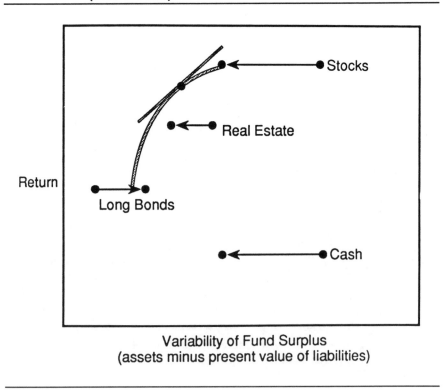

Variability of Fund Surplus
(assets minus present value of liabilities)

On the other hand, there is a danger in viewing all pension funds in these terms. Sometimes there is a temptation to go in that direction just because of the simplicity of relating the variability of the assets to the variability of the present values. Sometimes this temptation arises from a slavish devotion to the short run, where the desire for smoothness and consistency can easily dominate the acceptance of the variability that is inescapable in achieving high longer-run returns.

In reality, the size of the pensions that the corporation pays in future years will have relatively little to do with today's level of long-term interest rates. In reality, therefore, the future value of the pension obligation is going to be far more important than today's present value. The corporation that seeks to have a surplus in its pension fund in the future had better consider the risks likely to arise in the future, not just the immediate risks.

But that warning applies to all risk management. You do not buy life insurance on a building or fire insurance on a senior executive. You do not take out a 30-year term life policy on a 55-year-old executive or a 6-month maintenance agreement on a brand new mainframe computer. Insurance policies are matched to the nature and time horizon of the risks. The pension fund example is different from these examples only in its complexities, but then all corporations face many risks of equivalent complexity. They deserve equivalent analysis.

NOTES

[1] For more information on the ABO, see Chapter 14.

[2] The calculations assume that new money contributed each year was equal to 10% of the total asset value at the end of the preceding year, including interest earned in that year. This is a rough approximation of reality. If we had treated the bond simulation like the others, without any adjustment for fresh inflows of cash, the interest income number would never have budged above 1. This is what would have happened with a bond purchase in 1954 and no subsequent purchases at the higher interest rates that developed later.

CHAPTER 4

Managing the Asset Mix: Decisions and Consequences

ROBERT D. ARNOTT
PRESIDENT & CHIEF INVESTMENT OFFICER
FIRST QUADRANT CORPORATION

Asset allocation has been an enormously popular topic among institutional investors in recent years. On one level, we all talk about it, but, on another level, few of us are engaging in any systematic or deliberate asset allocation process, beyond setting a normal asset mix. If the asset allocation of a portfolio is not managed as a deliberate strategy, then it is drifting on autopilot, driven by the whims of the markets. This is the often overlooked fact of asset allocation: if we don't engage in asset allocation *management* on a continuous basis, the markets will do it for us. The markets will assure that we are overexposed at market highs and underexposed at market lows.

While it is often thought of as one decision, asset allocation really consists of several distinct and largely *independent* decisions.

- The *policy* asset allocation decision is a long-term decision aimed at assessing the appropriate *normal* asset mix. This mix represents a careful balancing between the often conflicting desires for return and for controlled risk.

- *Tactical* asset allocation represents an opportunistic strategy that seeks to enhance returns through deliberate shifts away from this normal policy allocation. The asset mix is shifted in response to the shifting patterns of return available in the markets.

- *Dynamic* strategies, such as portfolio insurance, represent a mechanistic attempt to reshape the return distribution. Typically, dynamic strategies are used to reduce risk in adverse markets, and to pay for that protection through lower returns in strong markets.

Many organizations invest significant time and expense to establish the appropriate long-term normal asset mix. After this mix has been established, the portfolio is often allowed to drift with the movements of the capital markets. This drifting mix is an important problem: it represents a significant drain both on the time of the investment officer and on investment results. It drains the time of the investment executive, because ultimately a drifting mix must be corrected. Rectifying a drifting asset mix requires a careful decision as to changes in the allocation of assets among managers. As we shall demonstrate, it also erodes investment performance.

RULE 1: DON'T EXCEED THE CLIENT RISK TOLERANCE

One of the most important rules in asset management is to never exceed the risk tolerance of clients. If we abide by this adage, then clients will show due patience when, inevitably, investment strategies are temporarily out of step. If the risk tolerance of clients is exceeded, then their patience will run out before a normal dry spell runs its course.

This adage holds as true for the pension sponsor as it does for the asset manager. The principle difference is in the nature of the customer. The asset manager's customer, most typically, is the pension officer, or perhaps the treasurer. For the pension officer, there is a very different (and often less predictable) "customer." Ironically, the pension officer's customer is *not* the pension beneficiary. The pension beneficiary does not determine whether the pension officer keeps his or her job! But, the CFO and pension committee most assuredly do.

If we are not to exceed the risk tolerance of customers, their risk tolerance must be understood. This is a multi-faceted problem. As Exhibit 1 suggests, there is no single measure of risk. In essence, risk might be loosely defined as any unpleasant and unanticipated consequence of any investment strategy. This might include losing money. It might include growing the assets more slowly than the liabilities (hence, losing surplus or falling underfunded). It might include failing to adequately educate the "customer" as to the patterns of risk and reward associated with chosen strategies.

Understanding Risk

Before we begin to manage the asset mix, it is imperative to first understand risk. Risk is not just portfolio volatility. It is not just the volatility of

EXHIBIT 1: WHAT RISKS MATTER?

I. How important is portfolio volatility?

    A. What role can be played by appraisal-based assets or "book value" assets, such as real estate or venture capital, in dampening volatility without forfeiting returns?

    B. How much volatility can be tolerated in an effort to achieve high returns?

II. How important is volatility in the surplus (actuarial liabilities minus assets)?

    A. Should we seek to match the duration of assets against an artificial definition of liabilities (the actuarial or accounting definition) to constrain surplus volatility?

    B. Should we seek high returns at a cost of surplus volatility?

III. How important is long-term business risk?

    A. Will my "customer" (the pension committee of the board) tolerate nominal portfolio volatility or surplus volatility in a quest for the high returns? High returns can ultimately reduce pension contributions and boost long-term corporate profitability, but only at a cost of short-term volatility.

    B. What is their "threshold of pain"? How much disappointment, in either nominal returns or diminished surplus, will they tolerate in this quest?

IV. How important is "maverick risk"?

    A. If our asset allocation strategies and policies differ sharply from the strategies and policies of other institutional investors, our results will differ sharply from our institutional compatriots.

        1. How tolerant will my "customer" be if this "relative performance risk" goes against us?

        2. How far can we safely stray from the pack?

funding ratios or of pension surplus. It is not just the long-term business risk of pursuing a strategy that moderates portfolio risk at a cost of increased long-term pension cost. More fundamentally, risk could be viewed as the likelihood of "doing something wrong."

There are widespread misunderstandings about asset allocation evident in its practice in portfolio management. These conceptions lead to errors which would be comical, were they not so terribly costly. Managers shuffle their asset mix and churn portfolios in an emotional response to the markets. Pension sponsors hire the recently successful manager, only to see that performance falter, then terminate the manager just before results turn. This pattern seems rooted in human nature.

Each of these errors can be quite expensive. They are costly for reasons that are also inherent in human nature. People want to do what is comfortable. In investments, what is comfortable is rarely profitable. Human nature conditions us to believe that what has been working will continue to work and that failure heralds failure.

It is *not comfortable* to employ a manager whose style has lead to recent disappointments. It is *uncomfortable* to take money from a manager who has been successful. It is *not comfortable* to move from the recently successful asset class into a market which has been dismal. It is *uncomfortable* to maintain one's own investment style in the face of disappointing results

But, to act in a comfortable fashion hurts results, *for the simple reason that it is comfortable. Uncomfortable* and out-of-favor investments are priced low by the markets, to reflect a demand for reward. It is the *uncomfortable* strategies that are priced to offer superior rewards. The investment world prices comfortable investments to reflect a *reduced* demand for reward. Those who invest conventionally, those who invest comfortably, reap correspondingly substandard rewards.

A Clash of Cultures

Part of the problem ironically stems from a fundamental dichotomy between the appropriate values and culture of a successful corporation and the appropriate values and culture of a successful investment manager. The successful business culture has long favored an "economic Darwinism," the survival of the fittest, depending on a pattern of aggressively rewarding success and ruthlessly punishing failure. In so doing, they grow and prosper by constantly weeding out those who cannot compete. The successful investment management operation ironically follows essentially the opposite pattern. Investments that have performed well should typically be viewed as candidates for liquidation, while investments that have performed poorly will more typically be candidates for purchase.

One of the most common errors in asset management is the assumption that what has been profitable will continue to work and what has performed badly will continue to fail. There are many manifestations of this. There are investment managers who, when their investment style is "out of synch" with the markets, hasten to correct it. There are the pension sponsors who are notorious for hiring an investment manager just after a spectacular 3 to 5 year run and just before the results collapse (then firing the manager just before the strategy rebounds). There are similar ad hoc "rear view mirror" shifts in the asset mix of a portfolio.

In 1984, Myra Drucker studied the performance results for the assorted markets used in the management of the Xerox pension fund. She tested two opposite strategies. In the first example, she shifted just 5% of plan assets from the most successful market over the last two years to the least successful market. Alternatively, she tested the more comfortable strategy of dropping 5% of assets from recent losers and moving them into the recent winners. The unfavorable approach surpassed the more comfortable one by an astounding 80 basis points per annum, *on the entire pension plan*, based on just a 5% shift in asset mix per annum! Few pension sponsors are comfortable in rebelling so openly against the comfortable strategy.

The Fiduciary Tightrope

Pension executives face an unusual tightrope walk. As fiduciaries, they know that performance will be improved by pursuing an often unconventional, often uncomfortable strategy. However, they also know that such strategies attract scrutiny and encourage second-guessing if the strategy goes awry.

In essence, the pension executive has a "customer." The customer is *not* the pension beneficiary; the customer is the group responsible for the pension officer's livelihood. This group consists of the top financial officers of the company, as well as the pension committee of the board of directors. Ironically, the most profitable strategies may exceed the risk tolerance of the customer. No one objects to risk or surprise when it is on the upside. However, any strategy that can generate favorable surprise can also generate unfavorable surprise. The unsophisticated or underinformed customer will be intolerant of adverse surprise.

One of the most valuable *responses* to this fiduciary tightrope is education. The educated board or CFO is less likely to be surprised. The educated board is more likely to tolerate contrarian disciplines. If the board is educated as to the importance of asset allocation, the nature of market movements, the peril of ad hoc shifts, and the impact that a few basis points can have on corporate wealth, that board will respond in an intelligent fashion to the choices that they face. The pension officer who fails to adequately educate the board does so at his or her peril.

So What Risk Matters?

Once we understand the client, we can better understand that *each* of these measures of risk matters. Portfolio volatility *does* matter. If the portfolio is volatile, it may suffer a drop in value which exceeds the risk tolerance of the customer. The mismatch between assets and liabilities (surplus volatility) *does* matter. A high volatility in surplus creates a risk that the surplus could disappear. This is a risk that most boards of directors would find distasteful at best.

The "maverick risk" associated with straying too far from the actions of our compatriots in the pension community is a risk which *should not* matter, but *does*. Like it or not, we are in a horserace. If our asset mix strategies lead to results that fall far behind those of other pension funds, our *judgment will be called into question*. This will happen *even if* portfolio volatility works to our benefit (i.e.—good returns), and surplus volatility works to our benefit (i.e.—an improved funding status). Maverick risk matters for an important business reason. If our pension fund offers inferior results relative to our competitors' funds, their cost of doing business will decline relative to ours. Therefore, in the short run, their competitive position will improve relative to ours.

Each element of risk is a two-edged sword. If we are willing to bear maverick risk, we create an opportunity to outstrip the results of our competitors' pensions. This improves our competitive position by lowering our costs for doing business. A willingness to bear surplus volatility may give us an opportunity to choose high-return asset categories that will boost our long-term returns and lower our long-term pension cost. The same holds true for portfolio volatility.

Each of these elements of risk has a direct bearing on the interplay between long-term and short-term business risk. Those who are willing to bear short-term risk, *and who bear that risk with intelligence*, will find that their long-term pension costs fall and their competitive position improves.

Many corporations behave as though a dollar made in the pension fund is worth less than a dollar made in incremental operating earnings. This is patently false. Indeed, it is worth much more than a dollar of operating income, due to the tax-sheltered nature of the portfolio. So, the quest for returns in pension assets should be as important to the corporation as the quest for operating profits. Most typically, it is not. The accounting and actuarial smoothing that makes pension volatility palatable also makes pension gains forgettable. But, the pension is *real money*, with a *direct* bearing on the long-term competitiveness, and even on the viability, of the corporation.

MANAGING THE POLICY MIX

The asset allocation decision cannot be avoided. If we choose not to make an asset allocation decision, the markets will do it for us. Only two rational positions exist in regard to asset allocation. Either market efficiency is assumed to preclude profitable shifts in asset mix, or else active shifts are assumed to add value. *Only a handful of investors behave in accordance with either view*! How many investors allow their asset mix to float with market impulses? This is a strategy that assures heavy exposure at market highs and low exposure at market lows. How many investors were selling bonds in 1980, 1981 and 1982, during a period of peak yields? How many were bailing out of stocks in late 1974 or immediately after the 1987 crash? *Such trades are hopeless attempts to escape from losses already realized.* A drifting mix and ad hoc *rearview mirror* shifts in asset mix are *not* consistent with either view of market efficiency.

For those who favor the view that markets are efficient, a simple process of rebalancing can reverse the damage done by a drifting mix. A simple mechanistic rebalancing strategy solves two problems at once. First, it means that the effort invested in choosing the appropriate long-term normal policy mix (see Exhibit 2) has not gone to waste. It does so by assuring that the normal mix is maintained in a rational manner. Second, it tends to enhance risk-adjusted performance. To be sure, it does not add value in every year, or even every market cycle. But, over the long run, it appears to add measurably to performance.

Systematic rebalancing merits consideration for many reasons:

- Simple rebalancing strategies do not require that the investor believe in "market timing."
- While an investment committee may tend to frown on active asset allocation strategies, it is far easier to persuade a committee to engage in simple rebalancing. This can be an effective way to steer an organization away from the ad hoc market timing that has plagued institutional performance for many years.

EXHIBIT 2:   WHAT IS OUR "POLICY" ASSET MIX?

I. How much exposure to illiquid or nontraditional assets is appropriate?

   A. Real estate.

   B. Venture capital.

   C. Non-U.S. stocks, bonds, real estate.

   D. Specialty categories:

      1. Limited partnerships.

      2. Energy partnerships.

      3. Timber leases.

II. How sensitive are we to funding ratio considerations?

   A. Avoiding the "four ills." Newly underfunded plans face:

      1. A new liability on the balance sheet.

      2. An earnings reduction due to a rise in pension expense.

      3. A cash flow cost due to sharply accelerated pension contributions.

      4. A cash flow cost due to increased PBGC insurance premiums.

   B. If well funded, how do we stay there?

      1. Reduce the volatility of funding ratios?

      2. Accept funding ratio volatility in the quest for high returns, thereby sustaining the funding ratios through strong returns?

      3. What is the risk tolerance of my "customer" (likely the pension committee of the board)? Will my customer permit a long investment horizon or not?

III. What mixture of stocks, bonds and illiquid assets offers the best long-term rewards, without exceeding our tolerance for risk?

- A simple rebalancing strategy is easy to implement and need not disrupt the existing managers.

- A rebalancing strategy will return control of the most important investment decision to the pension officer.

- A historical evaluation of returns indicates that a rebalancing strategy adds modest value. After compounding, this modest added-value can translate into significant incremental assets.

Each of these attributes of rebalancing is important and merits a detailed examination. Suppose we are skeptical about "market timing." Then, if a particular asset mix has been judged to best meet the long-term needs of the organization, a strategy that permits a drifting asset mix (or permits ad hoc shifts in mix) simply makes no sense. A skeptical view on market timing would rule out active shifts in the asset mix, based on a tactical asset allocation discipline. However, it would *also* rule out shifts in asset mix based on market drift or based on the whims of a pension committee. In short, a belief in the efficiency of markets would suggest a systematic strategy of rebalancing the asset mix to the target policy mix in response to any substantive market movement.

What Do We Do About the "Temptation to Tinker"?

One of the biggest challenges in managing institutional assets is the pressure to shift the asset mix in a reactive fashion after market movement. Such pressure inevitably is in the same direction as the recent market move. If a market has slumped, there is often pressure to slash our exposure. If a market has soared, there is a temptation to boost our exposure and to chase that market. These shifts in asset mix are often misguided efforts to prevent damage which has *already* occurred. One of the easiest ways to convince a committee *not* to engage in these ad hoc asset allocation shifts is to ask that committee to adopt a long-term policy asset mix and *stick with it* through systematic rebalancing. In other words, rebalancing can be an easy way to convince a pension committee not to disrupt a carefully crafted long-term policy for asset mix.

Can value be added by *ad hoc* changes in asset mix? Of course they can, but history suggests that most ad hoc approaches do not add value. In 1986, Brinson, Hood and Beebower looked at the 10-year results of 91 of the largest U.S. pension funds.[1] The results in Exhibit 3 demonstrate how the typical pension sponsor forfeited 66 basis points per annum through sloppy ad hoc shifts in asset mix. This is a huge difference; after 10 years, a $1 billion portfolio, growing at 10% per annum, would be worth $160

EXHIBIT 3: ANNUALIZED 10-YEAR RETURNS OF 91 LARGE U.S. PENSION PLANS, 1974-1983

Portfolio Total Returns	Average Return	Minimum Return	Maximum Return	Standard Deviation
Policy Mix	10.11%	9.47%	10.57%	0.22%
Policy Mix & Timing	9.44	7.25	10.34	0.52
Policy Mix & Selection	9.75	7.17	13.31	1.33
Actual Portfolio	9.01	5.85	13.40	1.43
Differential Active Returns				
Timing Only	(0.66)%	(2.68)%	0.25%	0.49%
Security Selection	(0.36)	(2.90)	3.60	1.36
Other	(0.07)	(1.17)	2.57	0.45
Total Active Return	(1.10)	(4.17)[*]	3.69[*]	1.45[*]

[*] Column not additive.

Source: Gary Brinson, Randall Hood, and Gilbert Beebower, "Determinants of Portfolio Returns," *Financial Analysts Journal* (July/August 1986).

million more without these ad hoc shifts! Historically, shifts in asset mix tended to be based on this kind of ad hoc decision process. In Brinson's study, the sponsor benefitting the most added just 25 basis points from timing, while the most unfortunate forfeited 268 basis points per annum over the span of a decade.

Although a disciplined framework for rebalancing has results that, like any other facet of investing, cannot be foreseen, clients who embrace it for the long run appear to prevail in the end. Investment committees tend to unite in order to avoid the unfamiliar and the uncomfortable. Persuading them to subscribe to a simple systematic process of rebalancing indicates that they will employ an extended portfolio management structure, thus offering the chance to adhere to the long-term investment policy consistently.

Let's assume that you want to maintain a policy mix of 60% stocks and 40% bonds. With the use of derivative securities (futures and options), trading costs will be minimal. It is likely that aggregate trading costs will be less than 10 basis points each way. No other trading vehicle can be traded so efficiently and economically. Indeed, it is impractical to consider ongoing active rebalancing without the use of derivative securities.

Over the 20 years from 1969-1988, simple rebalancing produced an average annual return of 9.25%, 16 basis points over the results for a drifting mix. Volatility has increased slightly: by rebalancing into the more variable-return assets in a declining market, the drifting mix stands to gain more than the portfolio.

Systematic rebalancing appears to enhance performance. But its most valuable attribute is likely the added control it gives over the asset mix of a portfolio. As is evident in Exhibit 4, it will not add value in every year or even work in every market cycle. But it does appear to work over time. Interestingly, this incremental return is earned with a turnover of less than 1% per month. Maintaining a policy mix on a consistent basis is supremely boring. Yet it makes sense. A belief in market timing is not necessary, it remains constant with the view that markets are efficient, and most important, can help to persuade the decision-makers to stick with the policy during unfavorable periods. Once they are committed to the idea, it is realistic to expect they will remain. Remember that the average pension fund in the Brinson study forfeited 66 basis points, not 16 basis points, due to untimely ad hoc decisions to stray from a long-term policy.

Too Much Cash!

A second element of policy mix that deserves attention is the large cash reserves maintained in most institutional portfolios. Idle cash reserves do not bear any resemblance to the liabilities served by the pension portfolio. In this context, cash can actually be a very high-risk investment. For example, substantial drops in interest rates reduce income on cash earnings, and we miss the bond and stock rallies that typify such markets. Similarly, if real wages rise, the returns on cash simply will not keep pace with real wage boosts that come from an increase in productivity.

Yet, while the risk implications of cash are subtle, the return implications are not. Over the past 60 years, the rate of return on cash equivalents has been less than that for stocks and bonds by roughly 6% and 1% per annum, respectively. Thus, cash equivalents will forfeit about 400 basis points annually on an average pension fund portfolio with a 60/40 stock/bond mix. For long-term investors (and pension funds should most assuredly be long-term investors), idle cash reserves produce low returns at a terrible cost in risk.

According to Federal Reserve data, some 11-15% of U.S. corporate pension holdings over the past decade have been cash equivalents. This

EXHIBIT 4: VALUE ADDED BY REBALANCING VS. A DRIFTING MIX

Results for Jan. 1969 to Dec. 1988	Drifting Mix Return	Rebalancing Return	Value Added
Average Return	9.09	9.25	0.16
Maximum Return	31.82	31.98	1.86
75th Percentile	20.12	20.59	0.52
Median	12.93	12.74	0.18
25th Percentile	1.78	2.98	0.01
Minimum Return	−14.59	−15.30	−2.17
Standard Dev.	12.80	12.96	0.86
Trans. Average	0.84% turnover/month		

	Summary of Annual Returns		
Year	Drifting Mix Return	Rebalancing Return	Value Added
1969	−6.86	−6.68	0.18
1970	7.24	7.36	0.12
1971	13.25	13.52	0.27
1972	13.40	13.41	0.01
1973	−13.17	−12.67	0.51
1974	−14.59	−15.30	−0.71
1975	22.23	24.10	1.86
1976	20.34	20.59	0.25
1977	−4.94	−4.92	0.02
1978	3.07	3.30	0.23
1979	10.01	9.57	−0.44
1980	17.91	15.74	−2.17
1981	−4.67	−4.53	0.14
1982	29.04	30.63	1.59
1983	13.83	12.81	−1.02
1984	9.12	9.77	0.65
1985	31.82	31.98	0.15
1986	20.12	20.64	0.52
1987	1.78	2.98	1.20
1988	12.93	12.74	−0.19

means that many pension funds may have forfeited as much as 60 basis points per annum just due to the cost of excessive idle cash reserves. Over the past decade, if U.S. pension funds were fully invested, then their aggregate value would be more than $100 billion greater than they are today. Endowment funds, similarly, continue to sustain large cash reserves, while still attending to commitments they hope will be lasting.

Most pension officers are not even aware of the magnitude of the problem. Few admit to cash reserves above 10%, yet Federal Reserve data suggests that the average is persistently higher than this. The problem is simple. Cash crops up in the portfolio in many spots. Equity managers maintain idle cash reserves, as do bond managers. Cash is contributed to the portfolio and lingers pending allocation to investment managers. The pension fund maintains a modest deliberate cash reserve in order to serve near-term pension benefits. It is the *combination* of these that represents such a huge number (and such a huge drain on investment results).

Yet, these idle cash reserves are necessary. Active stock and bond managers need cash to pounce on opportunities in the marketplace, cash is needed to serve near-term benefits. While the cash is needed in the portfolio, it doesn't have to *look like cash*. Futures and options can be used to *synthetically* create exposure to stocks or bonds, so that a portfolio can always be fully invested.

If we believe that the markets are efficient, then we cannot justify idle cash reserves; only a fully invested portfolio can be justified. Therefore, unless we choose to adopt a tactical framework for asset allocation, and unless that tactical framework suggests the use of cash in the face of vulnerable markets, then we have a *responsibility* to put idle cash reserves to work. Remarkably, this is more the exception than the norm, and at a terrible cost to the institutional investing community.

Exhibit 5 compares the rewards of disciplined rebalancing against the returns for a portfolio with a drifting asset mix and with 10% of the portfolio in idle cash reserves. As we already observed, cash reserves in the *average* pension portfolio are larger than this. In this example, a pension sponsor, with excess idle cash and with a drifting asset mix (*not even* suffering from the costly ad hoc shifts that so typify pension management), realizes returns some 33 basis points per year less than those provided by disciplined rebalancing. History suggests that the average sponsor actually does moderately worse than this.

Rebalancing and full investment of all idle cash reserves provides results that, over the long run, are measurably better than those achieved by the average pension sponsor. But, this is at the cost of somewhat more volatility. In 1974, rebalancing had us putting more and more money into a plunging equity market; worse yet, idle cash reserves performed far better than either stocks or bonds. So the combination of rebalancing and syn-

70   Arnott

EXHIBIT 5:   VALUE ADDED BY REBALANCING VS. A DRIFTING MIX WITH 10% CASH

Results for Jan. 1969 to Dec. 1988	Drifting Mix Return	Rebalancing Return	Value Added
Average Return	8.93	9.25	0.33
Maximum Return	29.49	31.98	3.92
75th Percentile	18.72	20.59	1.65
Median	12.33	12.74	0.40
25th Percentile	2.18	2.98	−0.92
Minimum Return	−12.12	−15.30	−3.18
Standard Dev.	11.51	12.96	1.75
Trans. Average	0.84% turnover/month		

Summary of Annual Returns

Year	Drifting Mix Return	Rebalancing Return	Value Added
1969	−5.55	−6.68	−1.13
1970	7.28	7.36	0.09
1971	12.33	13.52	1.19
1972	12.40	13.41	1.00
1973	−11.37	−12.67	−1.29
1974	−12.12	−15.30	−3.18
1975	20.18	24.10	3.92
1976	18.72	20.59	1.87
1977	−4.00	−4.92	−0.92
1978	3.44	3.30	−0.14
1979	9.96	9.57	−0.39
1980	17.22	15.74	−1.48
1981	−2.65	−4.53	−1.87
1982	27.17	30.63	3.46
1983	13.31	12.81	−0.50
1984	9.24	9.77	0.53
1985	29.49	31.98	2.49
1986	18.99	20.64	1.65
1987	2.18	2.98	0.80
1988	12.34	12.74	0.40

thetic investment of idle cash reserves hurt to the tune of 318 basis points. In 1975, the opposite occurred. Investment of idle cash reserves boosted returns wonderfully in a rising market. Rebalancing also had the portfolio move progressively out of stocks, which performed badly late in the year. The combination boosted returns by 392 basis points. In short, these disciplines make sense *in the long run*. They make sense because they provide an easy framework for enforcing a "buy low, sell high" asset mix into the overall portfolio process.

TACTICAL ASSET ALLOCATION: PANACEA OR PERIL?

Once the policy asset allocation has been prudently established, the sponsor can turn attention to the issue of active asset allocation. Here, once again, things are not as simple as they would appear on the surface, as we can see in Exhibit 6. Active asset allocation can include portfolio insurance and surplus insurance strategies, which reduce risk in plunging markets, but do so at a considerable cost. Alternatively, tactical asset allocation may be pursued. Tactical asset allocation seeks to opportunistically shift the asset mix in response to the changing patterns of reward available in the marketplace. Even tactical asset allocation is not a single, clearly defined strategy. There are many variations and nuances involved in the management of the tactical asset allocation decision.

Tactical asset allocation broadly refers to active strategies which seek to enhance performance by shifting the asset mix of a portfolio in response to objective measures of the reward available in various asset classes (e.g., stocks, bonds, cash, international assets, etc.). Notably, tactical asset allocation tends to refer to disciplined processes for evaluating the respective rates of return on various asset classes and establishing an asset allocation response intended to boost performance. The shared attributes of the various tactical asset allocation processes are several:

- They tend to be objectively driven, based on analytic tools, such as regression analysis or optimization. This is in direct contrast to the market timers of the 1960s and 1970s, who relied primarily on subjective judgment.
- They tend to be driven primarily by objective measures of *prospective value* among asset classes. We *know* the yield on cash; we *know* the yield-to-maturity on long-term bonds. The earnings yield (the reciprocal of the price/earnings ratio) on the stock market or a dividend discount rate of return on the stock market represent *objective and reasonable proxies* for long-term rewards available in stocks. In

EXHIBIT 6: DO WE PERMIT ACTIVE SHIFTS IN ASSET MIX?

I.   Should we employ tactical asset allocation to shift our mix in response to changing market conditions?

    A. What confidence do we have that tactical asset allocation will add value in the long run?

    B. What latitude should we permit in the asset mix and what discipline should be used to determine the appropriate mix within that range?

    C. What are the risks?

        1. What if the process stops working?

            a. A secular shift in the nature of capital markets behavior.

            b. A change in the equilibrium relationships between markets.

        2. What if we "lose our nerve"?

            a. The total return vs. relative returns paradigm.

            b. The episodic returns of tactical asset allocation.

II. Is my customer sufficiently risk averse that a mechanistic "insurance" approach makes sense?

    A. Should we insure nominal returns for a short span of time, such as a year?

    B. Should we insure pension funding status for a longer period, such as 5 years, using surplus insurance?

    C. What are the risks?

        1. Can we tolerate the long-term costs?

        2. Will the costs be in line with our expectations?

---

essence, the markets are *telling us* what rates of return are available.

•   These processes tend to rely upon a "return to equilibrium." If our objective models suggest that one market is offering greater return than normal relative to alternative markets, it is the *return to equilibrium* that is the most powerful source of profits. For example, if bond yields are 1% higher than normal relative to stock earnings yields, then there are two sources of return for this "disequilibrium." First, we garner 1% more return than we would normally expect from bonds relative to stocks. Secondly, if the markets return to their normal relationship, this will occur through either a 1% drop in bond yields (an impressive bond rally) or a 1% rise in stock market earnings yields (a mid-size decline in the stock market).

- Tactical asset allocation processes tend to buy after a market decline and sell after a market rally. As such, they are inherently contrarian. By objectively measuring which asset classes are offering the greatest prospective rewards, tactical asset allocation processes measure which asset classes are the most out-of-favor. These assets are priced to reflect the fact that they are neglected and the corresponding fact that the investment community demands a premium reward for an out of favor investment. Tactical asset allocation steers us into these unloved assets.

Tactical asset allocation processes cover a wide spectrum. Some are simple, objective comparisons of available rates of return. Others seek to enhance the timeliness of these value-driven decisions by incorporating macroeconomic measures, sentiment measures, volatility measures and even technical measures. We believe that the more sophisticated approaches are superior to pure value approaches. An undervalued stock can get more undervalued; by the same token, an undervalued asset class can grow more undervalued. The investor who buys an asset as soon as it becomes undervalued may earn attractive rewards. If an investor buys the same asset class when economic and sentiment conditions would favor a return to "fair" pricing, that investor will do even better.

The empirical evidence suggests that simple, quantitative measures of market attractiveness have impressive potential. Exhibit 7 suggests that the excess returns for stocks (stock market returns minus Treasury bill returns) are strongly correlated with several simple objective measures of the risk premium. The historic evidence, while it cannot assure future success, is compelling.

The Theoretic Underpinnings for Tactical Asset Allocation

If tactical asset allocation offers the hope of improved long-term returns without a corresponding increase in portfolio volatility, then it might seem

EXHIBIT 7: RISK PREMIUM AND MARKET PERFORMANCE

EX = Equity Risk Premium (Stock Market "Earnings Yield" – Bond Yield)
BX = Bond Maturity Premium (Bond Yield – Cash Yield)

	Subsequent Equity Return – Bond Return		Subsequent Equity Return – Cash Return		Subsequent Equity Return – Cash Return	
	One-Month	One-Year	One-Month	One-Year	One-Month	One-Year
Stage 1:						
EX	0.21[b]	0.47[b]	0.16[a]	0.24[a]	-0.08	-0.39[b]
	(3.1)	(7.4)	(2.3)	(3.4)	(-1.2)	(-6.0)
BX	0.14[a]	0.04	0.22[a]	0.20[a]	0.17[a]	0.34[b]
	(2.0)	(0.6)	(3.2)	(2.7)	(2.5)	(5.1)
Stage 1 Predication	0.25[b]	0.48[b]	0.27[b]	0.31[b]	0.20[b]	0.53[b]
	(3.6)	(7.4)	(3.9)	(4.4)	(2.8)	(8.5)

[a] Significant at 95% level.
[b] Significant at 99.9% level.

Source: Robert D. Arnott and James N. von Germeten, "Systematic Asset Allocation," *Financial Analysts Journal* (November/December 1983).

that we are violating finance theory. After all, we have long been taught that there is "no such thing as a free lunch!" The answer to this puzzle is found in utility theory.

As a market rises, so too does the "wealth" in a portfolio. Unfortunately, it is easy to forget that this is accompanied by a drop in *prospective subsequent* returns (Exhibit 8a). However, different institutional investors will exhibit different responses to changes in wealth. The appropriate asset allocation response to recent market moves differs for each of these investors:

- Exhibit 8b shows that some investors ("A") are blissfully unaffected by shifts in wealth. In other words, their tolerance for risk does not change with recent investment performance. As they become wealthier, their tolerance for investment risk is largely unchanged. These are the long-term investors. The long-term investors who have a tolerance for risk that is relatively independent of recent results will be inclined to pounce on the opportunities offered by a declining market (see Exhibit 8c). These sponsors will be naturally drawn towards tactical asset allocation. The improved return prospects that come with a newly fallen market increase the attractiveness of that market. In the absence of a change in risk tolerance, the investor should buy.

- Other investors ("B") will be somewhat sensitive to recent changes in wealth. As their wealth rises, their tolerance for prospective investment risk also rises slightly. The sponsors with slight sensitivity to market movements will find that a market drop reduces their tolerance for risk, but only slightly. For these investors, the newly improved return prospects for equities are just large enough to justify a return to a static mix. These are the "natural" candidates for a simple rebalancing process.

- Yet another class of investors ("C") shows somewhat more sensitivity to recent market behavior. Their aversion to investment risk rises sharply as the wealth of the portfolio declines. The "optimal" strategy for these risk-sensitive sponsors in category "C" would be to permit their asset mix to drift with the movements of the market. As the market falls, so to does their tolerance for risk. However, as the market falls, so too does their exposure to risky markets. So, these investors may find their tolerance for risk and their exposure to risk falling in parallel, so no trades are needed. These investors would permit their mix to drift with the whims of the market.

EXHIBIT 8: RISK TOLERANCE & RETURN PROSPECTS—ASSET ALLOCATION RESPONSE

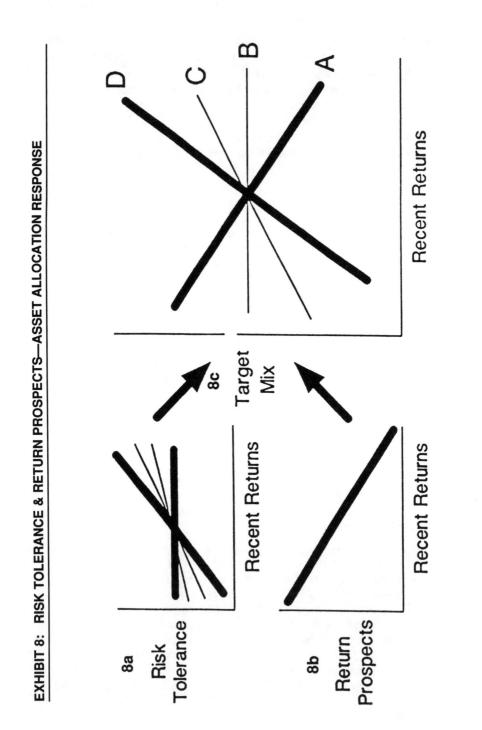

- Lastly, we have the investors ("D") who react strongly to recent behavior, i.e., if the market rises, their tolerance for risk soars. Investors with high sensitivity to recent market moves are natural candidates for insurance strategies. If the market declines, their tolerance for risk plunges. As a result, a market decline triggers a desire to bail out of the falling market.

Therefore, we have natural candidates for portfolio insurance or surplus insurance, for a drifting asset mix, for simple rebalancing to a static mix, and for tactical asset allocation. Tactical asset allocation is *not right for everyone*, for the simple reason that an improvement in long-term returns does not necessarily mean an improvement in "utility," or in the satisfaction of the natural human desires for *both* return and comfort. Tactical asset allocation historically has improved returns without increasing risk. Theoretically it can continue to do so. But it *does not* offer the long-sought "free lunch." It succeeds because total return and investor utility are not one and the same thing. When their wealth is declining, most investors seek the comfort of lower risk. Tactical asset allocation may enhance long-term returns without increasing objective measures of risk, but at a cost of lower comfort, hence lower utility, for many investors.

This recent work by Sharpe is a real addition to our understanding of asset allocation.[2] It provides an equilibrium framework, in which tactical asset allocation can *and should* enhance returns without increasing portfolio risk. This improvement in returns, without a corresponding increase in risk, can only hold true if tactical asset allocation is an uncomfortable strategy that certain investors will find unacceptable. We already know this to be true. Few investors were rushing to buy bonds during the peak yields of 1980, 1981 or 1982. Still fewer were buying stocks in late 1974 or immediately after the market crashed in 1987.

What Are the Risks in Tactical Asset Allocation?

The risks for tactical asset allocation can be broken into two categories. The first is the risk that the discipline may stop working. The second is the risk that a temporary period of disappointment may cause us to "lose our nerve."

Tactical asset allocation *can* stop working if our objective measures of prospective return are ill-conceived. For example, an equity risk premium, which is based on the difference between the earnings yield on the stock market and the yield available in bonds, may have the seeds of danger. If earnings soar, the earnings yield can rise, *even as the market is rising.* A secular shift in the earnings power of the market, in the relative risk of stocks and bonds, or of the normal tolerance for stock or bond risk in the investment community can each lead to an extended "dry spell."

These secular shifts in the nature of capital markets behavior are rare. It has often been said that the five most costly words in the investment world are, "Things are different this time." That statement is uttered far more often than it is true.

A more common risk in tactical asset allocation is that the equilibrium relationship between markets can change. In the 1950s, it was normal for equities to be priced at a *dividend* yield in excess of bond yields. This was to compensate the stock market investors for the fear that the Great Depression could recur. The gap between earnings yields and bond yields were still larger. As the fear of a renewed depression dissipated, so too did the *normal* relationship between stock earnings yields and bond yields.

A tactical asset allocation process, if it is predicated on a comparison of current market conditions with "long-term" normal relationships, runs the risk of being out of step for an extended period of time. For example, the 20-year *average* gap between the earnings yield of the stock market and long-term bond yields will not change quickly in response to a shift in the equilibrium relationships.

On the other hand, strategies that seek to respond more rapidly to changes in equilibrium relationships may be vulnerable to "whipsaw." If the equity risk premium soars, as it did in 1987 with the stock market crash, we run the risk of mistaking the jump in risk premium for a shift in the *equilibrium* risk premium. If we do that, we may buy stocks in response to the renewed opportunity, but may reverse those positions sooner (as many tactical asset allocation practitioners did in 1988 and 1989) as the markets return to their long-term normal relationships. History suggests that a "whipsaw" from seeking to adapt to a changing world is less common than the risk of falling out of step for a long period of time if the process is not responsive to changes in equilibrium relationships. Nonetheless, it is a risk that hurt many tactical asset allocation managers in 1989.

The more dangerous risk in tactical asset allocation may be the risk that we "lose our nerve." This risk is inherent in the contrarian nature of the process. Tactical asset allocation sells as the market rises. As a result, it is almost inevitably out of step for at least the final weeks or months of a bull market. The opposite happens at the end of a bear market. This makes the strategy profoundly uncomfortable at market turning points.

Tactical asset allocation objectively measures prospective rates of return and encourages purchase of the out-of-favor market. That market is priced to offer superior returns *because* it is out of favor, *because* it is profoundly uncomfortable. As a result, the temptation will always exist, particularly at market turning points, to "second guess" the tactical asset allocation process.

The temptation to give up on tactical asset allocation will be greatest as we approach market turning points. This holds true for any contrarian strategy, but perhaps more so for tactical asset allocation than most. One of the problems with tactical asset allocation is that its "episodic returns" will challenge our patience. Common sense and history tell us that it is very difficult to outpace a rising market with asset mix shifts.

If an equity manager is hired, we might reasonably hope that our stocks will fall less than a falling market, while, in a rising market, our stocks will rise more than the market. This pattern of reward might be termed an "index plus alpha" strategy. It is tempting to view any active strategy in this same context. But tactical asset allocation *cannot* outpace a strong market, and it *cannot* underperform a falling market.

Tactical asset allocation is best viewed as a *total return* strategy. It is tempting to view it as an "index plus alpha" strategy, but its performance is very different. If tactical asset allocation keeps pace with 2 out of every 3 rising markets, and keeps the institutional investor out of a like proportion of falling markets, then value will be added in the context of reduced risk.

The returns for tactical asset allocation are episodic. This will cause us to question whether the merits of the discipline have disappeared. We will face this question precisely as market turning points approach and when the model has been out of step for some period of time. Such is the nature of a contrarian process. Contrarian disciplines are uncomfortable, and so raise doubt when they fall out of step.

This is best illustrated in the series of diagrams shown in Exhibit 9. Here, we see the *simulated* performance of a simple stock/bond trading rule. This might be considered to be a crude form of tactical asset allocation. In this strategy, we buy stocks any time the stock market risk premium relative to bonds (earnings yield minus bond yield) has risen by more than 2% in the past year. We switch to bonds any time the risk premium has fallen by a like amount in the past year. This very crude tactical asset allocation discipline leads to surprisingly good results, as shown in Exhibit 9a. However, the rolling 12-month performance relative to a 100% stock portfolio is erratic, as shown in Exhibit 9b.

As noted previously, there are seeds of risk in tactical asset allocation. If equilibrium relationships change profoundly, if the fundamental pricing mechanism in the capital markets changes, then tactical asset allocation can underperform for extended periods of time. However, it is precisely at market turning points that we will be tempted to ask whether the process has "broken down." Such questions were asked in the third quarter of 1987, when tactical asset allocation practitioners around the country had un-

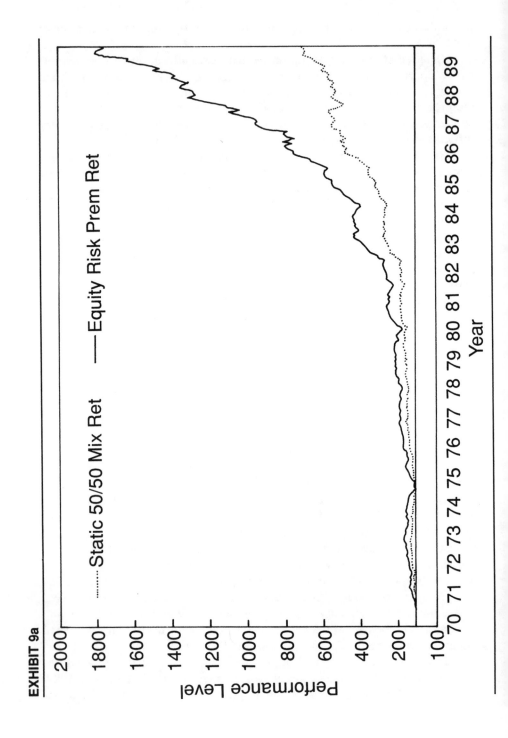

Static 50/50 Mix Ret ⋯⋯⋯⋯   Equity Risk Prem Ret ——

Performance Level

70 71 72 73 74 75 76 77 78 79 80 81 82 83 84 85 86 87 88 89

Year

EXHIBIT 9b

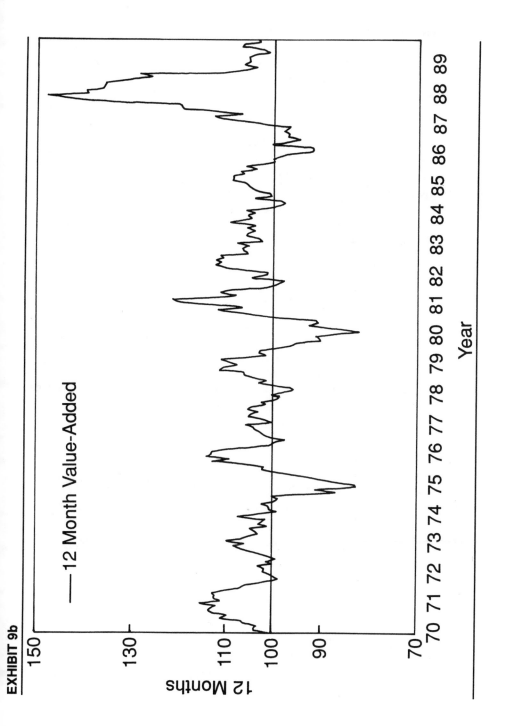

12 Months

150

130

110

100

90

70

——12 Month Value-Added

70 71 72 73 74 75 76 77 78 79 80 81 82 83 84 85 86 87 88 89

Year

derperformed by often large margins, and such questions recurred in late 1989 for the same reason.

It is worth repeating: tactical asset allocation is not for everyone. Long-term investors who wish to participate in a total return strategy may find the process occasionally uncomfortable but rewarding in the long run. Sharpe has demonstrated that the historic success of tactical asset allocation is *not* at odds with finance theory. However, pension officers and, more importantly, boards of directors who are not comfortable with large residual risk (relative to a static asset mix) or who are overly inclined to focus on recent performance will find themselves abandoning tactical asset allocation (and other contrarian disciplines) at inopportune times. Such investors would be well-served to adopt a persistent *rebalancing* strategy in order to avoid the risk of *forfeiting* value through inopportune shifts in asset allocation strategy.

INSURANCE STRATEGIES

For the few institutional investors without the nerve to "stay the course" on something as practical as rebalancing, insurance may make sense. Here, the key questions are those summarized in Exhibit 1 and reviewed earlier in the chapter, such as: *What risk matters?* How averse is the pension committee to declining markets? Will they tolerate nominal losses? How averse are they to funding shortfall? If liabilities rise faster than assets, will they exhibit patience? How much can our fund differ from the "average fund" without bearing a risk of an unacceptable shortfall relative to the competition?

All of these questions are important. The beauty of a rebalancing process is that it provides a mechanism for restraining the natural, but terribly costly, impulse to bail out after disappointment or to chase a rising market. If the board is insufficiently disciplined, and cannot tolerate even that risk, then an insurance strategy may make sense. Several points should be noted:

1. An insurance strategy carries a cost. Just as all insurance companies charge a fee, the capital markets exact a cost (and a fair cost) for synthetic insurance strategies designed to prevent unacceptable consequences. This could arguably reduce long-term returns by 1-3% per annum.

2. In addition to the implicit cost of an insurance strategy, there is also an explicit trading cost, which must be paid to effect the

strategy. This could arguably cut long-term returns 1% *in addition to* the cost of the insurance policy.

3. These strategies yield a *median* return which is dramatically lower than unprotected strategies. As an offset to protecting against unacceptable negative returns, the returns in rising markets can be clobbered, to the tune of 4-8% per annum.

For certain institutional investors, these consequences are quite acceptable. Suppose that an insurance strategy is deemed a prerequisite for significant equity market exposure. Then the net consequence may be improved long-term results. Suppose the board has shown a remarkable aptitude for pulling the plug after market declines and then chasing rising markets. Then insurance may be a way to dissuade (or at least moderate) these counterproductive moves. Better still, the "floor" (the minimum nominal return or minimum funding ratio, which forms the basis for the "insurance policy") can be adjusted from time to time. After a market decline, it might be lowered to permit reinvestment back into the market. Ironically, this can provide an ad hoc solution to the problem of ad hoc asset allocation shifts.

What Are the Risks in Insurance?

Insurance strategies are not without their own special set of risks. Let us first suppose that portfolio insurance and surplus insurance can be effected with negligible trading costs. If this is true, then we must still pay the "insurance premium." Just as an insurance company charges its customer a fee for bearing the risk of loss, so too do these strategies. For the very conservative customer wishing to eliminate the risk of loss in any calendar year, the cost may be high. For such investors, the long-term returns on the portfolio might be penalized by 2% to prevent that risk, as median returns fall 6-8%. A 2% cost, assessed against total portfolio value each year, is huge! The cost of funding a pension plan with 2% lower returns can, for many companies, be 50 to 100% higher as a result! Even a moderate insurance strategy, designed to penalize long-term returns by just 50 to 100 basis points, can substantially raise the cost of funding pension benefits over a long period of time.

Even so, these insurance strategies are useful for some investors. Notably, if the board of directors is intolerant of risk, and if the adoption of an insurance strategy can be used as a basis for boosting the overall aggressiveness of the fund, then it may have merit for some institutions. Such strategies must be adopted with a full recognition that the cost of insurance (whether portfolio insurance or surplus insurance) is high. Mean and median returns are lower than the returns for a more conventional investment strategy. The median return is actually lower than that of an immunized portfolio, and can be 4-8% below the median returns for a more conventional approach.

A second risk in insurance strategies is the implementation risk. Can it be implemented with negligible trading costs? The answer is probably "no." The reason for this is that insurance strategies buy after a market rise and sell after a market rally. When the market is rising, it is difficult to buy without further moving the market. If the market is plunging, it is difficult to sell without further depressing the market. Trading costs *are not negligible*, even if they are effected through the use of futures and options. The academics who have designed portfolio insurance (and now surplus insurance) dismiss some critical variables. The markets *do not* provide endless liquidity. Trading costs with a "trend-following" strategy, such as portfolio insurance, *are not* inconsequential. At times, such as the crash of 1987, the other side of the trade *may not even be available.*

That said, surplus insurance is a profoundly appealing product. It "promises" to prevent funding ratio shortfalls, while permitting participation in rallying stock markets. It accomplishes this objective at a modest *projected* cost. October 1987 showed us that the cost of effecting insurance strategies can be several hundred basis points greater than expected. However, in more normal markets, the cost can be manageable. Nonetheless, it is a cost which will be reflected in pension contributions year after year after year.

With recent regulatory and accounting changes, which heighten corporate sensitivity to funding ratios, it is likely that surplus insurance will become increasingly popular. On balance, the cost of surplus insurance is likely to exceed that estimated by its vendors, but not dramatically. Even though its intuitive appeal makes it almost certain to gain acceptance in the marketplace, it is not the right vehicle for most pension investors. Even a modest reduction in performance, compounded over many years, boosts the cost of funding a pension fund tremendously. Those who have disciplined boards, with the wisdom to look to the long-term, will find the costs associated with these strategies to be too large relative to the comfort that the strategy affords.

CONCLUSION

One of the most dangerous, and regrettably common, misconceptions about asset allocation is that the asset mix decision is a single decision. Indeed, it is not. The appropriate asset mix for *today* is dependent not only on market opportunities today, but also on our strategies for the long-term.

The first critical step is the assessment of the appropriate *policy* for the asset mix. What mix of stocks, bonds, cash, international assets, and illiquid assets, such as real estate or venture capital, represents the best balance between the desire for return and the desire for containment of risk?

Once this decision has been made, using whatever tools and wisdom can be brought to the decision process, we can turn our attention to active management of the asset mix. Of the two principal categories of active asset allocation, tactical asset allocation and dynamic strategies such as portfolio insurance, the objectives are different, as are the risks. One risk common to both forms of active asset allocation is the risk of having results far afield from the results of the average sponsor. As always, there is symmetry to risk. A risk of underperforming due to an inappropriate active mix carries with it the corresponding opportunity to outperform our competitors. Indeed, without some kind of disciplined framework for asset allocation, it becomes very difficult to outperform our competitors. Why is this important? *If* we can have results for the total pension fund that are better than the competitors in our industry, then pension costs will drop, pension contributions will drop, corporate profitability will improve, and competitive positioning (along with the ability to price products competitively) will improve.

One often neglected reality is that a dollar made in the pension fund is worth at least a dollar of operating earnings. Arguably, it may be worth more because of the tax-sheltered nature of the accumulation of assets. All too often, corporations act as if this is not so. The pension officer's role is a staff function, frequently with little promotion opportunity. The irony is all too clear. Pension funds often have assets approaching or even exceeding corporate net worth. As a result, a 100 basis point improvement in the return on plan assets can be worth as much as a 100 basis point improvement in corporate return on equity.

There is no element of the investment decision process that has a greater impact on long-term aggregate plan results than the policy asset mix decision. This decision *must* be made with all of the skill and wisdom that we can draw upon. History suggests that active asset allocation may offer opportunities to add measurably to portfolio returns. To do so, the active shifts in mix *must* be handled in a contrarian, hence uncomfortable, fashion.

Mechanistic insurance strategies for protecting against adverse markets are generally *not* devised to enhance returns. Indeed, as with an insurance policy, they exact a relatively predictable cost. The good thing about these kinds of strategies is that this cost can be softened by a more aggressive *normal* exposure to the high-return markets, such as equities. However, such strategies should not be undertaken without a *careful* evaluation of the long-term consequences of the insurance cost. Just as an individual or corporation may choose to self-insure, and thereby reduce costs, so too a pension plan can follow such a policy. The long-term costs of forfeiting just 100 basis points in total return can be startling.

For each element of the asset mix decision, there is no single "right" answer. Some investors should bear the risk of an aggressive asset mix policy. Others may jeopardize the competitive position of the corporation by doing so. Some organizations, particularly those with a willingness to focus on the long-term, may be in a position to seek enhanced returns through active management of the asset mix. Others may have a board of directors so sufficiently risk averse that costly portfolio insurance strategies are necessary. The intent of this chapter has *not* been to provide answers, but to provide a roadmap that may be useful for the pension sponsor to find their own answers.

NOTES

[1] Gary Brinson, Randall Hood, and Gilbert Beebower, "Determinants of Portfolio Returns," *Financial Analysts Journal* (July/August 1986).

[2] William Sharpe, "Investor Wealth Measures and Expected Return," *Quantifying the Market Risk Premium*, ICFA (September, 1989).

CHAPTER 5

Organizing Internal Asset Management for the 1990s

GARRY M. ALLEN, CFA
DIRECTOR OF INTERNAL ASSET MANAGEMENT
VIRGINIA RETIREMENT SYSTEM

MARK T. FINN
PRESIDENT
DELTA FINANCIAL, INC., AND
BOARD OF TRUSTEES, VIRGINIA RETIREMENT SYSTEM

T. DANIEL COGGIN, Ph.D.
DIRECTOR OF RESEARCH
VIRGINIA RETIREMENT SYSTEM

Much has been written about the characteristics of "successful" organizations. Indeed, entire college courses and even graduate degrees are offered in organizational behavior, organizational theory, and management. This chapter has a much more specific goal. In this chapter we provide a brief outline of an organizational structure for internal investment management in the 1990s. By *internal investment management*, we mean in-house investment units or groups charged with the task of investing all or part of the pension or investment fund of a corporation, governmental unit or foundation. We will refer to the sponsoring agent as the "sponsor" and to the investment fund as the "plan." To be sure, a number of important articles have been written on successful management of investment organiza-

We thank Dr. Ronald R. Sims at the College of William and Mary for his encouragement and helpful comments on this chapter.

tions. Recently, an entire monograph sponsored by the Institute of Chartered Financial Analysts was devoted to the subject.[1] This chapter seeks to contribute to this important literature by presenting what we believe is an innovative and flexible model of investment organizational structure.

There are two components of *any* organization (successful or unsuccessful): people (human resources) and structure. Both are critical to the successful organization. We readily agree that the human resource component is worthy of intense focus and study by the investment organization and its students. We dare say all investment organizations could benefit from more attention to such people-related activities as psychological testing, and employee training and development (e.g., sensitivity training, motivational training, etc.). However, that is not the focus of this chapter. This chapter will focus on the second component, the *structure* of the organization. We present an outline of an investment organizational structure that will allow the investment organization to deal with the challenges to successful internal investment management we foresee for the 1990s (and beyond).

The remainder of our chapter is divided into three major sections. The next section discusses the challenges to internal investment management in the 1990s. We follow with our model of an organizational structure to meet these challenges. The final section summarizes our presentation. While we focus here on internal equity management, our proposed model is applicable to asset management in general.

CHALLENGES TO INVESTMENT MANAGEMENT IN THE 1990s

It should be no surprise that the challenges to successful investment management in the 1990s are essentially the same as those in the 1970s, the 1960s, or any other period. The perennial challenges to successful investment management include: investment performance, maintaining a consistent investment process, creativity, organizational turnover and employee compensation.

Investment performance was placed first on the list of challenges for a specific reason. The cold hard fact of the investment profession is that, in the final analysis, performance is the most important factor. In the case of the internal asset manager, the specific investment objective is supplied by the plan sponsor. Whether the investment objective is to outperform the S&P 500 Stock Index (S&P 500) or some "normal portfolio,"[2] it must eventually be achieved if the investment management effort is to be deemed successful. An investment industry rule-of-thumb is three-to-five years and an outside manager is "up or out." While some sponsors have an even shorter time horizon, *very few* have a longer time horizon.

There is increasing evidence that the majority of active equity managers do not outperform the stock market (defined as the S&P 500).[3] Some have viewed this as evidence that active equity management is a "losers game" and that it is therefore fruitless (and even hypocritical) to attempt it. The organizational model presented here does *not* make such an assumption. In fact, our model is *neutral* on the issue. It can accommodate *both* active and passive investment styles. Our model does, however, make some assumptions about *human judgment*.

The noted investment consultant Richard Ennis was recently quoted as saying:

> Many of the best money managers are almost completely intuitive. You can use a computer to price certain standard instruments like options. But your best chance of beating the market by a meaningful margin is with *people of uncommon ability who observe subtleties, make judgments and weigh thousands of facts and observations in a powerful, analytical and intuitive way* (emphasis added).[4]

Mr. Ennis is quite confident of this opinion. Unfortunately, it is not supported by the evidence on the issue. Studies of human judgment consistently show that it is prone to *errors* and *biases* resulting from the selected overuse of information of limited and/or questionable validity.[5] Other studies consistently show that well-formulated statistical models outperform even trained professionals in making judgments.[6]

Recent studies have shown that a majority of investment managers do not use quantitative methods to value common stocks. A survey reported in *Pensions & Investment Age* (November 10, 1986) reported that only 8% of respondents use quantitative methods to manage stocks; and a survey conducted by Arthur D. Little, Inc. in March 1987 reported that only 30% of respondents indicated intensive use of quantitative methods in their overall money management effort. This small minority of quantitative managers spans a continuum from using analysts to provide input to quantitative models to using *no* analysts at all, relying instead on computers and "artificial intelligence" to process information, select and trade stocks.[7] Hence, 20 years after the "quantitative revolution" of the late 1960s, most money managers apparently continue to rely on conventional (i.e., nonquantitative) methods of investment management. In the case of stocks, this generally means that financial analysts perform fundamental security analysis and make recommendations to portfolio managers about which stocks to buy and sell. A relatively large *subjective component* is then applied to the final investment decision. No doubt, this process has been successful for *some* investment managers. However, it is our opinion that an increasing number of investment organizations will be forced by the pressure of underperformance to explore the use of quantitative investment models and techniques.

Maintaining a consistent investment process is high on the list of characteristics of successful investment organizations. Any investment management consultant will verify that one of the first things to look for in evaluating an investment organization is a consistent and well-defined investment process. *Creativity* is also crucial. The investment organization's ability to adapt to the ever changing market environment with new and innovative ideas is a major challenge in the 1990s. *Organizational turnover* is another variable high on the management consultant's list. The bane of sponsors is the all-too-frequent "here today, gone tomorrow" nature of investment management professionals. Last but not least, *employee compensation* is a key challenge to investment management. The ability to effectively link compensation to organizational goals and productivity is often lacking in investment organizations. The problem is especially critical in organizations characterized by the "star system." One or two key investment "stars" command high salaries while the "supporting cast" is significantly underpaid on a relative basis. Even so, the stars often move to another firm, tempted by an even higher salary.

The next section outlines an organizational structure that addresses each of these challenges. Our proposed structure is characterized by a quantitative, model-driven approach to investment management. In view of the facts and challenges listed above, we view our model as the "shape of things to come" in the ongoing evolution of investment organizational structure.

THE VALUE CHAIN ORGANIZATIONAL STRUCTURE

In the typical investment group, too little time is spent thinking about organizational structure. Most investment units are structured along the lines of the traditional, hierarchical pyramid organization model. Historically, the traditional pyramid is best applied in mechanistic, hierarchical, or bureaucratic organizations. In an established bureaucracy, with clear rules and operating procedures and chains of command, the static pyramid structure has a natural environment. Pyramids have survived because they are frequently applied in situations characterized by limited competition, simple environments, and predictable relationships. However, in the most *competitive* arenas of business enterprise (such as the investment arena), the traditional pyramid structure is *not* withstanding the test of time. The pyramid is today being challenged by such well-known management consultants as Ken Blanchard, who believes the pyramid should be turned upside down, with the customer (in our case, the sponsor) as the focal point of attention.[8] Peters and Waterman's now classic book, *In Search of Excellence* (1982), also emphasizes this basic point.

The investment world is characterized by high levels of uncertainty, complexity and nonroutine technologies. It lacks those static and predictable relationships found in traditional pyramid organizations. A wealth of real-time information must be effectively managed and quickly turned into usable investment knowledge. Investment units must, therefore, have a fluid organizational structure. That is, a form that is adaptive, flexible, and capable of managing information with a fast response time. More specifically, a structure that can quickly turn opportunity into knowledge, knowledge into action, and action into performance for the plan.

While the traditional pyramid allows a hierarchy of responsibility, talent, or even ego, rarely has it addressed the issues of strategy and competitive advantage. Our challenge is to apply creativity at the *organizational structure* level, not just at the investment process or product level. There is a revolution going on in the thought process of organizational design. The organization that sits back and holds on to mechanistic and bureaucratic form and symbolism will not survive in the investment arena.We believe that successful investment groups are already integrating form and function, and that pyramids will not be the structure of choice in the 1990s and beyond.

One of the basic principles of business policy is that strategy determines structure. At the core of strategic thinking is the pursuit of *competitive advantage*. We believe that competitive advantage can be built into organizational structure, just as competitive advantage has been built into the product level. There exists a tremendous gap between traditional organizational structures that resemble pyramids and the functioning of the organization as defined through job descriptions. In reality, the two can be linked in a manner that creates *sustainable* competitive advantage.

The Value Chain

The value chain concepts set forth by Michael E. Porter in his book on competitive business strategy[9] can be applied to organizational structure in ways that directly link human resource management with the economic value of the firm. The result is a *functional* organization structure for investment management; a structure that flattens the pyramid and aligns form, function, responsibility, and accountability into a single dimension.

That is, a structure that strikes at the heart of the key investment challenges of today and the future: performance, process, creativity, people, and compensation. Too often today's organizational structures pull apart critical success factors and never successfully reconnect them into a cohesive organization with competitive advantage. We believe the following value chain organizational structure provides a platform for managing a fluid investment organization.

The organizational premises behind the value chain structure are:

1. *Level the organizational structure.* Flatten the traditional pyramid into a form that symbolizes the fluid and dynamic character of investment management. A form that is dynamic, responsive and solution-driven fosters creativity and is results-oriented. Expect talented individuals to add value every day. Quantify and link performance with responsibility and accountability. The stock market chalks up gains and losses every day; the people that invest in it should know if their investment effort helped or hurt the plan in the short-run. The sponsor will know quickly enough! While short-run investment performance can be (and often is) *overemphasized*, reasonable attention to timely achievement of specified goals is highly desirable.

2. *Rebuild the structure around functional components.* At the conceptual level, the investment unit performs research & development, production, and monitoring. Our proposed structure should provide answers to such key questions and issues as: *Should* we build a new investment model? (Research Team); *Can* we build the model? (Systems Development and Data Management); *Build* the model (Production Systems Group); *Execute* the model (Trading); and *Monitor* the model (Investment Administration). The structure presented here provides *feedback loops* between the operating components so that no subunit is working in isolation, and the appropriate interchanges occur between them. There is a principle of continuous interdependence in place, while clear operating boundaries define lines of accountability. Our proposed structure is diagrammed in Exhibit 1.

   In our structure, the essential functions are carried out by organizational subunits called *teams*:

EXHIBIT 1: INVESTMENT ORGANIZATIONAL STRUCTURE

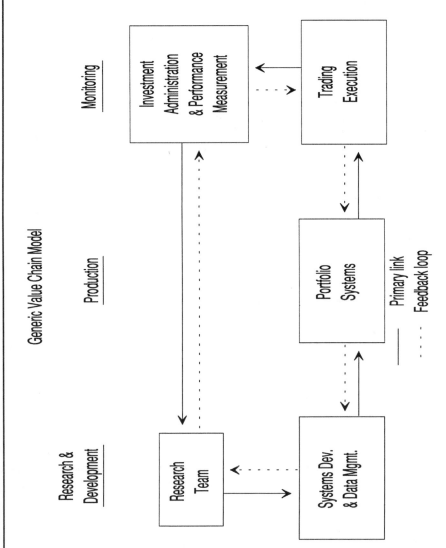

Generic Value Chain Model

Component	Function
Research Team	Ideas & Issues
Systems Development & Data Mgmt.	Database & Data Mgmt.
Portfolio Systems Team	Model-Building
Trading	Execution
Investment Administration & Performance Measurement	Monitor Process & Results

The Research Team is the primary forum for brainstorming, idea generation, and debating issues. The discussion of why a model should be built or enhanced occurs at this level. Once a decision is made to move forward with a model, the Systems Development & Data Management (SDDM) team obtains the necessary building blocks of data needed to construct the model. The SDDM team must turn the critical data over to the Portfolio Systems Team (PST) in a format readily usable by quantitative model builders. That is, the data should be structured and formatted by SDDM into the research format used by the PST. For example, SDDM would convert financial data (from COMPUSTAT) and expectational data (from IBES) into a relational database such as INGRES, which is them used by the PST.

The PST performs the model-building and quantitative task. This team transforms concepts into a real-world, operational investment model. Backtesting is performed to increase confidence in the model. Once built and tested, the model is launched via trading *execution*, and closely *monitored* by Investment Administration. The teams have been aligned in a value chain such that the previous tasks must be completed before the next group can add its value. Any weaknesses in the links will surface quickly via the monitoring and control process, and feedback.

3. *Redefine team portfolio management.* Team portfolio management is not the traditional investment management-by-committee process. In many cases, the management-by-committee approach has failed due to "groupthink" or the consensus instinct to "follow the herd."[10]

    An integral part of our team management structure is the concept of "designated experts." These designated experts handle assigned issues, areas of responsibility, and specific models. They act as *team leaders* of groups assigned to address specific topics and problems. The designated expert has ultimate responsibility for success or failure in the assigned area. This approach develops great depth and cross-training as different "special teams take the field" for different sets of challenges.

Benefits to the Value Chain Organizational Structure

The following set of benefits can be directly attributed to using the value chain investment organizational structure:

1. *Embeds competitive advantage into the core of the investment management structure.* When form, functionality, and accountability are creatively linked into a single investment system encompassing structure and process, the investment unit is operating at its maximum capacity for response to opportunity and crisis. To illustrate the benefits to timely analysis and appropriate response, some investment groups correctly assessed the 508-point DJIA plunge to 1738 on October 19, 1987 as an opportunity rather than a crash. With that assessment, those groups began buying stocks the following week and rejoicing as the DJIA recovered and rose to 2810 on January 2, 1990. Crisis and opportunity always stand side-by-side, framed by uncertainty and disguised with complexity. The highest reward will go to the investment unit that can quickly and correctly unravel events, isolate causal factors, and position itself accordingly. An organization can respond only as quickly as its structure will allow it to respond.

2. *Provides a model for engineered solutions to investment problems.* The investment world is evolving toward "structured" asset management. We believe that the structured investment process will gradually supplant the *ad hoc* approaches of the past. Engineered solutions to investment management involve decision rules based upon quantitative investment models. Engineered solutions serve to raise the information content of the investment processes to the highest level attainable. An engineered solution may stand alone or form the basis for an investment process which allows more human intervention.

3. *Problems will surface more quickly, enabling management to be proactive rather than reactive.* It would be enough if our structure only satisfied needs derived from investment-related demands. However, the structure is equally adept at flushing out problem situations in the *human resource* management area. The flattened organizational structure allows attitudes and egos not

conducive to team-building to surface and become visible more quickly than traditional pyramid structures. Management can then move to resolve issues before they become more serious.

4. *Insulates the investment unit from damaging turnover of key personnel with the team approach.* Professional turnover is a fact of life in the world of investment management. The investment unit requires stability of the investment process *independent* of key personnel turnover. Units with purely judgmental decision-makers and/or poorly structured processes are extremely vulnerable to the departure of key figures. A specific function or the *entire* unit may be placed in jeopardy because of turnover in key positions. While nothing can completely absorb the impact of a key person departing, the team portfolio management approach helps insulate the investment process from the damaging effects of key departures.

5. *Links strategy, accountability, and compensation into a single organizational structure.* The bureaucratic pyramid investment organization fights against atrophy, malaise, and inertia as much as it battles the stock market. The organization's response time is slowed by layer upon layer of procedures and rules. Few have final responsibility or can act alone. This is not an organizational structure designed for investment performance. Entrepreneurism and risk-taking have long departed this organizational climate. Our structure serves to streamline strategy, process, and accountability, as well as monitor the contributions of individuals.

6. *Develops depth and cross-training of skills.* Special teams headed by designated experts add natural depth and training to the organization and ensure that all essential skills are well covered. While there is sufficient room for individual creativity and growth, no one works in isolation; and the integration of form and function helps to provide continuity.

7. *The "star" is the system rather than the individual.* A prime example of this approach to investment management is Rosenberg Institutional Equity Management (RIEM) in Orinda, California. At RIEM, there are no stars, only team members. As if to emphasize the completely quantitative nature of the process, those who monitor portfolios are called "portfolio engineers."

8. *Makes it easier to match the right talent to the right position in the organization, since areas of expertise are well-defined.* Often in a purely generalist environment, it can be hard to determine who is adding value and who is along for the ride. Our structure recognizes the need to leverage special skills and talents, and yet maintain some boundaries of responsibility.

9. *Allows the investment unit to focus on who the competition really is—the S&P 500 or an appropriate benchmark, not each other.* In our system, performance comes first. The team is united in the belief that the opposition is the benchmark, and not other teammates. Rewards are based on team accomplishments as well as individual achievement.

10. *Requires interaction, which is the key to effective teamwork.* The value chain structure requires continuous interaction: first, through the natural progression of building value and second, through the feedback loop for reciprocal communication. Complex tasks can be segmented and apportioned based on specialized skills, and then brought back together for an overall evaluation.

CONCLUSION

This chapter has assumed an ambitious task—to provide a model of internal investment organizational structure for the 1990s and beyond. We see the investment management profession at a crossroads. The challenges of performance, consistency, creativity, turnover and compensation are now perhaps more pressing and intense than at any other point in the history of the profession. We do not believe that the traditional, static pyramid organizational structure will survive in this environment.

We have presented a flexible and dynamic organizational structure based upon the value chain principle elaborated by Michael Porter.[11] Our proposed structure is build around functional components headed by "team leaders" and "designated experts" who are responsible for the success or failure of each specific assignment. This structure embeds competitive advantage into the core of the management structure and provides a framework for engineered solutions to investment problems and challenges.

NOTES

[1]   J. R. Vertin, ed., *Managing the Investment Organization* (Charlottesville, VA: The Institute of Chartered Financial Analysts, 1988).

[2]   The normal portfolio is fully discussed in J. A. Christopherson, "Normal Portfolios and Their Construction," Chapter 17 in F. J. Fabozzi, ed., *Portfolio & Investment Management* (Chicago, IL: Probus Publishing Company, 1989) and in Chapters 6 and 7 of this book.

[3]   For evidence on this point, see T.D. Coggin, "Active Equity Management," Chapter 4 in *Portfolio & Investment Management*; A.S. Wood, "Fatal Attractions for Money Managers," *Financial Analysts Journal* 45 (May/June 1989), pp. 3-5; and M. Siconolfi, "More Stock Mutual Funds Fall Behind in Crowded Race," *The Wall Street Journal*, October 13, 1989.

[4]   "Richard Ennis on Getting Manager's Best Shots," *Pensions & Investment Age*, October 2, 1989, 62.

[5]   For a good introduction to this literature, see D. Kahneman, P. Slovic, and A. Tversky, eds., *Judgment Under Uncertainty: Heuristics and Biases* (New York, NY: Cambridge University Press, 1982).

[6]   The classic study is P. E. Meehl, *Clinical Versus Statistical Prediction* (Minneapolis, MN: University of Minnesota Press, 1954). Meehl's basic finding has since been supported by numerous studies in several different fields.

[7]   As a case in point, see the article on Rosenberg Institutional Equity Management, "Inside the Alpha Factory," *Institutional Investor*, September 1989, pp. 141-145.

[8]   K. Blanchard and S. Johnson, *The One Minute Manager* (New York, NY: William Morrow, 1982).

[9]   M. E. Porter, *Competitive Advantage* (New York, NY: The Free Press, 1985).

[10]   For a good discussion of this problem and the advantages of the model portfolio/team approach to investment management, see D. J. Forrestal, III "Control of the Investment Management Process Within the Large Organization," in J. R. Vertin, ed., *Managing the Investment Organization*.

[11]   An article published just as this chapter was completed discusses several investment groups that have already adopted the basic value chain organizational model presented here. See I. Schmerken, "CIOs

Orchestrate Trading, Teamwork As New Portfolio Analysis Theme," *Wall Street Computer Review*, November 1989.

CHAPTER 6

Benchmark Portfolios: The Sponsor's View

DARALYN B. PEIFER, CFA
MANAGER, BENEFIT FINANCE
GENERAL MILLS, INC.

THE SPONSOR'S ROLE

Today, the role of a plan sponsor in managing pension assets is a lot like that of the manager of a baseball team. A plan sponsor selects investment managers to fill assigned niches in an investment management structure in much the same manner as the baseball manager selects players to fill positions on the team roster. The baseball manager drafts and recruits players to cover the baseball field, while the plan sponsor hires investment managers, both internal and external to the sponsor's organization, to cover desired portions of the capital markets.

The baseball manager has one advantage over the plan sponsor in that the team's playing field is defined by league regulations. The baseball manager does not need to worry about the size and shape of the playing field, as this responsibility resides with league officials, but can simply focus on achieving good field coverage. In contrast to the manager, the plan sponsor must first decide what the dimensions of the playing field are to be before the field can be filled with players. That is, the sponsor must decide which portions of the capital markets should be covered to meet plan objectives before a team of managers can be hired.

Defining the appropriate playing field and filling the field with superior players are two of the most critical tasks faced by the plan sponsor. The sponsor defines the playing field by specifying the long-term policy asset allocation for the pension plan. The policy allocation lists the asset classes to be included in the total pension portfolio and target weights for each of the classes. The sponsor then fills the playing field by building an investment management structure, or a configuration of investment managers who will invest the assets. For each asset class in the policy asset allocation, the structure lists the investment styles or niches to be included in the asset class program, a policy weight for each of the styles, and the specific investment managers who will fill each assigned niche.

Plan sponsors and their consultants are finding that the tasks associated with defining and covering the playing field are becoming increasingly complex. In defining the field, the sponsor may now consider for inclusion in the total pension portfolio not only the traditional asset classes of stocks and bonds, but also the growing list of nontraditional asset classes such as real estate, resources, and venture capital. To further complicate the tasks, the sponsor may also include international securities along with domestic ones in each of the asset classes represented in the policy allocation. In covering the field, the sponsor must first determine the allocations to active and passive approaches. Today, the sponsor can choose from the extremes of purely passive and active approaches as well as a whole spectrum of structured approaches between the two extremes. Once the active/passive allocations have been established, the sponsor must select the specific investment styles and investment managers to be represented in the management structure. Here too, the list of styles and managers available for inclusion by plan sponsors in their pension portfolios has grown tremendously in recent years.

In this complex environment, plan sponsors have found benchmark portfolios to be very useful tools as they both define and cover their playing fields. Benchmark portfolios, also called "normal" portfolios, are quantitative descriptions of manager styles. We will focus first on the evolution of the use of benchmark portfolios by plan sponsors and the pension management trends that sparked the evolution. We will also discuss the application of benchmark portfolios to a specific portion of the sponsor's playing field, using the fixed-income asset class as an example and outlining some of the special challenges and opportunities associated with fixed-income benchmarks. Finally, we will address some of the more controversial issues that plan sponsors and their consultants and investment managers face with the use of benchmark portfolios in fixed income as well as other asset class programs.

GENESIS OF BENCHMARK PORTFOLIOS

Over the past fifteen years, pension plan management has been characterized by the shifting of investment responsibilities between the plan sponsor and the sponsor's investment managers. In the mid-1970s, many plan sponsors were concerned about the scope of their fiduciary responsibilities under the newly-passed Employee Retirement Income Security Act (ERISA) regulations. As a result, they hired external balanced managers and turned over to these managers the responsibility for allocating pension assets among the available asset classes, emphasizing primarily stocks, bonds, and cash equivalents. In addition, they charged the managers with selecting individual securities within each of the asset classes.

This balanced manager approach proved to be a very frustrating one for many sponsors. The limitations of this approach are easy to see when viewed in a baseball context. A team of balanced investment managers is a lot like a baseball team in which the players are allowed to choose their own positions and can change positions at any time during a game. Moreover, any number of players can cover the same position. Now, imagine a critical play-off game. The manager of the visiting team has shifted the responsibility for field coverage to the team players and is watching passively from the dugout. In the bottom of the ninth inning with the visitors one run ahead, the home team batter approaches the plate with two outs and bases loaded. The batter hits an easy fly ball to left field. However, the ball drops untouched and the winning runs score for the home team because all of the visiting players are over in right field. This situation is similar to that of a plan sponsor who, having given up the responsibility for asset allocation, watches helplessly from the sidelines as stocks perform well during a period, while all of the sponsor's balanced managers are invested in bonds.

In the late-1970s, many plan sponsors began to feel more comfortable with their fiduciary roles and took back the responsibility for making asset allocation decisions from their managers. These sponsors believed that they were better suited than their managers to make allocations to asset classes, based on their own understanding of plan characteristics and objectives. The sponsors terminated their balanced managers or restricted them to a single asset class and began to build configurations of multiple specialized managers within each of the asset classes represented in their pension portfolios.

There were two basic problems associated with sponsors' early attempts at building investment manager structures. First, the specialized styles of individual managers tended to be described solely in qualitative terms. For example, some common stock managers were labeled simply as "value," "growth," or "sector rotator" managers, while bond managers might be categorized as "interest rate anticipators" or "sector selectors." Because these simple descriptions did not convey the subtleties of an investment manager's investment process, sponsors could not be sure which area of the capital markets a particular manager covered. This meant that as sponsors put together teams of investment managers, they had no way of determining whether they had achieved full coverage in their desired segments of the capital markets.

The second problem resulted from the tendency of sponsors to emphasize strong recent performance as a manager selection criterion. Although most sponsors set out to hire managers with differing styles, their emphasis on short-term performance left them with teams of managers that were heavily weighted in the investment styles most recently in market favor. Again in baseball terms, this was a lot like a team manager who recruits the strongest players from the current season, putting a team together without regard for filling all of the positions. As a result of these two problems, sponsors who adopted the multiple specialized manager approach versus the balanced manager approach were able to achieve control over the coverage among available asset classes but experienced major "gaps" or "overlaps" in the coverage within each of the asset classes.

In the late 1970s and early 1980s, plan sponsors and their advisors began to search for better ways of defining and filling their playing fields. Benchmark portfolios began to be used for these tasks. As representations of manager styles, benchmark portfolios first served as useful tools in the evaluation of individual investment managers. However, sponsors and consultants quickly realized that benchmark portfolios could also serve as powerful tools in building manager structures. By providing more comprehensive descriptions of manager styles and quantitatively specifying managers' areas of focus, benchmark portfolios gave sponsors the means to reduce or eliminate the "gaps" and "overlaps" in their capital markets coverage.

PENSION MANAGEMENT: EMERGING TRENDS

Plan sponsors have demonstrated increasing interest in benchmark portfolios. This attention reflects several trends in pension plan management. First, sponsors have continued to assume more active positions, taking over some of the responsibilities for plan management they relinquished to managers in previous years. These active postures reflect a heightened awareness on the part of plan sponsors of the significant impact their policy decisions have on the value of pension assets under their care. In particular, sponsors have recognized that their allocations to asset classes and manager styles have a much greater impact on their pension portfolios than do the individual security selection decisions made by investment managers.[1]

As sponsors have assumed more responsibility for plan management, including allocations to asset classes and manager styles, they have also reassessed the allocations of resources within their own programs. Until recently, the focus of most sponsors was on the evaluation and monitoring of individual investment managers, and their staffs and budgets were devoted primarily to these functions. Today, many plan sponsors have shifted their focus from the individual manager level to the total portfolio level and have reallocated their resources accordingly. This shift is consistent with the major impact that total portfolio decisions have on plan assets.

Sponsors have also become increasingly aware of the need to clarify and prioritize plan objectives before making investment decisions. In addition, more sponsors are taking into account the unique characteristics of their own plans as well as the characteristics of their organizations in setting objectives. This new emphasis on objectives and characteristics has caused sponsors to redefine the risks relevant to their programs and to specify the tolerance of the sponsor decision-makers for bearing the risks. The liability streams represented by plan obligations have received greater attention in sponsor risk discussions; as a result, risks are being defined more frequently in an asset/liability context than in an assets only one.[2]

Along with these trends is an emphasis by plan sponsors on controlling risks at the total portfolio level. Many sponsors have acknowledged the importance of diversification in portfolio risk control and have adopted more sophisticated, quantitative approaches to diversification. As sponsors have constructed configurations of investment managers for each of their asset class programs, they have tended to diversify along a greater number of risk dimensions or factors.

Plan sponsors have also indicated the desire for more meaningful performance evaluation. As they have taken on more responsibility for investment decisions, sponsors have expressed interest in quantifying the value added to plan assets from their own decisions and from the decisions of their investment managers, and they have begun to hold their managers accountable for their assigned roles in management structures. To this end, sponsors have worked to clarify performance expectations for themselves and their investment managers. They have also expressed interest in tying the compensation of their investment managers to relative performance results, and this interest has been reflected in increased attention to performance-based fee systems.[3]

The shift to a total portfolio perspective, the emphasis on more sophisticated risk control, the desire for more meaningful performance evaluation, and the interest in performance-based fees have spurred pension sponsors, consultants and investment managers alike in their quest for "perfect" benchmark portfolios.

BENCHMARK PORTFOLIOS

Controlling the risk of the total pension portfolio requires that sponsors use benchmark portfolios at two levels in their long-term policy frameworks: the asset class level and the individual manager level. We term benchmarks used at the asset class level "asset class targets" and those at the manager level "manager benchmarks."

Asset Class Targets

Asset class targets are critical components of a plan sponsor's long-term policy statement. Sponsors must not only specify the asset classes to be included in the pension portfolio and appropriate weights for each of the classes, they must also define the role that each asset class is expected to play in the pension portfolio and the contribution the class is expected to make in achieving total plan objectives.

An asset class target is a universe of assets. As the benchmark for an asset class, the target represents the set of opportunities that best achieves the purposes for which the asset class is included in the portfolio. The target reflects the trade-offs between risk and return that are associated with the class and sets forth the performance expectations for the asset class program. By comparing the risk characteristics and the performance results of the actual asset class program with those of the asset class target, the sponsor ensures that the defined role of the asset class in the total portfolio will be met.

An asset class target can be a standard broad market index, a weighted combination of components of market indices, or a custom index. The selection of an appropriate asset class target depends on the objectives defined for the asset class. A broad market index may be appropriate for asset classes that are included in the portfolio for total return maximization. To the extent that the sponsor faces constraints or objectives for an asset class that differ from those of total return maximization, some deviation from a broad market index may be necessary in the construction of the asset class target to reflect the objectives.

In setting asset class targets, it is helpful to start with a broad market index as a base index and consider how that index should be altered in terms of characteristics or risk dimensions to reflect specific investment objectives. The deviations from a broad market index required to meet plan objectives may be identified by the sponsor through scenario analysis. In this type of analysis, the sponsor identifies a number of possible economic scenarios and determines which types of securities will behave in the desired manner under these scenarios to achieve plan goals. The selection of an appropriate index may involve trade-offs between investment objectives, as the deviations from a broad index required to achieve one objective may be counter to those needed to achieve another. In addition, the asset class target must have internal consistency. Because the risk characteristics of an asset class may be interrelated, in building a target it is important to check that all of the desired characteristics are mutually achievable.

Fixed-Income Targets

Fixed-income asset class targets are often more interesting to design than common stock targets because bonds are included in pension portfolios for a variety of reasons, while common stocks tend to be included in pension portfolios solely for total return purposes. As a result, sponsors tend to deviate very little from broad market indices in setting common stock targets. Where deviations occur, they reflect sponsors' investment constraints or opinions regarding long-term structural inefficiencies or opportunities in the stock market. Because bonds tend to be included in pension portfolios for reasons other than total return maximization and the reasons vary dramatically from plan sponsor to sponsor, the asset class targets selected by sponsors for their fixed-income programs vary as well.

In selecting a fixed-income asset class target, a sponsor might begin with one of the broad bond indices and consider how the index would need to be altered in terms of its duration, term structure, sector, quality, and embedded option exposures to meet the objectives for the asset class. For example, some sponsors include bonds in their pension portfolios to provide a hedge against unexpected and severe deflation. In order to design a fixed-income asset class target to reflect this objective, the sponsor needs to consider how various fixed-income securities behave in deflationary environments. The sponsor might then deviate from the broad index or "tilt" the fixed-income asset class target in favor of securities or characteristics of securities that provide the best protection against deflation. The resulting target might be weighted in favor of long-duration, high-quality securities with some additional protection against call and prepayment risks, as these kinds of securities can be expected to experience significant appreciation in declining interest-rate environments.

Other sponsors focus on the variability of pension assets relative to liabilities and the role of fixed-income securities in dampening pension surplus volatility. In establishing a fixed-income asset class target to reflect this role, a sponsor would need to begin with the pension plan liabilities as the base index and consider which types of fixed-income securities would respond in a similar fashion as the liabilities and provide the best hedge for the liabilities under various economic scenarios.

Risk Control

Sponsors control the risk in their portfolios by comparing the risk characteristics of each asset class target with the characteristics of the aggregate of the individual manager benchmark portfolios within the class. The sponsor designates a benchmark portfolio for each manager that reflects the manager's investment style. The sponsor then adds together the manager benchmark portfolios and compares the characteristics of the aggregate with the target. This comparison allows the sponsor to identify any mismatch or "gaps" between the aggregate manager benchmark and the target. In baseball terms, gaps in the aggregate benchmark represent areas of the playing field that the sponsor desires to cover that are not being served by the present players on the field. In investment terms, the gaps represent unintended or inadvertent bets in the portfolio for which no reward is expected. The objective of this use of asset class targets and manager benchmarks is to identify and eliminate all of the unintended bets, leaving only the managers' active bets, for which the sponsor expects to be rewarded.

Once gaps or unintended bets in the pension portfolio have been identified, a plan sponsor has several alternatives for reducing them. One alternative is simply to reallocate assets among the sponsor's current managers. This is equivalent to keeping the same players, but repositioning them slightly in the field. A second alternative is to add or subtract managers from the sponsor's current configuration. Yet another approach involves the addition of a completion fund, which essentially fills out the aggregate manager benchmark portfolio until it matches the asset class target.[4]

Manager Benchmarks

In order for a sponsor to effectively control the risk of the total portfolio by monitoring the "fit" between the aggregate manager benchmark portfolio for each asset class program and the asset class target for the respective program, appropriate benchmark portfolios must be created for each of the individual investment managers represented in the sponsor's portfolio.

A manager benchmark is a portfolio of assets that represents a manager's investment style. Manager benchmarks quantitatively describe manager styles. For plan sponsors, manager benchmarks represent a major improvement over the use of simple qualitative descriptors to categorize managers. Whereas qualitative descriptors tend to reflect only a single aspect of a manager's investment process and ignore others, manager benchmarks can reflect many aspects of the process. Manager benchmarks describe the numerous aspects of a manager's style in terms of the manager's typical exposures along a variety of risk dimensions or risk factors.

A manager benchmark represents a manager's baseline position. In this sense, a manager benchmark reflects the manager's exposures to risk factors under neutral investment conditions. A neutral condition exists when the manager has no strong opinions about misvaluations of sectors and/or securities in the manager's area of expertise. Another way to think about a manager benchmark is as a description of the segment of the capital markets within which the manager tends to position actual portfolios and upon which the manager focuses research efforts.[5]

Manager Benchmark Uses

From a sponsor's perspective, the most important use of manager benchmarks is in building manager configurations. Comparing aggregate manager benchmarks with asset class targets allows sponsors to understand and control the risk in their total portfolios. In addition to this use, however, manager benchmarks have a number of ancillary uses for sponsors as well as their investment managers.

Sponsors' expectations for portfolio risk and return can be communicated very clearly to managers using manager benchmarks. Benchmarks allow managers to better understand the assigned roles they are expected to play in the sponsor's portfolio. They also serve to communicate the division of responsibility between the sponsor and manager. The sponsor assumes responsibility for the performance of the manager benchmark and holds the manager accountable only for the performance of the manager's actual portfolio relative to the benchmark.

Manager benchmarks help managers to understand and maintain the constraints placed on their portfolio activities by sponsor clients. In order to control portfolio risks, sponsors may place restrictions on the types of securities that managers may hold as well as on the risk exposures managers may assume. For example, to ensure that overall fixed-income objectives are met, a sponsor may limit the amount of cash bond managers may hold and apply restrictions on the duration and quality of the managers' portfolios. By clarifying the role the manager is expected to play in a specific sponsor's portfolio and by communicating the division of responsibility, manager benchmarks facilitate adherence to sponsor constraints.

Sponsors also find manager benchmarks to provide a useful focus for reviews with managers. A sponsor can gain an understanding of a manager's current outlook for the capital markets by discussing the active "bets" or deviations in the manager's actual portfolio relative to the benchmark. Monitoring the risk exposures of a manager's actual portfolio relative to the neutral or benchmark position also enables a sponsor to gain a deeper understanding of the manager's investment processes and style. Astute sponsors can also detect shifts in a manager's style as well as identify any large and unusual "bets" present in the manager's portfolio.

Also, the identification of superior managers is aided by the use of manager benchmarks. With the randomness and uncertainty in the capital markets, it is difficult to identify, with any degree of confidence, which managers are skillful. Evaluating managers relative to appropriate benchmarks that reflect the managers' styles reduces some of the "noise" inherent in the performance measurement process. Manager benchmarks also enable sponsors to adopt performance-based fee systems and tie manager compensation to results relative to appropriate benchmark standards. In addition, manager benchmarks facilitate performance attribution, helping sponsors identify not only which managers are adding value to the total pension portfolios, but also the manner in which the "value added" is being generated.[6]

BENCHMARK PORTFOLIO CONSTRUCTION

The construction of a benchmark portfolio generally involves screening a broad universe for securities that represent a manager's style. For common stock manager benchmarks, the sponsor typically begins with a broad index of 200 to 1,000 stocks that represent the manager's research universe. The sponsor then screens the universe using risk parameters that reflect the manager's neutral investment position. The resulting manager benchmark may consist of several hundred stocks with weights assigned to each.[7]

In contrast, a cellular approach is often used in building fixed-income manager benchmarks. A broad bond index can be thought of as a series of cells that exhibit certain characteristics. The screening process involves focusing on cells that are consistent with the manager's area of emphasis. If, for example, a manager ignores certain sectors or segments of the broad bond market, cells representing those segments can be eliminated from the benchmark. Cells can be defined very narrowly or very broadly. All industrial bonds of a certain maturity, coupon, and yield might define a narrow cell. Or, the entire corporate segment of a published bond index might constitute a broad cell. Typically, we would expect a large number of a manager's actual holdings to be represented in the manager's benchmark portfolio. However, we would not expect all of the manager's actual holdings to be included in the benchmark, as managers are generally allowed to make bets or assume exposures that are outside their usual areas of focus.[8]

The construction process begins with a discussion of the manager's investment process and proceeds with an analysis of the risk exposures or characteristics of the manager's current actual portfolio. The process may also include an analysis of the characteristics of the manager's historical portfolios. The benchmark builder may examine the long-term average characteristics exhibited by the historical portfolios, as well as the range and trends of characteristics, to determine an appropriate way of describing the manager's style.

Once a preliminary manager benchmark has been created, it is helpful to compare the historical performance of the benchmark relative to the actual portfolio to see if the pattern of "value added" by the manager is consistent with expectations. Finally, the benchmark must be reviewed and possibly modified by the investment manager. Regardless of who constructs the benchmark, the manager must judge whether the benchmark truly reflects the investment process. Benchmark construction is an active process and often involves many trials before sponsor and manager agree that an acceptable representation of the manager's style has been created.

Benchmark building is a creative process, with elements of art and science. We believe the concept of benchmark portfolios becomes more difficult to apply as one moves from common stocks to the other asset classes, with fixed income lying somewhere between common stocks and the nontraditional asset classes such as real estate and venture capital, in the degree of difficulty associated with benchmark building. Fixed-income benchmark building represents several challenges not associated with the construction of common stock benchmarks. However, offsetting these difficulties are some unique features of the fixed-income markets which present opportunities for creative benchmark construction.

FIXED-INCOME BENCHMARKS: CHALLENGES AND OPPORTUNITIES

One of the most significant challenges in building fixed-income benchmarks is the overwhelming size of the fixed-income markets. While the construction process for a common stock benchmark portfolio may begin with a universe of only 500 to 1,000 stocks, a broad bond market index or universe may include well over 5,000 individual securities. Contributing to the complexity is the dynamic nature of the bond universes. Characterized

by the continual issuance and maturity of securities, the broad bond universes which must be screened to create bond benchmark portfolios, are
moving targets in themselves. In addition, unlike common stocks which
tend to be "plain vanilla" in nature, there is an ever-growing array of security types represented in the fixed-income markets. Compounding these
challenges are the complex embedded option features that characterize
many fixed-income instruments.

On the other hand, there are several characteristics of the fixed-income markets that facilitate benchmark building. First is the dominance of
interest rate sensitivity as the main risk factor in the bond markets. A common stock benchmark portfolio typically is described in terms of exposures
to many different risk factors.[9] In contrast, a sponsor or manager can make
a major step toward building a good fixed-income benchmark simply by
expressing an appropriate duration and term structure exposure. The large
number of published bond indices and sub-indices also facilitates the construction of fixed-income benchmarks. While a common stock benchmark
generally is specified in terms of individual securities, a bond benchmark
may be specified in terms of components of major bond indices and appropriate weights for the components.

Also, fixed-income portfolios lend themselves to consideration as distributions of expected cash inflows. As a result, sponsors have the opportunity to shape the expected cashflow distribution of a fixed-income
benchmark. On the asset class target level, the benchmark can be shaped to
reflect the objectives established for the fixed-income asset class. This
characteristic is particularly helpful in situations where the sponsor is focusing on the asset/liability relationship of the pension portfolio, as plan
liabilities can be thought of as distributions of expected cash outflows. On
the manager benchmark level, the benchmark can be shaped to reflect a
manager's style.[10]

BENCHMARKS: CONCERNS AND ISSUES

Despite the attractive features of benchmark portfolios, most sponsors and
managers have some concerns regarding their construction and use. One of
the most troublesome issues involves the separation of a manager's investment style from the active management. It is difficult to analyze the risk
characteristics of the manager's current and historical portfolios because
the manager's active bets are reflected in the characteristics along with the
manager's style. The task is to separate the manager's neutral style, for
which the sponsor assumes responsibility, from the manager's proprietary
"value added" processes.

There is some disagreement between sponsors and managers as to what constitutes proprietary "value added." Some managers maintain that the selection of the investment style itself represents value attributable to the manager. However, the availability of a wide variety of passive and semi-passive products has made it fairly easy for sponsors to replicate managers' styles at low cost, and therefore, sponsors have become increasingly unwilling to attribute the value added through style selection to managers. As a result, many sponsors will now pay active management fees only for value added above a manager's investment style.

Sponsors and their consultants also express concerns about the ability of managers to create easy performance targets or to game their benchmarks. While there is no question that managers have this ability, monitoring the characteristics of the manager's actual portfolio relative to the benchmark should make these problems apparent. The processes of building and using manager benchmark portfolios involve a high degree of interaction, negotiation, and cooperation between the sponsor and investment manager. Both parties need to agree that the final benchmark to be used for evaluation, and possibly compensation, is appropriate.

Some sponsors and managers question whether the benefits of benchmark portfolios justify the related costs. Resources need to be expended for the initial construction of benchmarks as well as for their ongoing maintenance and monitoring. This issue might be debatable from the perspective of an investment manager. However, from the sponsor's perspective, benchmark portfolios are integral components of the total pension management process. For a sponsor whose investment structure includes multiple active managers, the only way that the risk of the total portfolio can be identified and managed effectively is through the use of benchmark portfolios.[11]

As indicated earlier, sponsors and consultants are finding the application of benchmark portfolios to the nontraditional asset classes particularly challenging. In concept, benchmark portfolios are just as valid and important for real estate, venture capital, and resource programs, for example, as for common stock and bond programs. However, the implementation of benchmark portfolios for these asset classes has been problematic. Because investments in the nontraditional asset classes are often private ones, sponsors as well as consultants have had difficulties gathering enough information to form reasonable risk/return expectations for their programs and communicating their expectations to managers. Sponsors have been hampered in their efforts to establish asset class targets and manager benchmarks by the scarcity of acceptable published indices and sub-indices and the lack of formal risk models for these asset classes. This situation is improving gradually, but there is still considerable work left to be done.

SUMMARY

In the increasingly complex world of pension investing, plan sponsors are becoming more and more aware of the need to understand and control the aggregate risk of their pension portfolios. A growing number of pension sponsors are addressing this need by establishing clear objectives for their plans and translating the objectives into comprehensive policy frameworks. Benchmark portfolios have become key elements in many sponsors' policy frameworks.

Sponsors are using benchmark portfolios at both the asset class and individual manager levels of their frameworks. In essence, sponsors are defining their playing fields through the specification of asset class targets. Asset targets indicate those areas of the capital markets in which a sponsor intends to participate. Once the playing fields have been defined, sponsors are covering the fields with the use of manager benchmarks, which quantitatively describe individual investment managers' areas of focus. Manager benchmarks are very helpful because they enable a sponsor to send a team of players out onto the playing field and know the entire field will be covered. Manager benchmarks are also proving useful to sponsors in evaluating managers or identifying good players to put on their teams.

Building and maintaining benchmark portfolios require a significant commitment of resources on the part of sponsors. However, we believe the benefits of using benchmark portfolios, particularly in managing portfolio risk, are significant and justify the attention being given them by sponsors.

NOTES

[1]   The relative impact of various portfolio decisions on the value of pension plan assets is presented in the oft-quoted Gary P. Brinson, Randolph Hood, and Gilbert L. Beebower, "Determinants of Portfolio Performance," *Financial Analysts Journal* (July/August 1986), pp. 39-44.

[2]   The definition of risk and the recognition of liabilities in the pension planning processes are thoughtfully addressed in Robert D. Arnott and Peter L. Bernstein, "Defining and Managing Pension Fund Risk," and Keith P. Ambachtsheer, "Integrating Business Planning with Pension Fund Planning," in Robert D. Arnott and Frank J. Fabozzi (eds.), *Asset Allocation: A Handbook of Portfolio Policies, Strategies & Tactics* (Chicago, IL: Probus Publishing, 1988), pp. 17-39 and pp. 59-85, as well as in Wayne H. Wagner, "The Many Dimensions of Risk," *Journal of Portfolio Management* (Winter 1988), pp. 35-39. An inter-

esting approach to identifying investors' risk tolerance is presented in William F. Sharpe, "Investor Wealth Measures and Expected Return," Seminar proceedings from *Quantifying the Market Risk Premium Phenomenon for Investment Decision Making*, The Institute of Chartered Financial Analysts, September 1989.

[3]   Issues relating to the development and application of performance-based fee systems are discussed in Andrew Rudd and Richard C. Grinold, "Incentive Fees: Who Wins? Who Loses?," *Financial Analysts Journal*, (January/February 1987), pp. 27-38 and Jeffery V. Bailey, "Some Thoughts on Performance Based Fees," *Financial Analysts Journal*, forthcoming.

[4]   David E. Tierney of Richards & Tierney, Inc. is often credited with the development of the concept of a completeness fund. For discussion, see William S. Gray, III, "Portfolio Construction: Equity," in John L. Maginn and Donald L. Tuttle (eds.), *Managing Investment Portfolios: A Dynamic Process*, Sponsored by the Institute of Chartered Financial Analysts (Boston, MA: Warren, Gorham & Lamont, 1983). Also, see David E. Tierney and Kenneth Winston, "Dynamic Completeness Funds," *Financial Analysts Journal*, forthcoming.

[5]   One of the seminal works on common stock risk factors and benchmark portfolios is Barr Rosenberg and Vinay Marathe, "Common Factors in Security Returns: Microeconomic Determinants and Macroeconomic Correlates," Proceedings of the Seminar on the Analysis of Security Prices, University of Chicago (May 1976), pp. 61-225. Basic fixed-income benchmark concepts are presented in Martin L. Leibowitz, "Goal-Oriented Bond Portfolio Management," in *Total Return Management* (Salomon Brothers, 1979), pp. 3-20.

[6]   In Jeffery V. Bailey, Thomas M. Richards, and David E. Tierney, "Benchmark Portfolios and the Manager/Plan Sponsor Relationship," *Journal of Corporate Finance* (Winter 1988), pp. 25-32, the authors present a comprehensive overview of common stock benchmark portfolios, including a discussion of desirable properties of "correct" benchmarks and a case study of their application. An early application by a plan sponsor of common stock benchmark portfolios is described in Walter R. Good, "Measuring Performance," *Financial Analysts Journal* (May/June 1983), pp. 19-23. A current sponsor's approach to the construction and use of common stock benchmark portfolios is presented in Edward P. Rennie and Thomas J. Cowhey, "The Successful Use of Benchmark Portfolios," in H. Russell Fogler and Darwin M. Bayston (eds.) *Improving Portfolio Performance with*

Quantitative Models (The Institute of Chartered Financial Analysts, April 1989), pp. 33-42.

7   Basic benchmark portfolio construction techniques for common stock portfolios are described in Mark Kritzman, "How to Build a Normal Portfolio in Three Easy Steps," *Journal of Portfolio Management* (Summer 1987), pp. 21-23.

8   For presentations of fixed-income index and benchmark portfolio construction, see Sharmin Mossavar-Rahmani, "Understanding and Evaluating Index Fund Management," and Edward A. Robie, Jr. and Peter C. Lambert, "Fixed Income Normal Portfolios and Their Application to Fund Management," in Frank J. Fabozzi and T. Dessa Garlicki (eds.), *Advances in Bond Analysis & Portfolio Strategies* (Chicago, IL: Probus Publishing, 1987), pp. 433-449 and pp. 35-48. I am also grateful to Robert C. Kuberek of Wilshire Associates for sharing his insights on bond indexing.

9   At present, it appears that the majority of plan sponsors use the BARRA multiple-risk factor model for common stock benchmark portfolio construction.

10 The mechanics of shaping the cash flow structure of a bond portfolio are addressed in Philip H. Galdi, "Indexing Fixed Income Portfolios," in *Advances in Bond Analysis & Portfolio Strategies*.

11 For a more balanced treatment of the issues surrounding the use of common stock normal portfolios including the perspectives of investment managers and consultants, see Chapter 11.

CHAPTER 7

How Sponsors Can Use Normal Portfolios

ARJUN DIVECHA
DIRECTOR OF EQUITY SERVICES
BARRA

RICHARD C. GRINOLD, Ph.D.
DIRECTOR OF RESEARCH AND CONSULTING
BARRA

Two of the major issues facing pension plan sponsors today are the evaluation of investment management performance and the control of overall fund structure. The concept of a normal portfolio is helpful in addressing both of these issues and normal portfolios have applications in a wide variety of other areas.

This chapter addresses the strategic uses of normal portfolios by plan sponsors and some of their concerns about the use of normals.[1] We find that normals are extremely useful in performance evaluation and in controlling the sponsor's aggregate risk. We also find other uses for normals that have evolved, such as incentive fees, internal control in money management firms, and as a common language in the dialogue between sponsor and manager.

In addition, we examine the difficulties sponsors and managers have had with normal portfolios and comment on some of the sources of these difficulties and how they have been resolved.

In the first section we will define the concept of a normal portfolio and look at some of the reasons for using normals. We then look at normal portfolios from the plan sponsor's point of view, and aspects of normal uses by managers and consultants that effect the sponsor's role. After we have defined the players, their interests, and an example of the normal process, we turn to more controversial issues surrounding the use of normal portfolios and how they influence sponsors. In particular, do normals create more problems than they appear to solve? Is it appropriate to use normals for applications like incentive fees that were not anticipated when the concept originated? We will show how these questions have been resolved by sponsors who are using normal portfolios. Finally, we examine international normals to see if this concept holds promise for sponsors.

NORMALS AND THEIR USES

Before we get too far into the meaty stuff, we have to make sure we know what normals are and how the need for normals arose in the first place.

Normals—What and Why

A normal portfolio is a list of assets and investment weights. It is a portfolio like any other. What differentiates the normal from other portfolios is the way it is used.

Normal portfolios were originally conceived as benchmarks for investment managers whose investment habitats and styles were not adequately captured by a broad-based index or comparison portfolio like the S&P 500 or the Frank Russell 3000. It was recognized that the use of a broad-based index that did not accurately reflect the manager's style was unfair to both the sponsor and the investment manager. This need grew from both the changing nature of investment management and the theoretical difficulties in establishing universal performance evaluation benchmarks.

Diversification of investment style and growth in the use of multiple managers accelerated in the 1970s. By the late 1970s, multiple equity managers were standard in large pension funds, and a readily identifiable style, be it growth, yield, value, etc., was an accepted feature in the market for investment management services. Questions soon arose concerning the evaluation of growth managers. Was it fair to evaluate a growth manager against a broad-based index? Shouldn't the growth stock manager be evaluated in a peer group of growth stock managers? These types of questions naturally lead to the search for more appropriate benchmark portfolios.

As investment management became more specialized in the 1970s, the world of academe was also evolving. By the late 1970s the concept of the market portfolio[2] as a basis for performance evaluation was under attack, with no clear cut concept to take its place. This motivated the need for a clearly defined benchmark to be agreed upon by both sponsor and manager. The normal portfolio filled this role. Why a normal, rather than peer evaluation?

Normals Versus Peer Evaluation

The difficulty with peer evaluation is that it looks at only one aspect of a manager's style. Our experience with most of the larger institutional managers is that each is sufficiently idiosyncratic to warrant a customized benchmark or normal portfolio. Traditional classification schemes are one-dimensional, whereas manager styles are actually multi-dimensional. For example, within what is known as the "growth" style, we may find wide variations in the range of capitalizations of stocks that managers hold. In addition, certain "growth" managers like cyclical earnings while others prefer stable earnings. Therefore, it is necessary to use many dimensions to characterize a manager's style. A manager's investment habitat as described by an asset list cannot be adequately captured in one dimension.

Recall that a normal is a *weighted* asset list. Managers differ greatly in the way they weight their portfolios, so it is vital to capture their weighting scheme in the normal.

A broad-based index does not represent the weighting of a typical active manager. Most indices are capitalization weighted, while active managers vary widely in the manner that they allocate relative values to stocks in their portfolios.

Asset Weighting and Normals

Why is asset weighting important? Consider a manager who has a process that identifies 50 "superior" stocks. Assuming that the manager has no preference for any particular stock, he chooses to "equal" weight each stock. Thus, if both Apple Computer and IBM were among the chosen, each would represent 2% of the portfolio value. If the benchmark for this manager is the S&P 500, then IBM's weight in the S&P 500 is around 5%, while Apple's is near 0.2%. We would be making a negative 3% bet on IBM even when it made our "superior" list. Equal weighting (when compared to a capitalization weighted benchmark) systematically underweights larger capitalization issues and overweights smaller stocks. The overall effect is a bet on smallness. Given the fact that there are large differentials in the return to the size dimension, this may cause enormous differences in relative returns.

Exhibits 1 and 2 illustrate the smallness effect by showing the returns to the S&P 500 equal weighted as well as capitalization weighted.

Even though both portfolios contain the exact same stocks, their weighting is responsible for all differences in returns. During 1975-1983, when small stocks were doing well, the return to the equal weighted portfolio dominated. During 1984-1987, when larger capitalizations did well, the capitalization weighted strategy was better, although the equal weighted portfolio still dominated. Therefore, it is necessary to not only look at the sector within which the manager operates, but also at how the portfolio is weighted.[3]

A manager's style may be an important determinant of return, but do we have to focus on style, as captured by a normal portfolio, in evaluating performance or controlling the total fund? The answer is yes! We can view the normal as a way of dividing responsibility between the sponsor and the manager. The sponsor takes responsibility for the normal, the manager for active performance. By taking responsibility for the normal, the sponsor makes clear how the manager will be evaluated. For the normal to be a "fair" benchmark, it must be an investable portfolio that the sponsor could have held passively. As a result, the normal should be a list of assets with weights.

This section has argued, rather vociferously, for normal portfolios as a standard for the evaluation of a manager's performance. In the sections that follow, we will look at the concept of a normal from the perspective of sponsor, manager, and consultant. Their differing perspectives will give us additional insights into the use of normals.

THE SPONSOR'S POINT OF VIEW

The demand for normals grew out of the sponsor's need for more precise performance analysis. Like most innovations, there are unanticipated benefits to having normals. Sponsors have found several alternative uses for normals such as controlling the aggregate risk of several managers, monitoring the active risk in the manager's portfolio, establishing a quantitative communication channel between sponsor and manager, and setting incentive fees.

When a sponsor has more than one investment manager, the normal plays a crucial part in controlling the risk and return characteristics of the overall fund.

The *target* is like the sponsor's normal. This target may be a broad-based index, such as the Frank Russell 3000 or the S&P 500, or a customized target, reflecting the circumstances of the fund. This can de-

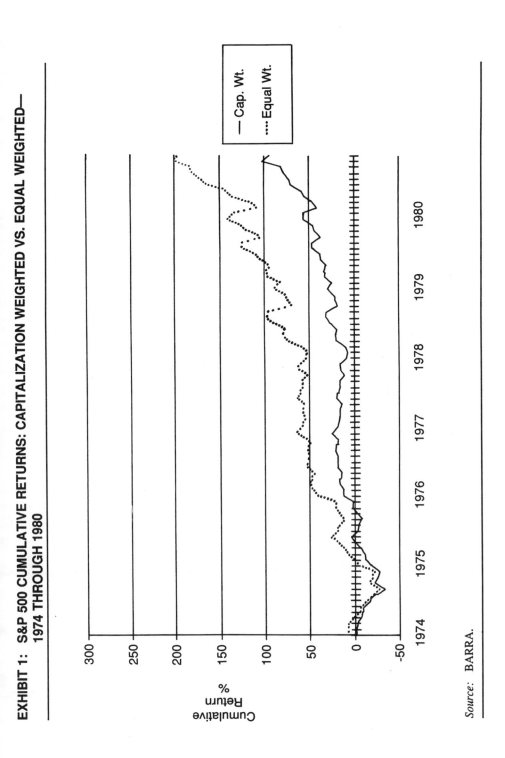

EXHIBIT 1: S&P 500 CUMULATIVE RETURNS: CAPITALIZATION WEIGHTED VS. EQUAL WEIGHTED— 1974 THROUGH 1980

Cumulative Return %

— Cap. Wt.
···· Equal Wt.

1974   1975   1976   1977   1978   1979   1980

300   250   200   150   100   50   0   -50

Source: BARRA.

EXHIBIT 2: S&P 500 CUMULATIVE RETURNS: CAPITALIZATION WEIGHTED VS. EQUAL WEIGHTED—1981 THROUGH JUNE 1988

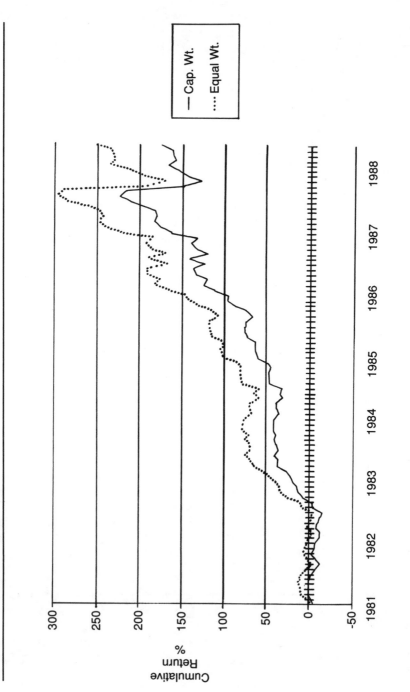

Source: BARRA.

pend on criteria such as under- or overfunding, the nature of the fund's liabilities, competitive position, restrictions on the fund assets such as South African-free investments, or beliefs in long-term structural inefficiencies in capital markets. The sponsor hopes to use his active managers to produce a return that is superior to the return of the target.

The *aggregate managed portfolio* is the sum of all actual assets held across all managers. The *aggregate normal* is the sum of all normal portfolios across all managers.

Thus, the difference in performance (and risk) between the aggregate managed and aggregate normal portfolios is termed the *active portfolio*. The active portfolio is where the sponsor looks for active returns to compensate him for the active risks taken *and* the active fees paid.

Therefore, when managers beat their normal portfolios, they will have fulfilled the purpose for which they were hired.

The Role of Misfit

The difference between the aggregate normal and target portfolios is the *misfit portfolio*. This misfit comes about when the normals of all the managers put together do not add up to the target. It is, in fact, difficult to match the target by making an asset allocation to, say, seven managers.[4] This is important because the sponsor may pick a number of excellent managers, each of whom delivers superior performance relative to his or her normal, yet the overall fund underperforms the target because a particular style (say, high yield) was underrepresented in the aggregate normal mix during a period when high yield stocks were doing well. Thus, the misfit represents the missing pieces in the aggregate pie.

Both the active portfolio and the misfit portfolio contribute to the difference in performance between the sponsor's target and the aggregate managed. The sponsor expects to be compensated for the active risks but cannot expect to be compensated for the misfit risk. The misfit risk is an incidental bet of the sponsor due to the selection and weighting of the managers. Misfit can, and frequently does, swamp the active risk in the aggregate portfolio.[5]

Normals as a Contract

The normal portfolio can be considered as the basis for an informal contract between sponsor and manager that specifies that the sponsor is responsible for the performance of the normal portfolio, and the manager is responsible for the performance of the active portfolio. This partitioning of credit (or guilt, as the case may be) is of crucial importance to the manager and the sponsor, so there is intense interest in having a "fair" normal. One by-product of this focus on the normal is the establishment of a fairly precise communications channel between sponsor and manager. The sponsor will gain additional insights into how the manager expects to add value, and will learn more about the manager's investment process.

The sponsor can also use the normal to monitor the active position of the manager. The sponsor can ask if the level of risk is consistent with historical levels, and, if not, why. The sponsor can also make sure there is a link between the manager's professed active strategy and the actual active positions in the portfolio. Nothing is more reassuring to a sponsor than to have a manager who says, "I can add value by doing X," then seeing the manager actually do X, and actually adding value. Nothing is more disheartening than to have the manager say X, do Y, and lose money.

Performance Fees

Performance fees as an option for sponsors concerned about the impact of fees on fund performance have become increasingly popular.[6] Normals can play a key role in performance fee implementation.

In the world of performance fees, monitoring the level of portfolio risk is necessary to make sure that the manager's bets are consistent with sponsor expectations as well as to prevent the manager from executing any "two minute drills" late in the fourth quarter of a bad year.[7]

The final role the normal plays from the sponsor's point of view is to help set the manager's fee. Certain styles are harder and more costly to implement than others. For example, a manager whose style includes some measure of momentum needs to turn over the portfolios more often than one who bets on high yielding utilities. The reason is clear; a stock that is doing well today is not the same as one that did well yesterday. However, a high yielding utility strategy is likely to have the same universe of stocks for a long time. As a result, one can use the turnover in the normal (during rebalancing) as a measure of how much turnover is necessary to manage that particular style. Managers that have high turnover should not be made to pay a price if that level of turnover is necessitated by their style. The turnover in the normal gives the sponsor an objective measure of how much trading is necessary to run that style passively.

In a performance fee context, some measure of how much it costs to maintain the normal should be taken out of the performance of the normal.

We've seen how sponsors view the normal as a useful tool in coordinating their overall investment strategy. How does it look from the other side of the table, and how do the manager's reactions to normals effect the sponsor's work?

THE MANAGER'S POINT OF VIEW

The evaluatee always feels differently from the evaluator. Teachers have a different view of exams than students. Players start arguments with officials, officials don't initiate arguments with players. Most managers would like to avoid the use of performance evaluation or at least be able to choose the comparison portfolio after the fact.[8] As a manager's performance is judged, he has an overriding interest in making sure that his performance is judged fairly and that any looseness or bias in the performance evaluation system favors him. If normals are going to form the basis for a performance evaluation system, then the manager, out of self-interest, should ensure that the normal is a fair representation of the manager's style. In fact, if normals are the language of sponsor-manager communication, then it is in the interest of the manager to master that language. Managers who have embraced the notion of a normal have, like sponsors, found additional uses for the normal.

The normal has two major impacts on a manager. Performance evaluation is one, and the representation of his style is the other. Since the normal represents a manager's style, it is like the manager's shingle. A sponsor may ask a manager search consultant to find a type X manager. If a manager has a type X shingle, then he is in the running. From that point on, the manager needs to demonstrate superiority. This can be done by having a finer differentiation of style: "I am a type X, model 3 manager, and model 3 is the margin of excellence." In addition, the manager can point to a track record of outstanding active returns, if it is available. The normal represents a manager's niche, and to some extent the degree to which a manager can demonstrate to a sponsor that he has grasped this concept, the more likely he will be able to convince the sponsor that he is on top of the situation. The normal will help in both respects. In fact, the normal can help the manager in other ways.

Normals as Opportunities

Some managers have seen the normal as an opportunity. Consider the sponsor's plight of trying to match his target by balancing the normals of his managers. The difference between the target and the aggregate normals is the misfit and represents a risk to the sponsor without any compensation in the form of higher expected return. A clever manager can build a special normal for that particular sponsor that rounds out his mix of managers and eliminates the misfit. Alternatively, sponsors can request a manager to build this type of normal. This type of fund is called a *fulfillment fund*. It gives the manager who can manage relative to any normal an additional marketing opportunity.

A manager's revenue is based to a large extent on the performance of the normal portfolio. If the manager has a flat fee or a base fee in an incentive scheme, then the portion of revenue he obtains from existing business will be mainly determined by the returns to the normal portfolio. By hedging the normal portfolio, the manager can eliminate a large amount of uncertainty in the revenue stream. Notice the manager is hedging the normal's performance. Sponsors should get edgy if managers start to hedge active performance.[9]

The manager can and should view the normal as the neutral position. If the manager temporarily has no exceptional market insights for a quarter, then it is in both the manager's and the sponsor's interest for the manager to hold the normal portfolio. The manager will benefit, since there will not be any poor performance. The sponsor will benefit for the same reason, and also because the sponsor's control of misfit risk will remain intact.

The manager can adjust the level of active risk in the portfolio. Sponsors should want different levels of aggressiveness from their managers and, by and large, the level of aggressiveness will depend on both the general level of active aggressiveness in the fund and each manager's share of the entire fund. The smaller the share of the fund the manager controls the more active the manager should be. This monitoring of active risk allows the manager to present the same style to all clients and still tailor the level of active risk to suit the special needs of clients.

This section has detailed several of the ways managers can use normal portfolios to benefit both themselves and their sponsor clients. We now turn to the third actor in this drama, the consultant who acts as intermediary between sponsor and manager.

THE ROLE OF THE CONSULTANT

We have seen that sponsors are interested in normal portfolios, and, although initially reluctant, managers have found important uses for normals. One obvious issue of importance to all those using normals remains.

Where does the normal come from? Who builds and maintains the normal portfolio?

The impetus in building the normal usually comes from a sponsor, although an outside consultant is generally in charge of the actual implementation. However with the increased use of normals, in particular with the use of normals as part of an incentive fee, some managers have started taking responsibility for their normals themselves. In any case, both sponsor and manager can be guaranteed fairness by having an independent third party construct and maintain the normal.

The normal portfolio construction process is part art and part science.[10] In building the normal, the consultant often serves as an intermediary between sponsor and manager. At this stage, the consultant may find that sponsor and manager have different ideas about what the normal portfolio should be and what assets it should contain. For example, the manager may want to have some cash in the portfolio, since he typically carries a small cash reserve. The sponsor may maintain that he pays the manager to manage equities, not cash. Another, and often more serious issue, is agreeing on which part of the manager's process is his style and which part represents his investment judgment. A manager may tend to prefer small growth stocks. The manager argues that this is part of his investment judgment and thus not part of the normal. The sponsor argues that there is a commodity "small growth stock management" and the manager should not expect to be paid active management fees for providing the commodity. In any case, the role of the consultant is to facilitate compromise. A compromise usually, but not always, turns out to be possible.

The consultant as an unbiased intermediary can facilitate the construction and use of the normal. In addition, the consultant can automatically ensure that the normal is kept up to date. Normals, like autos, need six-month checkups. As time passes, the characteristics of the normal portfolio will drift away from the desired characteristics. This is because both the market and the stocks change over time. For example, a growth-oriented normal would have contained oil stocks in the late 1970s and early 1980s; whereas in 1988 it would have very few oil stocks. Similarly, a normal with a tilt toward low p/e stocks would constantly change as the assets' p/e ratios changed. A six-month rebalancing of the normal is usually sufficient to control for this drift.

Normal Redefinition

A major change in the normal, called *redefinition*, is required when there has been a major change in the manager's style or when more data on the manager's process becomes available. These changes are usually motivated by personnel moves. In any case, the normal should be reviewed every two or three years to make sure it represents the current contract between sponsor and manager. One offshoot of the process is the creation of a normal portfolio library that allows the same normal to be used by multiple sponsors. In addition, the library benefits managers by marketing their skills to sponsors filling manager slots in-house as well as to consultants conducting manager searches on behalf of sponsors.

USING NORMAL PORTFOLIOS

The initial and most important use of normals as a tool for sponsors is to evaluate the performance of their investment managers. The importance of this is illustrated by the example shown in Exhibits 3 and 4.

In Exhibit 3, we see the performance of a growth stock manager and the S&P 500 over the period from mid 1984 to mid 1987. In that three-year period the manager underperformed the S&P 500 by 20%. Exhibit 4 shows a comparison of the manager's performance along with his normal, showing that the manager consistently outperformed the normal with a total active return of 40% in three years. The net difference of 60% in the evaluation points out in a rather dramatic way the difference a relative evaluation can make. Note that both parties benefit in this case. The sponsor has a skilled growth stock manager; he doesn't want to fire him. The manager, of course, has performed well and deserves recognition. The active return versus the S&P 500 shows erratic, poor performance. Many sponsors would be tempted to fire this manager for doing a poor job. However, when we look at the active return versus the normal, we clearly see that the manager consistently added value over the entire time period, while his sector did badly.

ISSUES

The example above shows a critical use of normal portfolios. But while many sponsors are using normals in this manner, there remain several difficult issues surrounding the use of normal portfolios. This section will detail these issues, starting with those we feel are the most significant.

EXHIBIT 3: CUMULATIVE HISTORICAL RETURNS

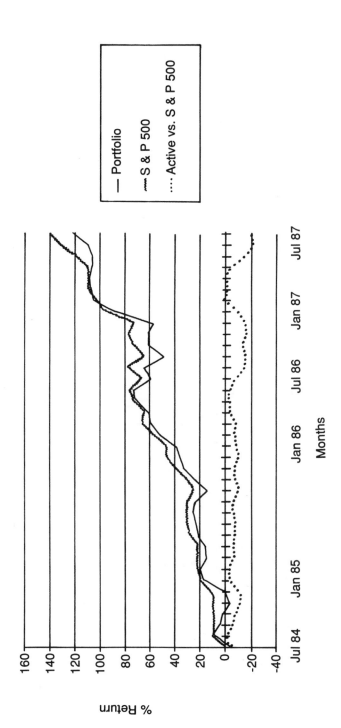

Source: BARRA.

EXHIBIT 4: CUMULATIVE HISTORICAL RETURNS

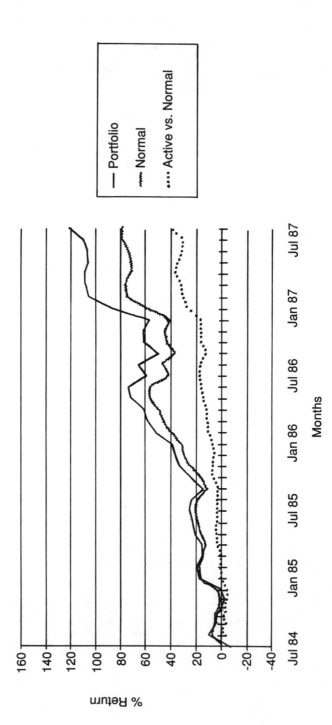

Source: BARRA.

The Ugly Normal?

Some managers feel that normals are an insidious assault on their domain. Part or all of the value added by the manager when compared to the S&P 500 is included in the normal. For example, if the manager habitually holds growth stocks and tends to equal weight his portfolio, then a significant part of his return relative to the S&P 500 will come from his growth and size biases. The normal takes that away from him. As normals become more refined and as knowledge of strategies becomes more precise, more and more sophisticated aspects of a manager's process will be reflected in the normal. In this way the normal represents a one-way street for the manager where his skills are gradually assigned to the sponsor and he is forced to find more and more refined ways of adding value. It is hard to deal with this criticism, since it accurately describes the situation. However, as sponsors become more sophisticated and the investment management business becomes more competitive, certain kinds of investment styles will be seen as "commodities" and, therefore, will not be able to command high fees. The normal is not the culprit here, it is merely the mechanism for implementing a new state of affairs.

Other managers may feel they are put in double jeopardy by the normal portfolio process. Plan administrators judge them relative to their normals, and plan trustees judge them relative to the S&P 500. They have to beat both indices to please both levels of management. Notice that the degree of jeopardy increases as the normal differs more and more from the S&P 500. A manager who consistently outperformed his normal, and who outperformed it by 2.50% in the past year, was recently fired, ostensibly because his performance was 5.00% below the S&P 500. Plan administrators who want their managers to have normals and manage relative to those normals must reassure managers that plan trustees have signed off on the normal idea and are familiar with all of its consequences.

Creating Correct Normals

To create a successful working relationship between sponsors and managers, sponsors must have a firm concept of the properly constructed normal. What is the correct normal? Some managers feel that their style is too eclectic to be captured by a normal portfolio. Others are never sure if the normal is correct. One of the major sources of contention is how assets in the normal should be weighted. We have seen in Exhibits 1 and 2 that asset weighting can make an enormous difference.

A mis-specification of the manager's size exposure could occur in several ways. One way is to quickly settle on a simple scheme such as capitalization weighting or equal weighting. Although a manager may sometimes feel that he is equally likely to choose an asset in his universe for his portfolio, the reality may be much different. Consider a manager who uses the S&P 500 as his universe and generally keeps about 100 assets in his portfolio equally weighted. Should the manager's normal be the equal weighted S&P 500? Maybe not. Suppose that we look at the manager's portfolio over several periods and see that in general, 30 of the stocks are in the top 100 in capitalization, 25 in the second 100, down to 10 in the last 100. In that case, we can see that the manager selects more frequently from the higher capitalization sector of his universe. A more representative set of weights would range from 30% in the top 100 down to 10% in the last 100.

In general, it is in the sponsor's and manager's interest to probe this type of issue to get as reasonable a normal as possible. Otherwise, part of the manager's active return will be return due to the mis-specification of the normal, and presumably represents a source of risk without any expected return. Thus, the risk of being judged on "normal mis-specification" drives the manager to be as precise as possible. However, the manager's need to have a normal that can be easily described to sponsors pushes the manager towards a simpler, perhaps less precise, version of the normal. To further complicate this issue, the more the normal moves away from the "simplicity" of the S&P 500, the more the manager is in danger of being in the double jeopardy referred to above.

The normal functions as an indication of the status of the relationship between sponsor and managers. The level of understanding and cooperation between sponsors and managers is reflected in their use of normals. In this regard, creating the most correct normal is critical for both parties.

The Normal as "Slow Rabbit"

Akin to the idea of correctly specifying the normal is the scheme of trying to choose a normal that is likely to do poorly, the so-called "slow rabbit." This is not such a great idea. First, sponsors will realize, as performance relative to the normal is monitored, that the normal is mis-specified. Second, the myriad of other uses mentioned for normals would be nullified. Third, it should be fairly difficult, and certainly counterproductive, to try and sneak a slow rabbit past the consultant.

As normals are used in more adventurous ways, particularly to measure return for sponsor-requested incentive fees, it will become more important to have precise measurements of the normal's returns. This means catching all corporate actions, a policy on the reinvestment of dividends, and some assumptions on the tendering of stock. This is more difficult than it appears. In a recent year, seven large institutions differed by as much as 72 basis points in their measurement of the S&P 500's performance for that year. There is clearly a need for precisely defined standards.

One assumption behind the use of normals is that the normal changes much more slowly than the active strategy. It is difficult to capture the normal for a manager who is a "sector rotator" with a low speed of rotation. There may not be enough data to determine the center of that manager's orbit.

A final difficulty that can emerge with the use of normals is when the manager has several normals for several sponsors. Notice that the manager could hold the average of the normals passively and still appear to be giving active management to each sponsor. In fact, at least one of the clients will be getting positive active returns. Multiple normals offer the manager a temptation to participate in a version of the old racecourse tout scheme.

INTERNATIONAL NORMALS

Up to this point, we have discused normal portfolios within the context of a domestic equity portfolio. How can sponsors use normals for other asset classes, specifically for international equities?[11]

With the soaring investment and interest in international markets, the concept of normal portfolios is being increasingly applied to international portfolios. In general, all of the issues applicable to domestic portfolios are applicable to international portfolios. In this section we will discuss the issues associated purely with international normal portfolios.

Issues

Most of the issues one must deal with in international normal portfolios involve their multidimensionality. Typically, international portfolios have been measured against one of the more widely-known and used international benchmarks, such as the Morgan Stanley Capital International, Financial Times/Goldman Sachs, and several others. Increasingly, however, these benchmarks are viewed as being less than ideal, often for reasons similar to their domestic counterparts'. Once one has decided that a custom normal portfolio is desirable, what must be done next?

At What Level Does One Create a Normal Portfolio?

An international portfolio is a multi-asset class portfolio. A portfolio can be invested in many different equity markets and have many different cash positions. Thus, the first decision involves at what level to specify the normal portfolio.

The simplest normal applies a revised country weighting scheme to one of the maintained international benchmarks, which are typically, but not always, capitalization weighted. However, international managers are typically very aggressive market timers. It may not be reasonable to assume that the average position always represents a long-term bias, so a normal country weighting position is very difficult to identify. As with all normals, the difference between a long-term active bet and a long-term bias (e.g. the persistent underweighting of Japan relative to the international benchmarks in the second part of the 1980s) must also be evaluated.

If it is decided that the normal portfolio should have a cash position, one has to decide the currencies in which the cash is held. As with equity market positions, cash positions, both total and individual currency, vary widely for international managers. This is another source of difficulty for those seeking to identify a "normal" position.

One may decide that the asset class normal portfolio is not adequate and that a normal portfolio on an individual asset level is necessary. One still has to decide issues like the following: Is the normal portfolio strictly an international portfolio with similar characteristics in every country? Or is the international normal portfolio the sum of several individual country normal portfolios, each with characteristics that reflect the manager's style within each country, characteristics which may or may not be the same for every country? Only a careful analysis of the portfolio will determine which of these two types of normal portfolios will be an adequate benchmark for the manager's portfolio.

Data Limitations

The lack of data on international stocks causes problems with creating an international normal portfolio on the individual asset level. One must have the data to identify the normal characteristics for the managed portfolio and also have the data to identify the characteristics of any asset that is considered for inclusion in the normal portfolio.

CONCLUSION

Normal portfolios play an important role in two areas key to sponsors—performance evaluation and risk analysis—and they provide various and diverse applications for managers and sponsors. Normals are useful in other respects as well. The sponsor uses them to control aggregate risk and monitor the manager's active strategy. The manager uses the normal to ensure quality control across portfolio managers, to devise incentive fees, and to build exotic new products like fulfillment funds. Consultants serve as useful intermediaries in this process by constructing and maintaining the normal portfolios.

With the advent of performance fees, there is an impetus to develop a fair benchmark from both the manager's and the sponsor's point of view. In addition, the normal plays an important role in managing the aggregate risk of a multiply-managed fund.

The construction process is frequently complicated and time-consuming, but offers great rewards for both sponsor and manager. One of the greatest benefits of normal portfolios, and their construction, is to help frame the new vocabulary sponsors and managers will increasingly use.

However, all is not roses in the world of normals. Normals are seen by managers as more of a stick than a carrot, and as an encroachment on their domain by appropriating parts of their skill into the normal. In this way, the normal acts as the messenger of a more sophisticated and aggressive form of sponsor.

NOTES

[1] Parts of this chapter are adapted from "Normal Portfolios: Issues for Sponsors, Managers and Consultants," which appeared in the March/April 1989 *Financial Analysts Journal.*

[2] The traditional form of the capital asset pricing model (CAPM) asserts that ex-ante expected asset returns can be determined by knowing the asset's beta with respect to the market and a consensus forecast of the market's return. If we use the CAPM's forecast as a standard, then we can judge whether an investment manager had information superior to the information that should be available to everyone through the CAPM.

The traditional form of the CAPM has been replaced by more complicated multifactor forms (which dovetail with the arbitrage pricing theory). While these new multiple factor theories of expected return are theoretically more robust, they unfortunately do not identify the "correct" factors and the expected returns that should be associated with each factor. Therefore, they are very subjective measures to use in evaluating investment performance.

3   Note that this "size effect" shows why crude evaluations of active managers (most of whom equal weight) go through periods where "the average active manager underperforms."

4   BARRA characterizes U.S. equity portfolios along 68 dimensions. To match the target exactly on all dimensions would, in general, take 68 equity managers.

5   For a further examination of this subject, see Chapter 8.

6   The topic of performance fees is the subject of Chapter 9.

7   See Richard Grinold and Andrew Rudd, "Incentive Fees: Who Wins? Who Loses?," *Financial Analysts Journal* (January/February 1987), pp. 27-38.

8   This may not seem apparent in the U.S. market, where performance evaluation is an accepted part of the industry. In international markets, performance standards range from respectability, to doing a good job, to an average of 15%, to 5% over risk free, to beating the local index. In all of these markets, the majority of managers are eager to preserve the status quo and will sigh when talking about the inevitability of more stringent forms of performance evaluation.

9   The topic of hedging the normal's performance and some related topics are treated in Andrew Rudd, "Business Risk and Investment Risk," *Investment Management Review* (November/December 1987), pp. 19-27.

10 In a related paper currently in preparation, the authors describe the normal portfolio construction process in some detail.

11 The use of normal portfolios for fixed-income securities is discussed in Chapter 6.

CHAPTER 8

The Sponsor's View of Risk

RICHARD C. GRINOLD, Ph.D.
DIRECTOR OF RESEARCH AND CONSULTING
BARRA

The whole is *not* the sum of its parts as far as investment risk is concerned. The same diversification of risk that makes portfolio management interesting at the individual manager's level also applies at the aggregate level and makes the management of managers a game that calls for skill and perspective. A sponsor can be as grossly misled by looking at the risk of each manager in isolation as a portfolio manager can be by considering the risk of each asset in isolation. The portfolio approach applies all the way up the line.

All too often, each manager in the sponsor's mix of managers gets an individual review either by the plan administrator or the board. When the manager is viewed in isolation, the cost-benefit ratios are distorted and the most aggressive manager can suffer in comparison to their less aggressive brethren. The plan suffers as well, because a manager by manager approach leads to the systematic undervaluing of the more aggressive managers.

A simple example illustrates this point. Consider the case of sponsor A with a single active manager whose expected active return is 2.00% per year with an active risk of 6.00%. Contrast this situation with that of sponsor B who has five managers, each with 20% of the fund, each with the same expected active return of 2.00% as Sponsor A, but an active risk of 8.00% for each manager. If we make the very reasonable assumption that the five managers' active returns are uncorrelated, then the active return for sponsor B has an expected value of 2.00% and an active standard deviation of 3.58%. Sponsor B is better off in terms of aggregate active risk than sponsor A. However, if the sponsors look at the manager(s) in isolation, each manager for sponsor B will be inferior to the single manager for sponsor A.

This chapter considers the problem of portfolio risk from the sponsor's perspective and argues that sponsors need to consider the impact of policy on the fund's overall risk. This line of thinking leads us to consider the problem of misfit risk that arises from the misalignment between the sponsor's overall target portfolio and the aggregate of the manager's benchmark portfolios. We also consider the question of passive managers and the trade-off between the transaction costs required to keep the passive fund in balance and the active risk (tracking error) of the fund.[1]

For active managers, we derive a simple rule of thumb that claims the sponsor's allocation of funds to each active manager should be *directly* proportional to that manager's ability to add value to the fund and *inversely* proportional to the manager's average level of active risk. From this rule we isolate each manager's added value contribution to the entire fund. This identification of value added points out the disparity between compensating managers based on their ability to add value and compensation plans based on a flat fee for assets under management. A technical appendix contains some of the derivations.

MISFIT AND ACTIVE RISK

A sponsor's strategic asset allocation defines an overall *target* portfolio. The target portfolio represents the sponsor's desired holdings over an horizon of three to five years.

When sponsors hire a group of managers spanning asset classes and investment styles, the aggregate of these styles and classes should be consistent with the overall target portfolio. Each of the managers should have their own version of a target or benchmark portfolio called the manager's *normal* portfolio. The normals can be widely quoted indices such as the S&P 500, EAFE, the Salomon Brothers Broad index, etc., or the manager's normal may be tailored to his or her particular style of management, be it growth- or value-oriented.

Misfit Risk

Ideally, sponsors want the target portfolio to be close to the weighted aggregate of the managers' portfolios. This is an admirable goal, but one that is difficult to obtain without special efforts. The sponsor's target can be considered a 'meta' portfolio that may consist of ten thousand individual assets. Attempting to match the target portfolio by adjusting the allocation to, say, twenty managers cannot hope to produce a perfect match. You can't control ten thousand dimensions with twenty.

There is a risk associated with the difference between the sponsor's target and the weighted aggregate of the manager's normals. This difference is called *misfit risk*. There are two important attributes of misfit risk:

- Misfit risk is a *permanent* feature of the sponsor's overall allocation; it will not change until either the allocation to the managers is adjusted or the sponsor's target changes; and
- Misfit risk is borne by the sponsor with no expectation of a compensating boost in return.

Active Risk

In addition to misfit risk, the sponsor is subject to the active risks taken by the managers. Each manager will maintain a managed portfolio that differs from the manager's normal. In contrast with misfit risk, the positions giving rise to the active risks change each month or each quarter. We assume that these changing active positions give rise to a nearly constant level of active risk; and for active managers we call this the manager's *aggressiveness*. For passive managers, we call this risk the manager's *tracking error*. The aggregate of all the differences between the normal and the managed portfolios is the *aggregate active risk*.

This allows us to write the sponsor's return as

$$R\{Sponsor\} = R\{Target\} + R\{Misfit\} + R\{Active\}. \qquad (1)$$

A representation of such a relationship is shown in Exhibit 1. In our experience, the risk associated with misfit and with active management—or active 'bets'—are roughly similar in magnitude.

The bulk of the sponsor's risk and return comes from the target portfolio, and its selection is an important strategic decision. However, life is led at the margin. Once the strategic choice of a target is made, it is the misfit and the active return that make the marginal difference.

Although the misfit and the active risk are usually similar in magnitude, active risk is generally the focus of attention. One can draw two opposing inferences from this: there should be more attention paid to misfit risk, or, if the aggregate active risk is of the same order as the misfit risk, then the aggregate active risk isn't very important either.

If more attention should be paid to misfit risk, there are three possibilities: Refine the definition of the target, rebalance the managers, or design special *fulfillment* funds to match the difference between the target and the aggregate of the other managers' normals. The notion of fulfillment

EXHIBIT 1: STRUCTURE OF AGGREGATE RISK

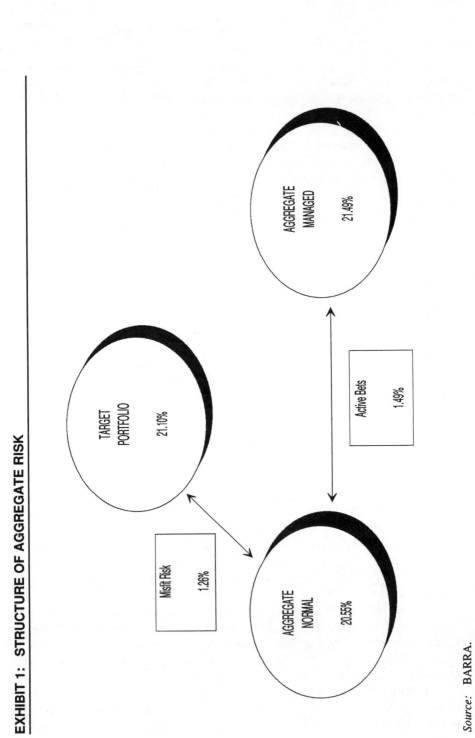

Source: BARRA.

or completeness funds has been around for a long time, and is gradually gaining acceptance among sponsors. The fulfillment fund can either work as a passive component of the overall mix or as a fund assigned to an active manager who is willing to add value relative to a normal portfolio that represents the gap between the target and the aggregate normal.

However, even if we are successful in eliminating misfit risk, the active risk will remain. A great deal of the sponsor's attention is paid to the active risk of individual managers rather than the aggregate active risk. The next two sections look at some of the implications of the sponsor's focus on this component of risk in both active and passive management.

PASSIVE MANAGEMENT

Passive management offers low fees, low transaction costs, and has proven effective in achieving its stated goals of providing returns linked to those of an index. If a sponsor believes that consistent positive (over and above fees and transaction costs) active performance is unlikely, then he will desire passive management. If the sponsor thinks that skillful active managers exist, but that he won't be able to identify them, then passive management makes sense. And if the sponsor wants to hedge his bets on active manager selection and control the residual risk of the aggregate, then passive management again makes sense.

One issue of concern with passive management is the trade-off between tracking error and transaction costs. Critics maintain that passive managers overemphasize tracking error as a performance criterion. We can check this contention by doing a brief analysis of the trade-off; to accomplish this we need some algebra. Here's the terminology:

$R(P)$ = the managed portfolio's return

$R(B)$ = the benchmark portfolio's return

TC = transaction costs

TE = tracking error

The variables are related by the equation

$$TE = R(P) - R(B) - TC. \tag{2}$$

It is generally assumed, to be consistent with the ideal of passive management, that the expected return on the managed and the benchmark portfolios is the same. The expected level of tracking error is then

$$E \{TE\} = - TC. \tag{3}$$

Transaction costs have three components: commissions, the bid-ask spread, and market impact. Most benchmark returns are measured from close to close; if passive managers trade with closing prices, they can ensure that the market impact of their trades is reflected in the benchmark return as well as the portfolio return. Whether this is wise is another matter,[2] but the upshot is that there will be no contribution to tracking error from market impact.

The active risk is

$$\sigma\{TE\} = Std \{R(P) - R(B)\}. \tag{4}$$

This forecast of the standard deviation $\sigma\{TE\}$ is also commonly called *tracking error*. The choices open to the manager are described by a passive efficient frontier of the sort shown in Exhibit 2. The frontier F-F′ shows the combinations of expected tracking error and standard deviation of tracking error that are obtainable. Note the vertical scale for transaction costs is in percent. The horizontal scale is in terms of tracking error *squared*. The exhibit is drawn so that the existing portfolio (at F′) has a 1.00% tracking error. The minimal tracking error portfolio (at F) has 0.22%, or 22 basis points, of tracking error; and the transaction costs for moving from F′ to F are 37 basis points.

In order to choose a point on the passive frontier F-F′ we need a way to choose between the certain component of tracking error (the transaction costs TC) and the uncertain component as measured by $\sigma\{TE\}$. We do this by minimizing the function

$$TC + \lambda \bullet \sigma^2\{TE\}. \tag{5}$$

Exhibit 3 shows how the point along F-F′ will vary with the choice of the parameter λ that measures the trade-off between the certain transaction costs and the uncertain components of tracking error. This choice of objective is consistent with trading off expected returns versus active risk for an active manager. We call λ the aversion to active risk or active risk aversion. Point A is optimal if $\lambda=0.5$. At point A we have 0.10%, or 10 basis points, of transaction costs and 0.50%, or 50 basis points, of tracking error. Point B is optimal for a higher level of aversion to active risk ($\lambda=2.0$), and, at point B, transaction costs are 26 basis points with 28 basis points of tracking error.

BARRA's experience has shown that an active risk aversion of 0.1 to 1.0 is reasonable for the active risks a plan sponsor faces. For example:

EXHIBIT 2

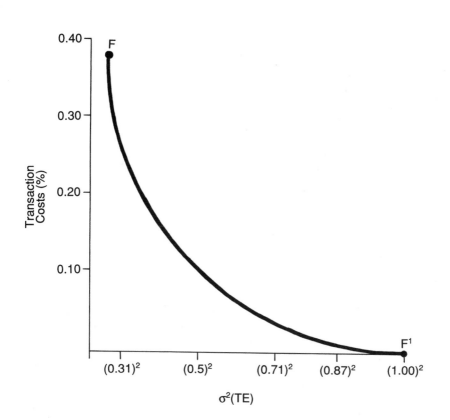

EXHIBIT 3

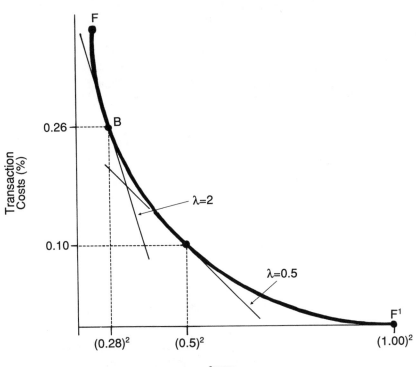

$\sigma^2(TE)$

with an active risk aversion of 0.5, and $\sigma\{TE\}=0.75\%$, there is a cost of $0.5 \bullet (0.75)^2 = 0.28\%$ or 28 basis points.

With an appropriate cost associated with $\sigma\{TE\}$, it is possible to look at the transaction costs and tracking error choices. The way we view those choices depends on whether we look at the passive fund in isolation or in the context of the entire fund. If we look at the passive fund in isolation, then it takes reasonably high levels of active risk aversion on the sponsor's part (about 2.0) to imply a strong intolerance of tracking error. At a more realistic level of sponsor's active risk aversion, say 0.5, the sponsor will tolerate relatively large amounts of tracking error in order to avoid transaction costs.

The analysis is different if only a fraction of the fund is invested passively. Suppose, for example, that 50% of the fund is invested passively. To formulate this analysis, we make the quite reasonable assumption that the *tracking error* in the passive fund is uncorrelated with the *active* returns of other managers. The transaction costs are multiplied by 0.5 to measure their contribution to the total fund. The contribution to the active variance of the entire fund is multiplied by the fraction invested passively squared, or 0.25 in this case. When viewed from the perspective of the entire fund, transaction costs are half as large, and the cost of the tracking error is only one-fourth as large. For a fund with 31.62% passive, the transaction costs would be .3162 of their value in isolation, and the cost of risk would be only $0.1 = (.3162)^2$ of its value in isolation.

We can make this point another way. Consider a passive fund that costs 10 basis points to rebalance to a point with 50 basis points of tracking error, $\sigma\{TE\}$. If this passive fund is 100% of the sponsor's fund, then the cost is $0.10 + \lambda (0.50)^2$. If the passive fund is a fraction, f, of the total fund, then the cost to the sponsor is $(f \bullet 0.10) + \lambda f^2 (0.50)^2$. As the fraction invested passively, f, decreases, we see that the contribution of the risk term, $\lambda (0.50)^2$, becomes less and less significant.

An extreme intolerance for active risk would be needed to induce very small levels of active risk. In Exhibit 4, we look at the cost of passive management where 50% of the sponsor's assets are in a passive fund.

The 50% passive allocation reduces the transaction costs by half and the risk by one-quarter. We can view tracking error and transaction costs from the perspective of the entire fund by asking how our choice would change if we retained the same level of active risk aversion we used in analyzing the passive fund in isolation. Point C in Exhibit 4 shows the optimal rebalancing strategy with risk aversion equal to 0.5. This should be compared to point A in Exhibit 3, where risk aversion is also equal to 0.5. Tracking error for the passive fund is 0.50% at point A in Exhibit 3, and 0.64% at point C in Exhibit 4. The contribution of point C's tracking error

EXHIBIT 4

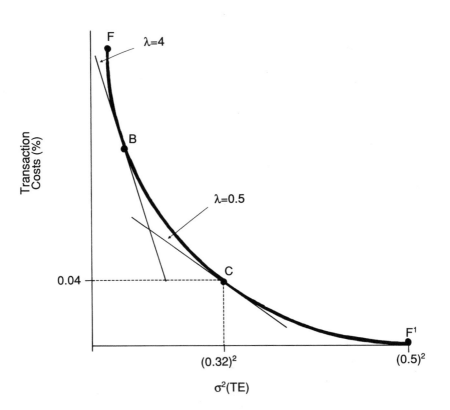

in the passive fund to the total fund is $(0.5) \bullet (0.64) = 0.32$, because we are 50% passive.

Another way to measure the effect of looking from the aggregate perspective is to ask what level of active risk aversion would be required to maintain a policy. Point B from Exhibit 3 will remain optimal only if the risk aversion increases to 4.0, as shown in Exhibit 4. A risk aversion of 4.0 would place a cost of 2.25% for an overall, or entire, fund with an active risk of 0.75%; $4 \bullet (0.75)^2 = 2.25$. This is an extremely large penalty for active risk.

There is clearly a double standard by which the active risk (tracking error) that stems from passive management is not tolerated to the same extent as the active risk that stems from the aggressiveness of active managers. The reason for this different treatment *is not* that there is an anticipated active return from the active managers. Recall the level of optimal level of tracking error, $\sigma\{TE\}$, was obtained through a trade-off with the certain loss in active return due to higher transaction costs.

ACTIVE MANAGEMENT

Active managers pose a similar problem for the sponsor, and the difficulty again is the perception and control of risk. The sponsor who views each manager's contribution to risk at the overall fund level will reach different conclusions from the sponsor who judges each manager in isolation. The situation is analogous to the relationship between individual assets and portfolios. Assets are to portfolios as managers are to the stable of managers. When portfolios are evaluated on an asset by asset basis, diversification plays no role. In order to emphasize the importance of diversification, we look at the managers from the perspective of the entire fund.

In the best of all worlds, sponsors see each active manager as an opportunity. That opportunity is measured by the manager's information ratio, or the ratio of expected active return to the standard deviation of active return.

$\alpha(n)$ = Manager n's expected active return (% per year).

$\omega(n)$ = Manager n's level of active risk or aggressiveness (% per year).

$IR(n)$ = Manager n's information ratio; $IR(n) = \alpha(n)/\omega(n)$.

$y(n)$ = The fraction of funds allocated to manager n.

$VA(n)$ = Manager n's contribution to value added.

λ   = Sponsor's aversion to active risk.

In the technical appendix we examine a very simple case to reach a rule of thumb that relates the sponsor's allocation of funds to the manager's aggressiveness and information ratio. The relationship is

$$y(n) = IR(n)/[2{\bullet}\omega(n){\bullet}\lambda].   \tag{6}$$

Sponsors are concerned about the product of their allocation to the manager and the manager's active risk; notice that $y(n){\bullet}\omega(n)$ is constant across managers. The reason is clear; the contribution to active return from the manager is proportional to the product, and the contribution to active variance of the manager is proportional to the product squared. If a sponsor has an aversion to active risk of 0.33 and gives 15% of the fund to a manager with 8% active risk, the "cost" of the active variance is $0.33{\bullet}(0.15{\bullet}8.0)^2 = 0.48\%$. If the sponsor gives 40% of the fund to a manager with 3% active risk, the cost is $0.33{\bullet}(0.4{\bullet}3.0)^2 = 0.48\%$. If both managers have an information ratio of 0.79, then the expected active return of the first manager will be $0.15{\bullet}0.79{\bullet}8.0 = 0.95\%$ and the second manager's expected contribution to the sponsor's active returns will be $0.4{\bullet}0.79{\bullet}3.0 = 0.95\%$ as well.

Value added is defined as expected active return less the cost of the active variance. In the example above, the value added of each manager is 0.95% - 0.48% = 0.47%. This is consistent with a more general rule that the manager's contribution to value added depends only on the manager's information ratio. If we assume that allocations are made according to rule (6), then the manager's contribution is given by

$$VA(n) = IR(n)^2/[4{\bullet}\lambda].   \tag{7}$$

To illustrate (7) let's consider an example; the results are detailed in Exhibit 5. Suppose there are three good managers. Each has an information ratio of 1.0, and each has different levels of active risk while the sponsor's risk aversion is 0.33. The allocation rule, (6), states that allocation to the manager times the active risk level should be $1.5 = (0.5{\bullet}1.0)/.33$ times the manager's information ratio. Manager A has an active risk of 4%, manager B of 6%, and manager C of 8%. The allocation of the sponsor to each of these managers would be 37.5% for manager A, 25% for manager B, and 18.75% for manager C. The remaining 18.75% is managed passively.

Clearly, when fees are proportional to assets under management, manager C suffers from having a higher level of active risk! In addition to getting a smaller piece of the pie, manager C has a larger chance of having an extremely bad year and thus less in the way of client relationship security. The probabilities of an annual active performance under –5% for managers A, B, and C are respectively 1.2%, 3.3%, and 5.2%.[3]

EXHIBIT 5: ALLOCATION OF FEES AND VALUE ADDED

Manager	Info Ratio	Active Risk (%)	Allocation (%)	Contribution to Alpha (%)	Contribution to Value Added (bp)	Fee (bp)
A	1.0	4	37.50	1.50	75	19
B	1.0	6	25.00	1.50	75	13
C	1.0	8	18.75	1.50	75	9
Total	1.73	2.60	81.25	4.50	225	41

Assumptions: Sponsor's Active Risk Aversion 0.33
Fees are 50bp.
Manager's Actice Risks are Uncorrelated

Source: BARRA.

From the sponsor's point of view, each of these managers adds the same amount of value, 45 basis points per year (recall they all have the same information ratio). However at fees of 50 basis points per dollar under management, managers A, B, and C get 18.75, 12.5 and 5.6 basis points based on the value of the entire fund. There is an inconsistency between their ability to add value and their compensation.

The allocation rule (6) is somewhat in line with current practice. More aggressive active managers tend, on the whole, to have smaller portions of fund assets than less aggressive managers. But as we see from (7), it is in the sponsor's interest to have the managers be more aggressive so the sponsor can capture the same level of value added while allocating a smaller portion of funds to the manager to save on fees. At the same time, it is usually in the interest of managers to have a low level of aggressiveness. This will tend to garner larger accounts and the associated larger fees. Low aggressiveness has the added benefit of reducing the manager's business risk since the less aggressive manager has a smaller chance of having very low performance over any period of time.

It is easy to calculate the effect on value added of a manager using less (or more) than the desired level of aggressiveness. If the sponsor's allocation to the manager is y, then the desired level of aggressiveness from (6) is

$$\omega^* = IR/[2 \bullet \lambda \bullet y]. \tag{8}$$

With ω^* as the desired level of aggressiveness, and w the actual level of aggressiveness, let f be the ratio of ω to ω^*. The value added that the sponsor receives will be

$$VA = \{2 \bullet f - f^2\} \bullet IR^2/[4 \bullet \lambda] = \{2 \bullet f - f^2\} \bullet VA^* \tag{9}$$

Exhibit 6 shows the impact on value added for various levels of f.

EXHIBIT 6: EFFECT ON VALUE ADDED OF REDUCED AGGRESSIVENESS

ω / ω^*	VA / VA^*
0.25	0.44
0.50	0.75
0.75	0.94
0.90	0.99

This is good news. Relatively large deviations from the desired aggressiveness ω^*, say 10% or 25%, imply small losses of 1% and 6% in the manager's value added.

PUTTING IT ALL TOGETHER

The earlier sections discussed misfit risk and the management of active risk separately to derive some insight into the relationship between the manager's ability as measured by the information ratio and the sponsor's aversion to active risk.

It is possible to do a more sophisticated computer analysis that takes into consideration the following:

- misfit risk;
- active risk;
- management fees;
- the cost of reallocating between managers;
- the active manager's ability to add value; and
- constraints on the amounts allocated to the managers.

This optimization analysis will look at the trade-offs between each of the factors listed above and, as such, can provide a sponsor with an analytical framework for managing risk.

SUMMARY

The message of this chapter is that sponsors should look at portfolio risk in the aggregate. An aggregate view makes the implied cost of tracking error for passive managers, and the cost of aggressiveness for active managers, far smaller when viewed in the aggregate than when each manager is viewed in isolation. Multiple managers offer sponsors great diversification benefits; but sponsors need to adapt policy to take advantage of those diversification benefits.

The allocation of funds to active managers should, in general, be directly proportional to the sponsor's assessment of the manager's ability to add value as measured by the manager's information ratio, and inversely proportional to both the sponsor's level of risk aversion and the manager's level of aggressiveness. Under this allocation scheme, each manager's contribution to value added will be proportional to the manager's information ratio squared and independent of the amount of funds allocated to the manager. This suggests that compensating managers on the basis of assets under management is at odds with compensation based on value added to the overall portfolio.

NOTES

[1] For an earlier view of these topics, see Barr Rosenberg, "Institutional Investment With Multiple Portfolio Managers," *CRSP Proceedings* (November, 1977), pp. 55-160.

[2] Conventional wisdom and some evidence (Lawrence Harris, "A Day-End Transaction Price Anomaly," *Journal of Financial and Quantitative Analysis* (March 1989), pp. 29-45) say that closing prices tend to be biased on the high side. This would argue for a clever passive manager to do the sell programs at the close and try to work the buy programs at other than closing prices.

[3] We are assuming that the *active* returns are normally distributed.

APPENDIX

This appendix derives the results cited in the main text. Here is a list of variables and their definitions.

Notation:

n	=	Index for the managers
y(n)	=	Amount of funds allocated to manager n
IR(n)	=	Information ratio for manager n. This is a measure of the ability of manager n to add value.
ω(n)	=	Residual (active) risk of manager n. Called the aggressiveness.
α(n)	=	Alpha of manager n
μ(n)	=	Expected excess return from manager n at a zero level of aggressiveness. This is the expected excess return of the normal.
r(P,n)	=	Portfolio return of manager n
r(B,n)	=	Benchmark return for manager n
r(P)	=	Aggregate portfolio return
r(T)	=	Sponsor's target return
r(M)	=	Misfit return
r(A)	=	Aggregate active return

Let the return on the nth manager be

$$r(P,n) = \alpha(n) + r(B,n) + \omega(n) \bullet z(n) \qquad (A1)$$

where z(n) is random with mean zero and standard deviation equal to one.

If we use the definition of the information ratio,

$$IR(n) = \alpha(n)/\omega(n), \qquad (A2)$$

then we can rewrite manager n's return as

$$r(P,n) = \omega(n) \bullet IR(n) + r(B,n) + \omega(n) \bullet z(n). \qquad (A3)$$

The aggregate portfolio will give us

$$r(P) = \Sigma_n \ y(n)\bullet r(P,n). \tag{A4}$$

The aggregate return r(P) can be broken down into three terms: target return, misfit return, and active return.

$$r(P) = r(T) + r(M) + r(A). \tag{A5}$$

The misfit return, r(M), is defined by

$$r(M) = \Sigma_n \ y(n)\bullet[r(B,n) - r(T)], \tag{A6}$$

and the active return, r(A), by

$$r(A) = \Sigma_n \ y(n)\bullet \ \omega(n)\bullet\{IR(n)+z(n)\}. \tag{A7}$$

Assumption #1: The target return and the benchmark return coincide for all managers. This implies that the misfit risk is identically zero. This is usually not the case in practice, however, this assumption will help us focus on the active component of return and ignore the interaction of the misfit return and the active return.

Assumption #2: The active risks, z(n), across managers are un-correlated with each other and with the target return r(T). The zero correlation of the active returns z(n) and z(m) is not a very strict assumption. The observed correlations tend to be very small. If each manager maintains a beta equal to 1.0 with respect to the target portfolio, then the active returns will be uncorrelated with the target.

These assumptions let us calculate the active variance as

$$\text{Var}\{r(A)| \ y,\omega\} = \Sigma_n \ y(n)^2 \bullet\omega \ (n)^2. \tag{A8}$$

The expected active return will be

$$E\{r(A) \ | \ y, \ \omega\} = \Sigma_n \ IR(n)\bullet\omega(n)\bullet y(n). \tag{A9}$$

For the given level of sponsor aggressiveness $\omega(n)$, we can solve for the optimal allocation, y, by maximizing the mean variance criterion

$$VA\{r(A) \ | \ \omega,y\} = \Sigma_n IR(n)\bullet y(n)\bullet\omega(n)-\lambda\bullet \ \Sigma_n \ y(n)^2\bullet\omega(n)^2. \tag{A10}$$

where λ is a risk aversion parameter.

The first order conditions in this optimization are

$$IR(n) \bullet \omega(n) = 2 \bullet \lambda \bullet y(n) \bullet \omega(n)^2, \text{ or} \qquad (A11)$$

$$y(n) = IR(n)/[2 \bullet \lambda \bullet \omega(n)] \qquad (A12)$$

Note this formula indicates, as one would expect, that we are more aggressive where we have the more skill and that we are more aggressive if risk aversion, λ, is lower.

If we substitute the first order condition (A11) back into our expression (A10) for the optimal level of value added, VA^*, we get

$$VA^* = \sum_n IR(n)^2/[4 \bullet \lambda]. \qquad (A13)$$

The optimal level of value added is independent of both the allocation, $y(n)$, to the managers, and the level of aggressiveness, $\omega(n)$, of the managers.

CHAPTER 9

Manager Fees from the Performance Viewpoint

ARJUN DIVECHA
DIRECTOR OF EQUITY SERVICES
BARRA

NICK MENCHER
CONSULTANT
BARRA

This chapter discusses methods for the compensation of investment managers. We look at current techniques, examine some commonly used performance fee schedules, and discuss some of the pitfalls involved in the use of both traditional and performance fees. We examine the basic conflict between sponsors and managers, offer our own performance fee scheme which may mitigate this conflict, and summarize the experiences two sponsors have had using performance fees.

We also present a discussion of how some of these schemes can be gamed, as well as some of the undesirable option-like effects caused by floors and caps. Finally, we look at who stands to gain and lose if the industry moves to a performance fee standard.

Most proposed schemes, including our own, are variants of performance fees; i.e., the fee increases as the manager's active return beyond the benchmark return increases. One impact of such arrangements, we argue, is that they increase the business risk of money management, leading to higher capital requirements for managers and, perhaps, to a fundamental change in the ownership structure of the industry.

CURRENT SCHEMES AND NEW INCENTIVES

The industry standard for the compensation of active investment managers is a fixed-fee based purely on the amount of assets under management. This fee is often combined with a volume discount, and the resulting arrangement might look as follows:

Assets Under Management ($)	Annual Fee (%)
0 - 10 million	0.50 of assets
10 - 20 million	0.40 of assets above $10 million
20 - 100 million	0.35 of assets above $20 million
over 100 million	0.25 of assets above $100 million

These fees are usually payable quarterly in arrears.

This type of fee schedule has led to dissatisfaction in the sponsor community because it neither rewards good performance nor penalizes bad manager performance.

The current fee arrangement, however, creates a number of performance incentives for managers; the most important is probably the reputation of the manager, which helps maintain current accounts, garner new accounts, and increase his or her funds under management.

In addition, assets under management grow when portfolio value goes up, thereby increasing the manager's fee. As the asset base grows, good performance in any one period effectively increases the present value of future fees.

Current fee schedules do give managers an incentive to perform as effectively as possible. The primary disadvantage of asset-based fee schedules is that the fee is for *promised* performance rather than for *delivered* performance. Performance, or "incentive," fees address this issue by setting the fee ex-post rather than ex-ante. But while there are benefits to performance fees, there are also pitfalls that need to be avoided. We will discuss a few of these issues after a brief review of performance fee methods.

PERFORMANCE FEE SCHEMES

Most performance fee schemes, either implemented or proposed, are based on some sort of linear fulcrum fee with floors and caps. This is illustrated in Exhibit 1.

Usually, the manager earns the equivalent of his or her fixed fee for providing 200-300 basis points of performance above an agreed upon benchmark. Performance above or below that fixed fee generates more or less additional fees. However, the fee has a minimum and maximum amount, called the floor and cap, since sponsors do not want to be overly generous nor put their managers out of business.

The slope of the linear fee shown in Exhibit 1 varies. We have seen cases where the manager gets $1 for every $20 the sponsor earns, as well as "one-for-every-five-dollar" ratios. Clearly, the steeper the slope, the more "performance" based is the fee, and the flatter the slope, the more it resembles the traditional "flat" fee. The slope's profile is clearly a crucial issue in negotiations between managers and sponsors. There are currently no industry-wide standards for the process of setting these fees, but we believe some consensus will emerge if and when performance fees based on "normal"[1] portfolios become widely accepted.

BENEFITS AND DISADVANTAGES OF PERFORMANCE FEES

The primary goal and benefit of performance fees is to reward the manager's good performance. In addition, performance fees force sponsors to concentrate on the value-added performance of their managers in terms of its effect on the entire fund, rather than market or sector performance.

Another advantage is that performance fees, unlike traditional fee structures, allow sponsors to keep poorly performing managers in their stables until conditions change and performances improve. Under traditional methods, the only alternative is to terminate these managers, as they will continue to earn fees despite performing poorly. It is easier to tell a board of directors that you want to give a manager another chance to prove his strategy when he worked for free last year, than to tell them the manager will continue to bill the fund for losing its money. Unfortunately, as we will discuss later, those managers best able to function under a system where they may have to forgo income for several years will most likely

EXHIBIT 1: PERFORMANCE FEES WITH FLOORS AND CAPS

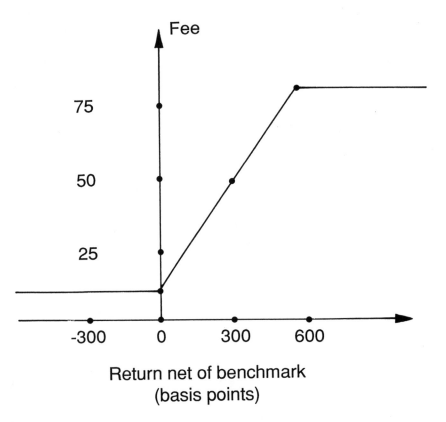

Return net of benchmark
(basis points)

have ownership and capital structures that rule out the innovative styles which may take longer to bear fruit.

Other advantages for sponsors of performance fees are that they increase flexibility and create options for differing fee arrangements between sponsors and managers. Some also see performance fees as more fair than current schemes, and, to many in the industry, performance plans have a strong common-sense appeal. Manager searches and hiring should also become easier—as the greater information available on performance should enable sponsors to more effectively comparison shop for management services. The drawback to performance evaluation is an impaired ability to comparison shop, but as performance measurement reaches consensus, sponsors should be able to compare performances by comparing fees awarded to managers.

Barriers to Entry

What are some disadvantages to these systems? One is that performance-based fees create barriers to entry into the money management business. These barriers occur because performance fees tend to increase the need for a proven track record, which is the single largest impediment to those entering the business. These barriers would also increase if performance fees awarded become part of manager search methods.

A track record is not the only barrier performance fees exasperate. Performance fees also effectively make the manager a financial partner of the sponsor by making the manager's cash flows dependent on performance. This inevitably will lead to greater volatility in the manager's earnings, requiring him to be more highly capitalized in order to ride out bad periods.

These capital needs may well drive the small boutique managers out of business and hinder the success of new and innovative firms. Reducing the choices of managers and manager styles available may, in the long run, not be desirable from the sponsor's point of view.

If in-house manager searches using performance fee information increase, the trend would also create a business risk for traditional consultants. This business risk, like many others, creates an advantage for part of the industry and a disadvantage for another part. While search consultants will suffer as a result of less income, sponsors will save money usually spent on consultant services.

It might also be argued that current assets-under-management systems already provide many of the benefits of performance-based fees, and that performance fees will increase costs to sponsors by adding the expenses of monitoring performance and maintaining appropriate benchmarks. We would argue that the expenses of monitoring performance and maintaining benchmarks are tiny when compared to the benefits of having better information about one's managers. And, of course, for those managers who find their fees reduced by performance fees, the whole concept is a disadvantage. It seems inevitable that equity managers as a group will receive lower fees, given their collective underperformance vis-a-vis broad market indices over the last few years.

Floors and Caps

Another disadvantage to performance fees is that their use of floors and caps can create option-like effects that are undesirable for sponsors.

For example, say a manager reaches his cap during the month of February. He then has no further incentive to do a good job for his client and, in fact, has every reason to retreat into an index-like portfolio to lock in the gains. Such a retreat is a disadvantage for the sponsor, however, because he or she is now not benefiting from the manager's ideas.

Similarly, the manager that is 700 basis points behind in November has an incentive to take extreme risks in December, the equivalent of a 90 yard "Hail Mary" pass.

Both of these problems can be addressed by the sponsor's monitoring of the level of risk in the manager's portfolio and ensuring that it remains within an acceptable range. Another solution is to do away with a fixed one-year contract and move to a rolling three-year scheme. Every quarter, using this rolling scheme, one new quarter's performance is added and the oldest quarter's performance is dropped. Such an approach leads to two desirable effects: it will reduce the option-like effects of floors and caps, as well as reduce the quarter-to-quarter cash flow volatility of the manager.

Benchmark Confusion

In the context of performance fees, the selection of a benchmark is clearly a sensitive and crucial issue for both sponsor and manager. Some benchmarks are clearly inappropriate—for example the S&P 500 is not the correct benchmark for an aggressive growth manager. It is because cf the unsuitability of broad-based indices like the S&P 500 that normal portfolios, despite their flaws, are still the best friend of sponsors seeking to use performance fees.

One of the problems with performance fees is the lack of widely accepted standards for measuring return to the benchmark and, thus, fees due to the manager. For example, the S&P 500 had a range of 50 basis points in the measured return for 1988 across 10 large institutions. Unfortunately, using a customized normal portfolio, in and of itself, does not completely solve this problem, because there may also be discrepancies in the computation of return for normal portfolios.

A more serious criticism of performance fees is that they increase the possibility of manager gaming. This potential abuse is examined below.

Performance Gaming

The current system of paying fees based on assets under management represents a relatively simple method. Performance fees are more complex, and, as with many new and complicated processes, the possibility of undesirable outcomes exists.

One scenario whereby managers might be tempted to game the process calls for the manager to consistently keep the beta of his or her portfolio above that of the benchmark. Because in the long run markets go up, there would be a premium to holding a higher beta. This would lead to portfolio returns above the benchmark returns and, thus, to the awarding of unearned performance fees since the manager actually made no active judgements to earn the fee.

One way to avoid this type of gaming problem is for sponsors to monitor the level of beta in the portfolio and benchmark on an ongoing basis. Over time, this monitoring leads to discussions between the sponsor and manager about the appropriateness of the benchmark. Such discussions, while not always exactly cordial, are crucial in the effective running of a fund which uses performance fees.

Another possible gaming ploy is to run what we call an "alphabet fund." Under this scenario, the manager charges active management fees but actually runs the S&P 500 passively, allocating all companies whose names begin with letters A-F to the first sponsor, G-L to the second sponsor, and so on.

By using an alphabet fund, the manager collects an active fee for what is, in effect, passive management. In up markets, when many active managers find it difficult to beat indices like the S&P 500, the temptation to sneak such a game past the sponsor is strong. To avoid such subterfuge, sponsors and search consultants should be wary of managers bearing multiple normals, unless the normals truly represent different strategies.

Again, close monitoring of risk levels over time will also reveal problems arising from the alphabet game. The common thread to these problems is that performance fees clearly require a greater level of vigilance on the part of sponsors.

Performance fees also represent a business risk for managers. An approach which converts this business risk into a shared contract between sponsor and manager may help both parties and encourage the increased use of performance-linked fees.

BUSINESS RISK, INVESTMENT RISK AND A NEW APPROACH

A fundamental conflict exists between the sponsor and manager: the sponsor wants the manager to be as aggressive as his best ideas warrant, while the manager wants to diversify his portfolio to reduce the risk of losing clients and fees. This tension is expressed as the investment risk of the sponsor versus the business risk of the manager.[2] The financial contract between sponsors and managers, here expressed as the performance fee arrangement, should attempt to bring about a convergence of these two opposing goals while maximizing each party's utility.

In recent years, a new field of inquiry called "agency theory" has received increased attention. Agency theory examines how principals can structure contracts with their agents in such a manner that the agent performs in the principal's best interest.

The proposed performance fee plan, based on agency theory, seeks to resolve the business risk/investment risk conflict by forcing managers to reveal the best assessment of their own skills to the sponsor as part of the fee-setting process. Exhibit 2 shows an example of such a scheme.

In Exhibit 2, the two lines, A and B, show the fee schedule for two managers. Line A represents the payoff pattern of a manager who promises sponsors an active return, or alpha, of 1.00% over the benchmark. Line B represents the payoff pattern for a manager who promises 2.00% over the benchmark.

According to this proposed system, the fee is set up so that the following occurs:

1. The manager who promises 1.00% but delivers 0% receives *less* of a fee than an index fund manager.

2. The manager who promises 1.00% and delivers 1.00% receives *more* than the manager who promises 2.00% but delivers 1.00%.

EXHIBIT 2: PROPOSED SCHEME

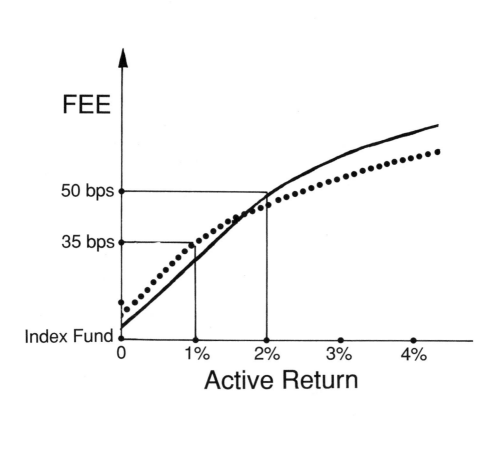

3. The manager who promises 2.00% and delivers 2.00% gets *more* than the manager who promises 1.00% but delivers 2.00%.

As a result, a manager *maximizes* his or her fee by promising *only* what he or she thinks is possible to deliver, not more or less. Grandiose marketing or negotiating ploys that overestimate what the manager thinks is possible thus carry a penalty which works in the sponsor's favor. This scheme also gives the sponsor more information than he or she would have under other fee methods. The added information is the major benefit of this proposed scheme, because forcing managers to reveal information they would not have revealed under other systems allows sponsors to assess and rank managers as part of the search process.

To deal with the problems inherent in caps, this scheme has no cap. Rather, the incremental fee keeps getting smaller, i.e. the slope of the line keeps getting smaller, but never becomes flat. There is always an incentive, therefore, for managers to perform better.

While not active in the scheme proposed above, two sponsors have used performance-based fees for several years. The experiences of the Rockefeller Foundation and the Minnesota State Board of Investment may be of interest to those considering embarking on a similar campaign.

THE EXPERIENCES OF TWO SPONSORS

The Rockefeller Foundation is pleased with the results of their foray into the world of performance fees. One reason is that the fee arrangement wound up lowering the managers' transaction costs. This occurred because the managers, when confronted by the need to improve performance to maintain and increase fees, targeted transaction costs as a main area where savings could be garnered.

It is interesting to note that the managers looked to transaction costs as an area where savings in trading fees could be translated into performance gains for clients and fee increases for themselves. The role of transaction costs in active management is an increasing area of focus, and we anticipate more managers and sponsors viewing transaction costs as the most logical place to begin cost savings and performance boosting. If we agree with Abel and Noser that "trading costs are the reason overall performance of all professionally managed portfolios lags the S&P 500,"[3] trading costs and, more generally, transaction costs are clearly areas for attention.

In any case, The Rockefeller Foundation found that overall management fees were slightly higher due to the good performance of their managers. While the prospect had occurred to the Foundation that fees might *increase* rather than decline under performance fees, they were happy to pay the higher fees.

When asked why they feel performance fees are not catching on industry-wide, the Foundation replied that the lack of good normal portfolios and problems with the precise measurement of returns are slowing the growth of the scheme. In addition, the lack of a widely accepted pricing source for fixed-income assets discourages fixed-income managers from participating in performance-based fee plans.

Another sponsor using performance fees is the Minnesota State Board of Investment, which also reports good experiences with the method over the last three years. An overall result of using performance fees is that most of the Board's managers focus more clearly on their normal portfolios, allowing the sponsor to control misfit risk. In addition, there was no observed change in the managers' aggressiveness that might have occurred as the managers became more concerned with their business risk.

The result of the Board's experiment with performance fees was that overall fees remained about the same, the majority of managers earned less money, and a few received substantial fee increases over those they had earned using the assets-under-management system. The top and bottom of the performance spectrum are represented by one manager who maxed out at plus 9% and two who bottomed out at –7%. The later two managers worked free during 1988.

The nine managers currently working for the Board had no complaints, and in fact, did not want to change the scheme during renegotiation of their contracts.

These two examples have happy endings. But it is clear from their slow progress in the sponsor community that performance fees are not universally loved. One reason may be that the benefits of performance fees can depend on the skill of those using them.

UNEQUAL BENEFITS

Who benefits and who suffers under performance fee arrangements, including the one we've proposed? It is clear that good managers will benefit, as their performance will boost fees. Average and poorly performing managers will clearly suffer under the system.

On the sponsor side, performance fees actually hurt skillful sponsors who hire good managers who then perform well—under this arrangement, total fees, like those paid by The Rockefeller Foundation, actually went up. This appears to be a reason good sponsors shouldn't embrace the scheme, but other considerations may apply: for example, it may be that not all of the managers hired actually performed well. Average and poor sponsors will come out ahead, as the poor performance of their managers will lower fees the sponsor must pay.[4]

THE IMPACT OF PERFORMANCE FEES

We've discussed the concept of performance fees for investment managers and their impact on managers and sponsors. Other than the potential for lower manager profits, what would be some of the industry-wide effects of adoption of this system?

One result might be that managers would become financial intermediaries, thereby forcing them to sustain losses during periods of poor performance. In situations like this, where reserves of capital become key to continued operations, the marketplace clearly favors large firms like banks and insurance companies. In fact, the specter of performance fees may lead to boutique managers being bought out by people with deep pockets—perhaps, in particular, well-capitalized Japanese firms. Is such a state desirable?

While this question cannot be answered fully here, it should be noted that a shift in ownership of managers would increase the business risk of the manager without increasing (substantially) the return to the sponsor. This, in our opinion, is the main drawback of performance fees.

CONCLUSION

This chapter examined current and new manager fee schemes and their problems, suggested a new method for performance fees, and examined the experiences of two sponsors. From our experience, performance fees have had mostly positive reports from sponsors; they are happy to pay the higher fees when performance is good, and happy to pay lower fees when performance is bad.

We have also looked at some other possible results of performance fees—particularly the possibility that this fee arrangement may result in a money management industry that is dominated by large, corporate-owned firms rather than small, independent boutiques.

NOTES

[1]   For a detailed discussion on normal portfolios, see Chapters 6 and 7.

[2] These issues are discussed in detail in Andrew Rudd, "Business Risk and Investment Risk," *Investment Management Review* (November/December 1987) , pp. 19-27.

[3] Stanley S. Abel and Eugene A. Noser, Jr., "Trader to Broker," in Wayne H. Wagner (ed.), *The Complete Guide to Securities Transactions* (New York, NY: John Wiley & Sons, Inc., 1989), p. 63.

[4] For a detailed examination of these issues, see Richard Grinold and Andrew Rudd, "Incentive Fees: Who Wins? Who Loses?" *Financial Analysts Journal* (January/February 1987), pp. 27-38.

CHAPTER 10

Structuring Managers Using Fundamentals

RONALD J. SURZ
PRINCIPAL
BECKER, BURKE ASSOCIATES INCORPORATED

Structuring an investment management team is a complex process involving decisions in the following areas:

1. Asset allocation, or commitments to:
   stocks
   bonds
   real estate
   foreign
   etc.

2. Manager types, or criteria such as:
   active or passive
   generalist or specialist
   bank, counsellor, insurance
   location
   etc.

3. Number of managers

4. Allocations to managers

Fortunately, a plan sponsor can obtain a lot of assistance in the process of structuring a managment team. Asset allocation consultants help to determine the appropriate risk and diversification guidelines for the plan, based on the plan's emerging liabilities. Manager search consultants help to determine the number and types of managers, based on experience and judgement. Unfortunately, the linkage between the asset allocation decision and the manager search decision is frequently weak. Manager positions are often filled by the best-performing managers, without regard to the style, or orientation, of the managers. Asset allocation studies are frequently performed as a result of poor performance. The sponsor fixes the problem by reevaluating the entire investment program, from policy on down. The poorer performing managers are subsequently terminated as part of the resulting restructuring. The replacement managers are often those whose styles have been in recent favor, rather than those with superior skills.

This chapter addresses this linkage problem by focusing on manager allocations. It assumes that asset allocation and manager type decisions are in place, and that the sponsor currently has an investment management team. An approach is developed that can materially improve the investment program through better allocations to the managers. The approach is fundamental, in that it does not rely on sophisticated models or formulas, but rather uses some straightforward concepts of skill and diversification.

CONCEPTS

The investment community generally acknowledges the importance of asset allocation. The commitments to stocks, bonds, real estate, etc. are powerful determinants of investment return and risk. In light of this importance, another aspect of asset allocation is frequently overlooked; this aspect is the allocation to managers within an asset class. With the proper attention, risks and returns can be improved through better allocations among investment managers.

There are two central considerations involved in determining manager allocations—diversification and skill. Good diversification means investing in a wide range of asset classes with all categories of each asset class held in their market proportions. Put another way, diversification means avoiding concentrations in any one asset class or any one segment of an asset class. Unless you believe that some asset or some segment of an asset class will perform better than another, your best course of action is to be well diversified. However, you may want to deviate somewhat from perfect diversification if you believe your managers have skill, weighting the better managers more heavily. Generally speaking, you ought to employ active managers for the market segments where you think value can be added, and employ passive, or index, managers where you do not have such beliefs. Passive managers should receive passive weights, while active managers may receive active weights. The trade-off thus becomes maintaining diversification while concentrating investments with the more skillful manager. You might find the world's best growth stock manager, but you would be foolish to entrust him with all of your assets; growth stocks might someday experience devastating losses.

APPROACH

A framework is needed to simultaneously maintain diversification while capitalizing on the managers' skills. The framework described here concentrates on one asset class at a time. That is, the approach is applied sequentially to stocks, then to bonds, then real estate, and so on. This focuses attention on diversification and skill within an asset class. Diversification across asset classes is the glue that pulls these individual allocations together into a total program, as established in the plan's investment policies. That is, investment policy is overlaid on the allocations within each asset class to create an overall plan, as exemplified by the following:

Policy Overlay on Asset Class Allocations

	Asset Allocations % of Asset Class		Policy Overlay: 70% Stocks/30% Bonds % of Total			% of Manager's Assets	
	Stocks	*Bonds*	*Stocks*	*Bonds*	*Total*	*Stocks*	*Bonds*
Manager A	20%	40%	14%	12%	26%	54%	46%
Manager B	80		56		56	100	
Manager C		60		18	18		100
	100%	100%	70%	30%	100%		

In this way, balanced manager guidelines "fall out" of the process as a reflection of relative skills, and specialty managers are similarly funded as a result of their respective skills. This contrasts to the practice of having balanced managers operate within the overall policy guidelines, and allocating to specialists to "fill in" the overall policy allocations.

A fundamental allocation approach thus evolves from two graphics—one to control diversification, and a second to capture skill. The diversification graphic is shown in Exhibit 1. The market for an asset class is broken into two dimensions: the horizontal scale measures aggressiveness, and the vertical scale measures company size. For example, a stock manager with a large company growth orientation would appear in the north-

EXHIBIT 1: MANAGER STYLE MATRIX/DIVERSIFICATION

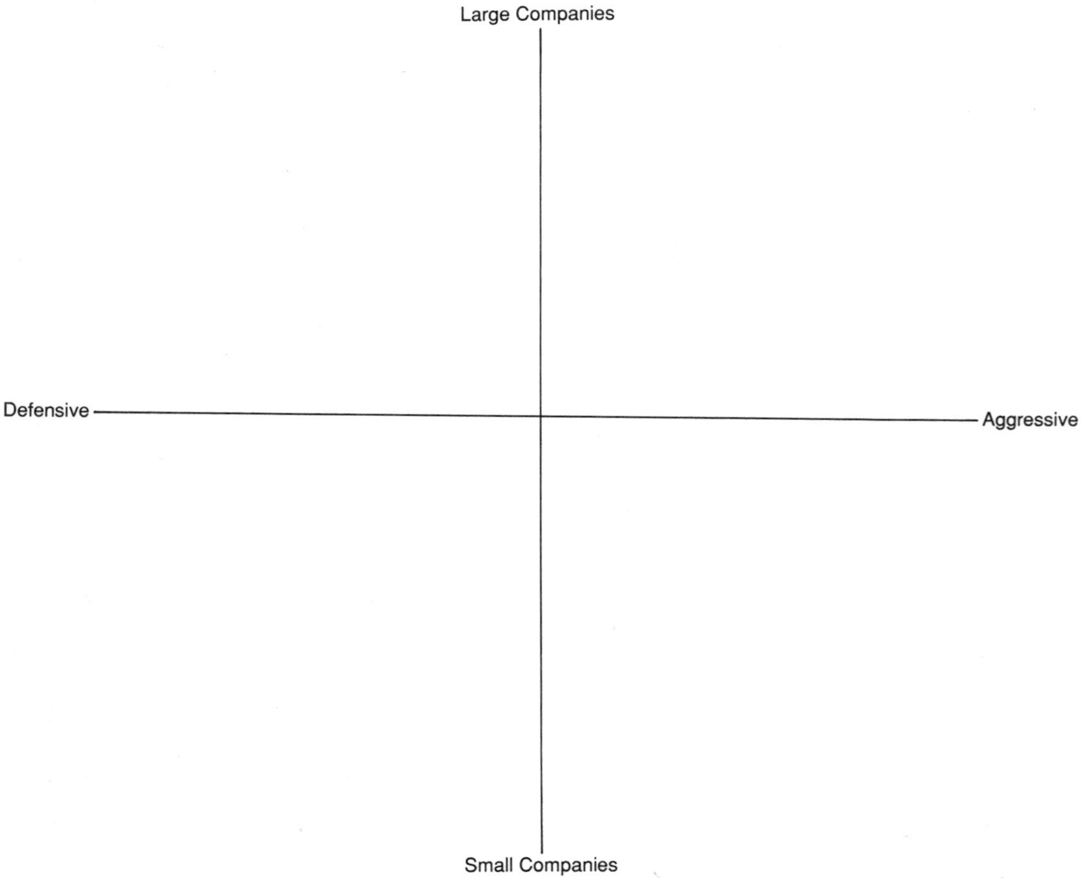

Large Companies

Defensive ——————————— Aggressive

Small Companies

east quadrant; if instead we were working with bonds, a bond manager with short duration and low quality would appear in the southwest quadrant. Good diversification in the context of Exhibit 1 is defined as being near the middle, which is average aggressiveness and average company size. Stated another way, diversification is maintained by staying near the middle of Exhibit 1. Accordingly, the family of allocations that meets this criteria can be carried to the next phase, which is capitalizing on the managers' skills.

Exhibit 2 shows how the skills of the managers can be located. The horizontal axis measures risk, and the vertical axis measures return. Risk is typically measured as the standard deviation of returns. Exhibit 2 is the traditional picture used in optimizations; you want to find the allocation with the best possible return for a given level of risk. However, here we constrain the optimization to only consider allocations that conform to the Exhibit 1 criterion of being well-diversified in a fundamental way. Like other optimizations, this constrained optimization has a family of solutions (analogous to the efficient frontier) that can be examined by the decision maker to arrive at the final allocation.

Unlike other optimizations, diversification is controlled explicitly, rather than assumed away as part of the solution; that is, standard (unconstrained) optimizations assume that the solutions are diversified because they have the risk-reward characteristics of a well-diversified portfolio. The approach described here allows judgement and common sense to override some of the theoretical constructs to arrive at a solution that is much less "black box." This flexibility can best be demonstrated with a few examples.

SOME EXAMPLES

Exhibits 3 and 4 show how the approach has been used in an actual situation involving allocations to equity managers. Exhibit 3 shows the diversification aspect while Exhibit 4 shows the skill consideration. In Exhibit 3 the sample plan's eight managers and the total plan are located within the overall stock market on the basis of company size and aggressiveness. Company size is the value-weighted average capitalization of the securities held by each manager. Aggressiveness is a composite of value-weighted yield and value-weighted price/earnings ratio; aggressiveness is associated with a tendency to hold low yielding securities with high price/earnings ratios. To achieve good diversification, we want the composite to be near the center of Exhibit 3; the center represents median size and median aggressiveness. As can be seen in the exhibit, this plan did not employ any

EXHIBIT 2: MANAGER RISK AND REWARD/SKILL

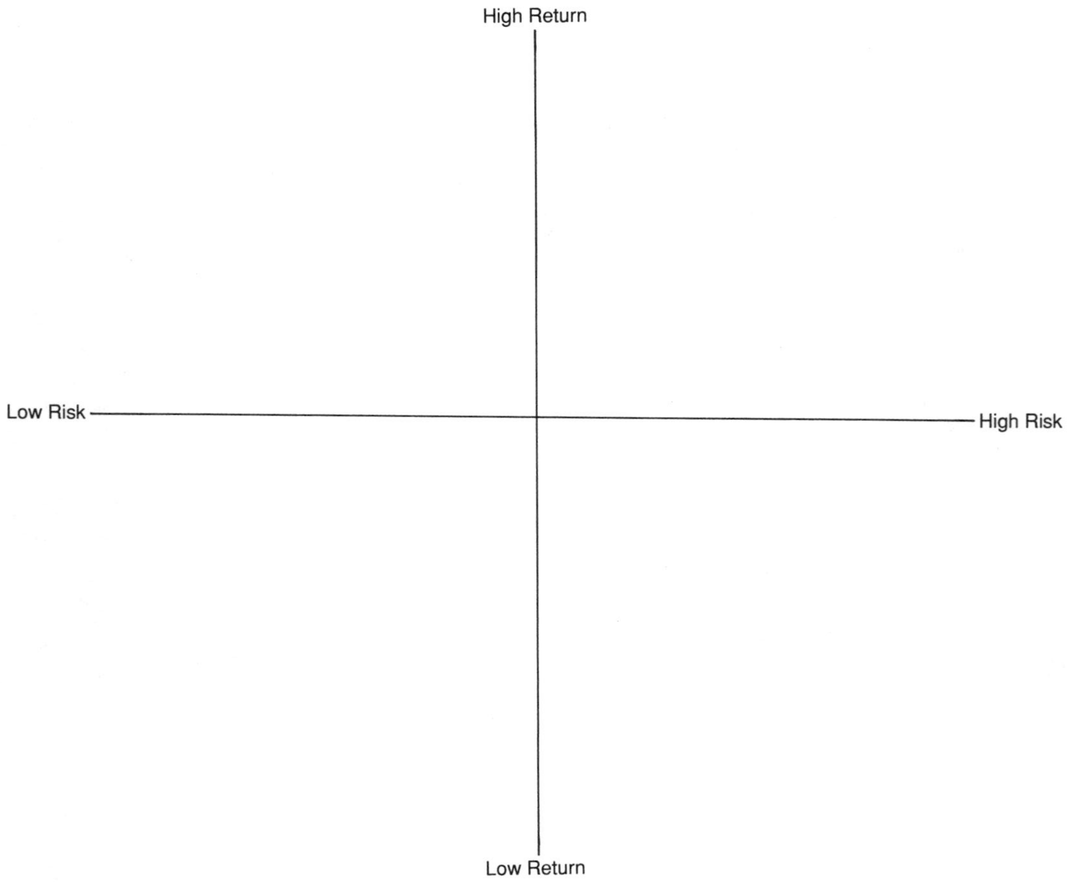

High Return

Low Risk ——————————————————————— High Risk

Low Return

EXHIBIT 3: EQUITY MANAGER STYLE MATRIX/DIVERSIFICATION

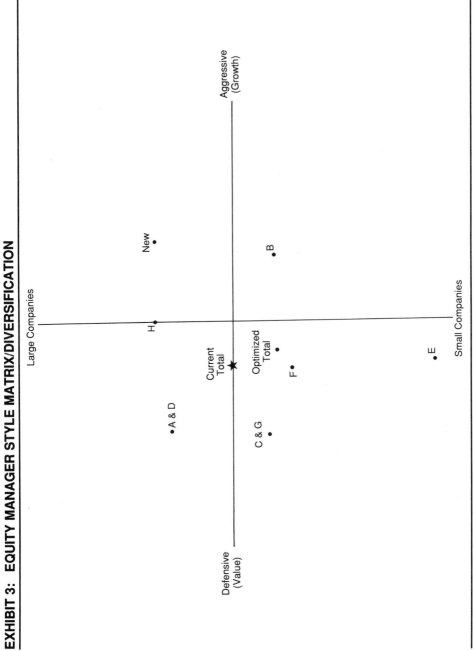

EXHIBIT 4: EQUITY MANAGER RISK AND RETURN/SKILL

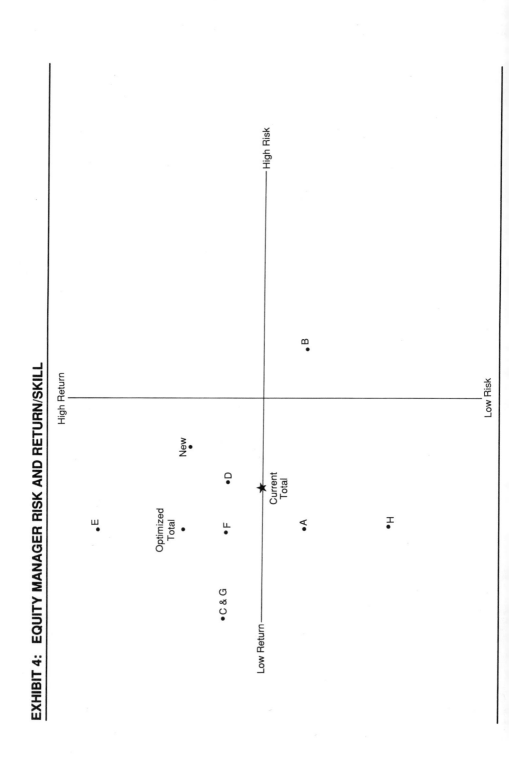

managers in the large company, aggressive segment of the stock market. The allocation approach identified this deficiency, and added a hypothetical manager denoted "NEW" in the exhibit to enhance the final solution. The solution to the allocation approach is shown as the "Optimized Total." This solution evolves from a maximization of the reward-to-risk ratio, subject to maintenance of good diversification. Exhibit 3 shows that the Optimized Total maintains good diversification by remaining near the center of the exhibit, although some movement off-center is permitted to capitalize on the superior skills of manager E. This trade-off against manager skill is shown in Exhibit 4.

Exhibit 4 locates the managers in risk and return dimensions. As can be seen, some managers are more skillful than others, offering higher returns at a given level of risk. At this point, consideration can be given to replacing the less skillful managers, but care must be taken to maintain adequate diversification. For example, you wouldn't want to replace all of your large company managers with small company managers. The exhibit shows the improvement that has been achieved in risk-reward by moving to the optimization. This optimization may be summarized as follows:

Manager	Optimized Solution Optimized Allocation (%)	Original Allocation (%)
A	10	30
B	10	38
C	10	3
D	10	10
E	30	3
F	10	8
G	0	6
H	0	3
New	20	0

This process can also be applied to other asset classes. Exhibits 5 and 6 show how the approach has been used with bond managers. The diversification dimensions for bonds become duration and quality. Thus, Manager B is a manager who concentrates in low quality, longer maturity bonds. With this change in diversification dimensions, the process follows along the lines described above for stocks.

Another example is shown for real estate in Exhibits 7 and 8. Here the diversification dimensions become stage-of-development and property

EXHIBIT 5: BOND MANAGER STYLE MATRIX/DIVERSIFICATION

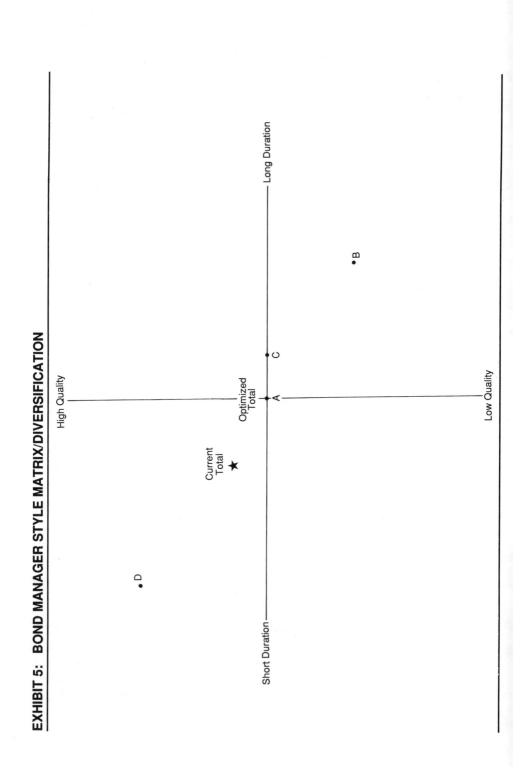

EXHIBIT 6: BOND MANAGER RISK AND REWARD/SKILL

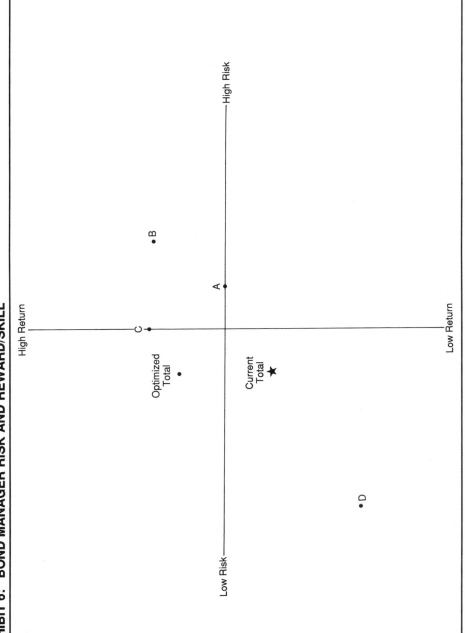

EXHIBIT 7: REAL ESTATE MANAGER STYLE MATRIX/DIVERSIFICATION

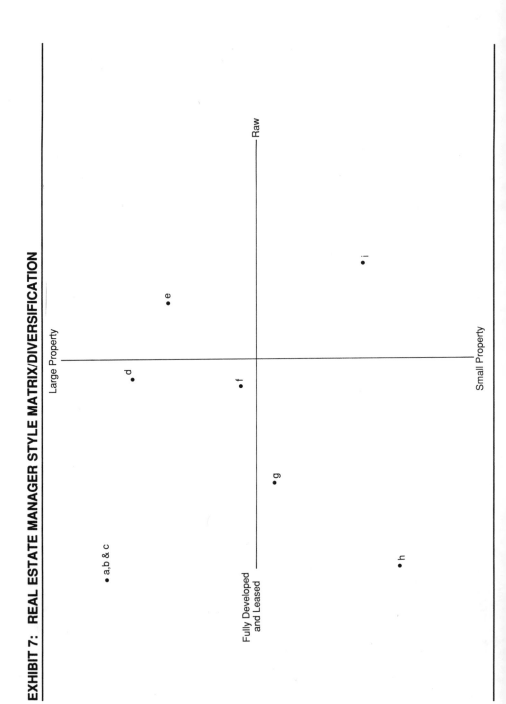

EXHIBIT 8: REAL ESTATE MANAGER RISK AND REWARD/SKILL

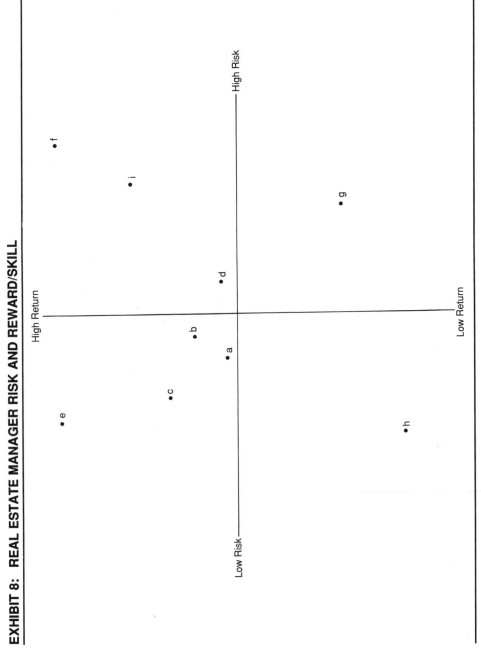

size. Again, the process finds allocations with good diversification and a high reward-to-risk profile.

After all asset classes have been dealt with in this fashion, investment policy can be overlaid to arrive at overall allocations. Exhibit 9 is an example of such an overlay. This optimization causes substantial improvement in expected return plus a significant reduction in risk, without sacrificing diversification. Furthermore, it achieves this improvement with the current managers given priority; some additional improvement could have been achieved if substitutes were considered for some of the managers, but the plan's relationships with the managers were valued highly.

SUMMARY

The process described in this chapter causes each asset class to achieve its full potential within the overall policy guidelines. Also, balanced managers can be assigned guidelines that recognize how the individual stock style and bond style of the managers fit into the overall diversification and performance framework. It's customary to give all balanced managers the same guidelines that govern the total policy of the plan. The optimized allocation process recognizes differences in skills and investment styles among all of the managers, both specialty and balanced, and structures the management team to take full advantage of the managers' collective skills without jeopardizing diversification.

Fundamentally optimized manager allocations provide the plan sponsor with a tool for getting the full benefit of his managers' collective skills. Care is exercised to ensure that the theoretical optimum doesn't depart too much from a common sense measure of good diversification. Even if the "solution" isn't implemented in totality, the insights gained from the analysis benefit the overall plan structure.

EXHIBIT 9: ALLOCATIONS TO U.S. STOCKS AND BONDS

Optimized Allocations

	U.S. Stocks	Bonds	40% Stocks/45% Bonds
A	10%	0%	4%
B	10	25	14
C	10	45	22
D	10	30	16
E	30	–	12
F	10	–	4
G	–	–	–
H	–	–	–
New	20	–	8
	100%	100%	85%

Revised Guidelines

	% of Assets		Stock Target		Bond Target	
	Proposed	Current	Proposed	Current	Proposed	Current
A	4%	25%	100%	45%	0%	55%
B	14	22	25	60	75	40
C	22	4	20	30	80	70
D	16	21	25	20	75	80
E	12	1	100	100		
F	4	2	100	100		
G	0	3				
H	0	1				
New	8	0	100			

CHAPTER 11

Money Manager Selection: A Top-Down Approach

VEENA A. KUTLER, CFA
VICE PRESIDENT
T. ROWE PRICE ASSOCIATES, INC.

The purpose of this chapter is to offer a methodology for selecting money managers. In general, the suggestions will be geared to the needs of multi-manager defined benefit plans, although they can be applied to single-manager defined contribution plans.

OVERVIEW

The approach advocated is top-down, and based on a detailed analysis of the plan's needs and objectives, with manager selection positioned as an important final component within the overall context of plan management. This contrasts with the more commonly used bottom-up style, in which manager selection is made with little reference to the total plan. Bottom-up style is based on external criteria, such as a manager's recent performance, rather than on internal plan requirements. Just as ad hoc security selection by an individual investor can lead to an unbalanced portfolio, bottom-up manager selection may create an undiversified plan with risk that is not necessarily compensated by its expected excess return.

Is a top-down approach generally used in plan management? Too often it is not. An asset allocation is generally made, based on some variation of the 60/40 equity/bonds theme, not necessarily tied to a determina-

The author wishes to acknowledge the assistance of George J. Collins and Jane F. Nelson, of T. Rowe Price Associates and Eugene M. Waldron of Fidelity Investments.

tion of the plan's unique needs. Sector decisions within asset classes may not receive much consideration. This leads to undiversified plans that behave in a volatile fashion and at some point become an unpleasant surprise to the sponsor. For example, multiple growth managers may be retained as equity managers, not because the sponsor wishes to establish a heavy position in the growth area, but because these particular managers outperformed the market over the most recent period. Needless to say, the forthcoming period may not favor growth stocks, leading to underperformance by the sponsor's aggregate equity portfolio and a growing disappointment with the newly retained managers. Conversely, a current manager may be discharged because he or she underperformed the market over a period of time. If sectors within asset classes were considered, there may have been indications that the manager was, in fact, doing a good job within an out-of-favor sector and should be retained—provided continued exposure to the sector was desired. *Since markets tend to be cyclical, hiring and firing managers after their market sectors move in and out of favor, will, by definition, be a self-defeating process.*

The top-down approach, on the other hand, should lead to an efficient plan by ensuring that the decisions that have the greatest impact on the plan—asset allocation, followed by sector choice—would be made first. Then managers whose expertise offered the best fit within a sector could be retained. Both manager and sponsor would have a good understanding of why the manager was retained and what his or her role is within the overall structure, leading to a potentially smoother and longer lasting manager-sponsor relationship.

The approach advocated here begins with a thorough analysis of the plan's asset-liability mix and ends with the funding and subsequent monitoring of the selected money manager(s). The broad steps advocated include:

- Asset-liability analysis
- Setting investment policy and strategy
- Establishment of target asset and sector allocations
- Establishment of benchmarks
- Manager search and funding
- Ongoing monitoring

ASSET-LIABILITY EQUATION

An understanding of the relationship between the plan's asset mix and its projected liabilities ideally forms the underpinning of its investment strategy, whether this relationship is stated explicitly or implicitly. Typically, this type of analysis is performed infrequently in a plan's life, perhaps once per market cycle or whenever either component of the asset-liability equation changes significantly. Frequency of analysis should depend on the relative complexities of the plan.

The plan actuary will typically serve as the best source on the liability side by supplying both the data and the analysis required to determine current and projected liability levels. Additionally, the actuary can often prove helpful on the asset side in evaluating the present mix and in providing projections of asset growth based on capital market forecasts and projections of contributions. Alternatively, a consulting firm, a current money manager, or the plan's custodian bank may be preferred as a source of asset data. In any event, the asset and liability sides are ultimately matched against each other to derive current and projected funding levels. The analysis should answer the following key questions:

1. What is the plan's funded status? That is, what are its assets as a percentage of liabilities (on a present value basis)?

2. What is the plan's funding horizon?

3. What is the plan's risk sensitivity, or its ability to withstand funding volatility? To a great extent this will depend on the employer's financial strength, outlook for the industry and company, and the profile of the participant group. The plan of a declining or cash-strapped company with an older workforce may be sensitive to a drop in funding, which would require an increase in contribution levels. Conversely, a young and growing company may be willing to take on some funding volatility in return for a greater probability of asset growth and lower required contributions down the road.

4. To what extent are the assets and liabilities mismatched? Are assets invested in a manner appropriate to the liabilities? For example, are long liabilities matched to equities, long-term bonds, or other assets projected to have a fairly long duration? Or is the funding source a short asset such as cash or money-market securities? A mismatch of this type can lead to severe shifts in funding levels over time.

INVESTMENT POLICY AND STRATEGY

The plan's overall policy and strategy should be a natural outgrowth of the asset-liability study findings. Once the sponsor has determined the plan's funding status and risk tolerance, evaluation of the current investment policy as well as the plan's strategy and structure should begin. Scenario analysis is a method of projecting the long-term implications of asset mix versus projected liability growth. This is done by constructing a series of hypothetical portfolios and market conditions and by deriving long-term returns and volatility measures through computer simulation. A variety of asset allocation and simulation models are available through consultants and actuaries to facilitate this process, and we will not discuss all the methodologies available. Common to all methods, however, is their use of assumptions that tend to allow subjective bias. An example would be the tendency to use past patterns to predict future returns. There is nothing wrong with using assumptions (indeed without them, analysis would be impossible) provided the sponsor is alert to biases that may result. One frequently used method of asset allocation is the mean-variance approach. The following are the main inputs to this process:

1. *Universe of asset classes.* Equity, bonds, cash and real estate are the broadest categories. There are sophisticated models available that provide more detailed categories such as large-capitalization stocks, small stocks, intermediate bonds, long bonds, junk bonds, international, and commodities. Any asset class for which data are available, and which is believed would be a possible fit for the plan, can be included.

2. *Correlations between asset classes.* Correlation measures the overlap of return patterns between two asset classes. For instance, corporate bond returns are highly correlated with government bond returns but significantly less so with small capitalization equity returns. Correlation data are derived from historical return patterns. In choosing an efficient asset mix, all other things being equal, low correlated assets are preferred because they offer diversification on the total portfolio level.

3. *Return projections.* Each asset class will require a projected real growth rate over the horizon period of the study. While this can be based on historical return patterns, it would be equally valid to use forecasts of returns or some combination of projections tempered with historical experience.

4. *Volatility of asset classes.* Each asset class should have a projected return standard deviation. Typically, historical data are used to derive these values, although these may be modified based on outlook.

5. *Constraints.* These would be based on the plan's risk sensitivity, the sponsor's particular preferences, or the plan's explicit needs, such as the need for certain income levels to meet near-term liabilities. They would take the form of limits on individual asset classes, such as at least 10% in cash; or in other constraints, such as maximum allowed volatility levels.

ASSET ALLOCATION RESULTS

The outcome of this analysis will be a single portfolio or a series of alternative portfolios that are termed optimal because they combine the highest returning assets with the lowest expected risk (volatility) measures at the portfolio level, given the liability stream and other unique needs and preferences of the plan.

An example of the analysis and its output is shown in Exhibits 1 and 2. It was compiled using a PC-based asset allocation model, Asset Allocation Tools™ (Ibbotson Associates, Chicago, IL). Other vendors such as CDA Investment Technologies Inc., a consulting firm based in Rockville, MD, also produce asset allocation software. The sample case illustrates a fairly straightforward case, in which the current portfolio is a 60/40 equity/bonds mix. Our universe consists of small cap equity, S&P 500 equities (large cap), long-term government bonds and money market instruments. The assumptions used for expected return, volatility, correlations, and percentage limits are shown. The output suggests that over the horizon period (10 years), the current mix is suboptimal. The optimal mix has an expected return of 10.05%, an average risk tolerance level (50), and is comprised of 67% large cap equities, 10% small cap equities, 12% long bonds, and 10% money market instruments. It must be emphasized that the assumptions going into this analysis determine its outcome, and a change in the assumptions will alter the result. Again, this underlines the importance of the sponsor's understanding and approval of the assumption values.

An optimal portfolio derived from this type of analysis would then be used as the plan's "normal" target allocation, with ranges established around the target to allow for tactical shifts or to allow asset fluctuations without triggering frequent rebalancing to the original target. The next step is to establish targets for sectors within asset classes. These targets need not be rigid and may, in fact, contain more flexibility than the ranges around the target asset allocation. The advantage to explicitly choosing sectors or styles is that it avoids the random bets created by selecting manag-

EXHIBIT 1: ASSET ALLOCATION INPUTS AND ASSUMPTIONS

	S&P 500	SmCap Equity	LT-Gov't.	Comm Paper
Expected Ret.	13.349%	18.034%	4.881%	5.952%
Std. Deviation	17.156	26.794	10.187	3.319
Corr. S&P 500	1.000	0.772	0.084	–0.265
Corr. SmCap-Eq	0.772	1.000	–0.081	–0.101
Corr. Lt-Gov't	0.084	–0.081	1.000	0.252
Corr. Comm Paper	–0.265	–0.101	0.252	1.000
Upper Bound*	100.0	10.0	100.0	10.0
Lower Bound*	30.0	0.0	0.0	0.0
Starting Portfolio	60.0	0.0	40.0	0.0

* Percentage minimum and maximum allowed by asset class.

Source: Ibbotson Associates, Asset Allocation Tools[TM], Chicago, IL.

EXHIBIT 2: ASSET ALLOCATION MODEL RESULTS

	Current Mix	Optimal Mix for Risk Tolerance				
		10	30	50	70	90
Characteristics						
Expected Ret.	9.96%	8.15%	10.05%	11.99%	13.08%	13.82%
Std. Deviation	11.39	8.58	10.56	13.76	15.81	17.59
Utility	7.37	6.68	7.81	8.20	8.08	7.63
Assets						
S&P 500	60.00	30.00	44.20	67.17	80.00	90.00
SmCap-Eq	0.00	4.74	10.00	10.00	10.00	10.00
Lt Gov't-Bd.	40.00	55.26	35.80	12.83	0.00	0.00
Comm Paper	0.00	10.00	10.00	10.00	10.00	0.00
Utility						
Expected Ret.	9.96	8.15	10.05	11.99	13.08	13.82
– Risk Penalty	2.59	1.47	2.23	3.79	5.00	6.19
= Utility	7.37	6.68	7.81	8.20	8.08	7.63

Source: Ibbotson Associates, Asset Allocation Tools[TM], Chicago, IL.

ers ad hoc for equity, fixed income, etc., without reference to style. This is a point that cannot be overemphasized. *Like it or not, managers tend to operate within preferred sectors and, therefore, sector bets will be placed in any multi-manager portfolio.* The question each sponsor must answer is: Should these bets be defined to some extent by the plan strategy or should they be allowed to develop randomly through the manager selection and funding process?

INVESTMENT STYLES AND APPROACHES

Many styles and approaches are available within selected asset classes including the following:

1. *Equity*—growth, value, small capitalization, high technology, international, market timing (cash/stock), sector rotation, or passive.

2. *Fixed income*—interest rate anticipator, sector rotator, defensive, international, specialist-mortgage, high yield, derivative instruments, or passive.

3. *Real estate*—equity ownership, diversified product, leveraged, product or geographic concentration (e.g., Sunbelt, warehouses or shopping centers).

4. *International*—equity, fixed income, currency-hedged, country or area concentration, such as the Pacific Basin.

MANAGER REVIEW

Following the identification of acceptable sectors or styles, each sector's allocation should be determined. As mentioned, sector allocation need not consist of rigid values; fairly wide ranges allowing for tactical strategic shifts in allocation are acceptable. Lastly, the number of managers to be hired should be considered and ballpark estimates made at this time, subject, of course, to the results of the manager search. This determination is a function of the sponsor's preferences, the size of the plan, and its allocations. Some sponsors believe that a large pool of managers offers greater insight to the markets. Lack of administrative staff requires others to maintain a limited line-up. Plans with large asset bases may employ numerous managers, although these may be reduced by employing passive strategies or managing a portion internally. Additionally, plans with numerous sector strategies, or overlays such as options and currency hedging, will tend to have a large manager stable.

At this stage, sponsors should evaluate existing managers. Managers who are clearly doing a satisfactory job within their sector may be earmarked as retention candidates. Managers who are poor may be considered for termination or, if mediocre, included in the new search as candidates on equal footing with other managers. Managers in sectors that are now inappropriate for the plan's investment strategy may be evaluated for termination or, depending on the manager's strengths, viewed as a candidate for a different sector. Manager retention is to be encouraged. The time and effort already expended by the sponsor in establishing the working relationship is of real value and should be one of the factors in the termination decision.

PLAN BENCHMARK

Lastly, some benchmark(s) for the restructured plan should be established at this stage, to be used later on in the monitoring process. The benchmark may be a weighted average of market indices, a ranking within a total plan universe, or some combination. An example would be an index composed of 60% S&P 500, 30% Salomon Broad Investment Grade index, and 10% Frank Russell Real Estate index or other bogey, with the weightings representing the plan's "normal" but not tactical asset mix. Over a three- to five-year period the plan's objective might be to beat this benchmark and to rank in the top half of a plan universe. Some sponsors will be reluctant to tie themselves to this type of measurement, citing a variety of reasons. Obviously, each sponsor is best aware of the issues confronting his or her plan and may not choose to be measured in this way. However, establishing performance standards at the plan level appears a logical step in the effort to "professionalize" the plan sponsor role and to achieve the recognition and compensation levels commensurate with the effort and expertise required to run a well-managed plan.

SELECTION OF MANAGERS

The final step of the plan management process is to hire and to fund managers. At this point, assuming the preceding steps have been followed, the sponsor has chosen an investment policy, and long-term and tactical strategies have been adopted. Allocations at the broad asset class level have been determined, and ranges have been set for sectors within asset classes. In addition, some estimates of the number of managers required for each asset class and sector have also been made. Selection requires sampling a broad group of managers, identifying several from this group who meet the plan requirements and hiring those who offer the best fit.

Creating a Universe of Managers

We begin by creating a universe of managers meeting the primary requirements of each asset class of the plan. For a given plan, for instance, this may imply an equity universe comprising growth, value, and small capitalization managers. The fixed-income portion may contain only defensive intermediate-maturity managers. To create this specialized universe of managers, we must access a comprehensive database of manager information. Data included would be the firm's history, operating details, its principals, assets under management, styles or specialties, client relationships and performance records. The data can be culled from in-house files, from a consulting firm's proprietary data base, from a local or regional plan sponsor group's pooled information or a combination of these. In-house research is often an excellent starting point for developing a manager pool. By establishing an open-door policy, even when no new hires are contemplated, a sponsor can build a group of those managers who appear to have promise, and also keep up with developing trends. Offsetting these advantages, of course, is the vast amount of time required to maintain a truly open-door policy. However, this can be controlled by limiting the frequency and duration of manager visits.

Consulting firms offer vast resources of manager data, as they are in the business of maintaining up-to-date and screened databases. Generally, many of the managers included have had their performance track records and other relevant data verified by the consultant, who has also identified any particular areas of expertise. To be on the safe side, make sure before subscribing to the database that performance data has indeed been validated by the vendor. Rankings within styles are often provided. In other words, candidates will be pigeon-holed for the convenience of the user. Consultants offer an invaluable service—timesaving, but this service may be costly. The other negative is that the consultant's objective is to retain the sponsor as a client, and therefore he may adopt a conservative view and eliminate candidates with somewhat radical ideas, or start-up operations without long track records. A combination of consultant data and in-house or sponsor group data should result in a comprehensive database.

The specialized universe is created by screening the larger database by asset class and sector or style and selecting those managers who fit the requirements. Incidentally, the database and screening method do not require elaborate computer equipment or expertise. The sponsor can do much of the work manually, or on a Lotus 123 spreadsheet, using the data sorting options. Most of the work will consist of creating manager records that are consistent and can be readily referenced and sorted. In the example given, the screened universe would consist of all equity managers who specialize in growth, value, and small capitalization, and all fixed-income managers who specialize in defensive, intermediate portfolios. This group may be quite large because many managers will list multiple specialties.

Screening the Universe

The next step is to screen the universe even further, based on the unique requirements of the plan, or sponsor. For instance, all managers without five-year track records may be eliminated. Or for large plans, which tend to allocate sizeable portfolios, managers with less than $500 million under management may be eliminated. The net result of this screening should be to reduce the universe to a reasonable size, perhaps of 20 managers per category.

Evaluating the Candidates

Next comes the important step of evaluating the candidates to come up with a list of semifinalists. This requires analyzing each candidate to get a clear understanding of the firm and its history. The questions to be answered involve the firm's financial status, asset base, client list, principals and their commitment to the firm, the firm's philosophy, performance record, and staffing with respect to depth, experience and form of compensation. From this should evolve semifinalists who will be invited to meet with the sponsor and board, or with the investment committee. The data required to perform the detailed evaluation can come either from the information available in the manager database, or from a comprehensive questionnaire sent out to each candidate eligible for inclusion in the semifinals list. Questionnaires are fairly standard tools used by most consultants and sponsors in the search process. If the sponsor does not have a questionnaire, the best way to develop one is to obtain a standard one from a consultant, plan sponsor network, or fellow sponsor, and customize it to suit the plan's needs. The time expended in developing a good questionnaire should be considered an investment. Remember, the more comprehensive the questionnaire, the less effort expended later evaluating facts and obtaining meaningful analysis.

The basic components of a questionnaire should include:

1. *The firm*—years in existence, ownership, financial status, financial statements, an annual report if available. Employee ownership status—generally an equity interest is a good sign. Are earnings diversified, or dependent on just a few clients? Plans for growth or to limit growth should also be discussed.

2. *Asset base*—total assets under management, assets by asset type, breakdown of *Employee Retirement Income Security Act* (ERISA) vs. other accounts, average account size, representative client list, recent terminations and hirings and, if excessive, some explanation.

3. *Staffing*—breakdown by job function—portfolio managers, analysts, back office, etc. Length of tenure with the firm, experience and qualifications. Account load per manager. Turnover at the professional level (high turnover indicates turmoil at the firm). Your manager should be managing your portfolio, not worrying about keeping or finding another job. Compensation—is there some incentive system to encourage good people to stay on? What back-up do the professionals have? This is especially important at small shops where lack of depth can leave the sponsor in a difficult or embarrassing position should the sole manager leave. Also important, although not as critical, is an experienced and adequately staffed back-office area, as this promotes a smooth operation both for the sponsor and the custodian bank.

4. *Approach and philosophy*—what are the fundamental themes and ideas that drive the firm's investment approach and make it unique? Is the philosophy thought out and articulated? Is it reflected in the investment style, in the type of accounts managed, and the performance achieved over a significant period of time? How are accounts managed—by individual managers, or teams? What are inputs to the investment approach? What resources are required?; how much research is generated internally? How is outside research purchased? (The soft dollar issue is becoming important to many sponsors.)

5. *Performance*—this topic can be a minefield. There are many different ways of calculating performance and in displaying it to its best advantage. There may not be anything inherently wrong with any one method as long as it is consistent and clearly identified by the sponsor. Some issues to keep in mind include:

- Is the performance a total rate of return, which includes principal as well as income changes? Is it dollar-weighted or time-weighted? Time-weighting reduces the impact of cash flows, which are generally beyond the manager's control. Does the return include the effect of residual cash in the account? If not, why not? If the manager is permitted to hold cash, then a way of measuring the cash decision should be available.

- Is performance based on simulated results (backtesting) or on accounts managed prior to the formation of the firm? Is the performance a composite of similar accounts, and, if so, how exactly is the composite formulated? Are terminated accounts included in the composite, as well as the performance of past portfolio managers? Are all portfolio manager accounts included in the composite—or are you being shown a "star's" results, which may have very little to do with the portfolio manager assigned to your account?

- It may well be impossible to obtain meaningful answers to all the questions you generate, particularly at the questionnaire stage. At the next stage, where a handful of semifinalists are chosen, it is worth the follow-up effort to verify performance. One of the best approaches is to first ascertain which portfolio manager or team is to be assigned to your account. Then obtain complete performance records for that manager or team by account, with relevant benchmarks for each account. Next, reference calls can be made (to clients selected by the sponsor) to verify that the returns as well as the benchmarks shown are in agreement with the reference client's records.

- Finally, performance, while important, should not be the only criteria in choosing the semifinalists. As stated previously, performance numbers can be misleading, and more importantly, prior outperformance is no guarantee of future results.

6. *Reporting*—what reports are available to the client on a regular basis? To what extent will the manager customize to the sponsor's needs?

7. *Fee schedule*—is there a standard fee schedule based on account size or objective? Often there is room for negotiation, if you persist.

Selecting Semifinalists

The next step is to select semifinalists who offer the best fit for the plan, based on the questionnaire analysis and perhaps in-person presentations by managers. The method of choosing these managers will vary depending on the sponsor's preferences and needs. One method would be a simple scoring system, such as the example shown in Exhibit 3.

Semifinalists should be invited to make formal presentations to the board or committee responsible for the hiring decisions. This gives the sponsor the opportunity to evaluate their presentation in relation to what was learned in the analysis. Specific questions in any area that is not clearly understood should be planned for this session. Lastly, the personal chemistry or rapport established between the manager and sponsor is an important element in the final decision. Of course, the rapport established must be with the portfolio manager, not a marketing representative who may have little to do with the relationship once it is established.

Checking Candidate References

A last step before finalizing the decision to hire a candidate, and prior to notification and start of contract and fee negotiations, is to check references. This is extremely important. Use contacts in a local sponsor network, or follow up on the references provided by the manager. No one knows the manager as well as a current client. While a sponsor in a search is being wooed by the potential manager, a fellow sponsor has nothing to

EXHIBIT 3

Semifinalist Rating Sheet

	Maximum Score	Actual Score	Comment
Firm (Size, longevity, asset base, etc.)	15	12	
Approach & Philosophy	25	20	
Performance	25	25	good long-term
Staffing	20	10	"star" manager
Administrative Strength	15	13	
Total	100	80	

lose by being objective, and, in general, they will be candid. Among the topics to discuss would be performance. Have the client's returns been in line with others provided by the manager? Who is responsible for the client's portfolio? How good is the servicing? Are reports on time and phone calls returned? Has the client noted any problems or causes for concern, such as frequent changes in personnel or an abrupt change in style? By asking general questions, without demanding specific portfolio information (which the reference may be reluctant to provide), the sponsor will be able to reconcile manager-presented information with actual experience.

MONITORING

Monitoring should be an on-going process both at the manager and the plan level. On at least an annual basis, the sponsor should evaluate the fund versus its assigned benchmark and its peer group. At the same time, the sponsor should measure asset growth, relative to liability growth and relative to capital market conditions, to determine whether the investment policy and strategy still makes sense. Tactical strategy shifts may be made at this time without changing the long-term investment policy. You will recall the earlier suggestion that broad ranges be established for tactical allocation. Some rebalancing will be needed from time to time as asset proportions change with varying market movements. For instance, a sharp rise in stock prices may result in an overweighted equity component, which could then be reallocated to fixed-income or another asset class.

Manager review is equally important. As a part of the hiring process, the sponsor has hired the manager for a particular style or sector expertise, has assigned objectives and benchmarks (which should be agreed upon with the manager) and has established a horizon period over which the manager is expected to achieve the objectives. The purpose of periodic reviews over the horizon period is to continuously evaluate the manager against these objectives.

Performance can be reviewed quarterly or semiannually versus the benchmark established at portfolio inception and also against peer groups. Several performance databases, including TUCS (Trust Universe Comparison Service), track peer groups by style or sector—for instance, small capitalization managers. This is very helpful as it allows the sponsor to see how a particular sector or style is doing relative to the broad market and also how a particular manager ranks within a peer group. As mentioned before, it is important to differentiate between a poor sector or style and a poor performer within a sector.

The manager's approach should also be reviewed. Is the manager following the strategy for which he or she was hired? An unexpected change in style, even if it results in good performance, should be questioned. Changes within the firm also need to be investigated.

Communication is the building block of a good manager-sponsor relationship. Periodic meetings and phone calls are to be encouraged. An open dialogue is particularly important during poor performance periods, when efforts should be made to allow the manager to explain what happened and to offer projections for the future.

CONCLUSION

Manager selection should be viewed as an important component of a comprehensive approach to the overall plan. The top-down process advocated here is both complex and time-consuming, but once complete should lead to lower manager turnover and to a more efficiently structured plan.

CHAPTER 12

Attributing Performance to Sponsors and Managers

RONALD J. SURZ
PRINCIPAL
BECKER, BURKE ASSOCIATES INCORPORATED

Performance measurement and evaluation of sponsors and managers has evolved over the past quarter-century to incorporate certain widely accepted disciplines. The time-weighted rate of return is accepted as the appropriate performance measurement, and peer group comparisons, of various sorts, are accepted as appropriate evaluation backdrops. Furthermore, it is generally accepted that some form of performance attribution is essential to the evaluation process. Attribution answers the question "why?" performance is good or bad, thereby providing direction for change.

Because of this central role in decision making, performance attribution ought to be very important. Yet we find that attribution is commonly performed qualitatively rather than quantitatively. That is, there are few, if any, generally accepted principles of performance attribution. Part of the reason for this deficiency rests in the difficulty of separating the effects of the sponsor's decisions from those of the manager. The approach described here achieves this separation and, in so doing, leads to better decision making. The sponsor's role in the "why?" question is a major one: the sponsor establishes policies, selects managers, and allocates assets. To properly identify where change is necessary, the sponsor needs to take responsibility for his role and to evaluate the strengths and weaknesses of his investment program. This is the purpose of performance attribution.

The first step in performing attribution analysis is to identify the key investment decisions and who is responsible for them. There are three key decision-areas, all related to asset allocation: (1) managers, (2) asset types

219

(stocks, bonds, etc.), and (3) individual securities. Responsibility for each decision area breaks out as follows:

Investment Decision Responsibility		
Investment Decisions are Allocations to:	Persons Responsible are:	
	Sponsor	Managers
Managers	X	
Asset Types	X	X
Individual Securities		X

Accordingly, the sponsor should receive full attribution for how assets are allocated to managers, and the managers should receive full responsibility for the securities they select. The grey area arises in asset type allocation, since the sponsor knows how the managers are committed to asset types when he allocates assets to them. This grey area can be broken down into black and white areas with the proper methodology, as described in this chapter. As you will see, the effects of manager and sponsor decisions manifest themselves as performance differentials away from a neutral, or central, situation.

This chapter presents some tools for attributing performance to both sponsor and manager. The tools fall into three general categories:

1. *Benchmarks* are developed that describe control states (or so-called "neutral" references).

2. *Attribution measurements* are calculated from the benchmarks.

3. *Attribution evaluation* is described.

It is hoped that these tools will find their way into the toolbox of widely accepted disciplines.

THE BENCHMARKS

Benchmarks are tools for measuring control states—what would have happened in the absence of a particular event. For example, the S&P 500 is frequently used as a benchmark for what would have happened in the absence of active management decisions. To achieve performance attribution, we need six such performance benchmarks. Two are directly sponsor-related, two are directly manager-related, and two are hybrids since they are related to both sponsor and manager decisions. We develop these performance benchmarks by having three control variables, against which we apply either the actual situation or a neutral situation. Since there are 3×2 (three variables times two "states of nature") such combinations, there are six benchmarks.[1] The neutral situations are those developed by the plan sponsor in establishing investment policies; accordingly, they are called policy states. The control variables are (1) allocation of monies to the managers, (2) manager allocation to asset classes, and (3) asset class performance.

The form of each benchmark is:

$$S_1 (A_{1,1} r_1 + A_{1,2} r_2 + A_{1,3} r_3 + ...) + S_2 (A_{2,1} r_1 + A_{2,2} r_2 + A_{2,3} r_3 + ...) + ...$$

where
$$S_m = \text{sponsor allocation to manager m}$$
$$A_{m,a} = \text{manager m's allocation to asset a}$$
$$r_a = \text{return on asset a}$$

The six performance benchmarks and their symbols (which we'll use throughout the rest of the chapter) are as follows:

Performance Attribution Benchmarks

Type	Name	Symbol	Sponsor Allocation to Managers	Manager Allocation to Assets	Return
Sponsor	Policy	P	Policy	Policy	Passive
	Allocation	A	Actual	Policy	Passive
Manager &	Tactical	T	Actual	Actual	Passive
Sponsor	Strategic	S	Actual	Actual	Actual
Manager	Tactical	t	Policy	Actual	Passive
	Strategic	s	Policy	Actual	Actual

These benchmarks are used to calculate attribution measures, as described in the next section.

THE MEASUREMENTS

There are two forms of attribution measurement—timing and selectivity. Timing measures the effect of changing allocations, while selectivity measures the effect of deviating from passive, or index, management. Both forms measure the value added or subtracted relative to strict adherence to policy guidelines.

Some basic, or fundamental, measurements can be calculated and used to derive more complex, or derivative, measurements. The derivative measures serve to further delineate manager and sponsor effects. These measurements are as follows:

Performance Attribution Measurements

Basic Measures		*Rationale (Benchmark Composition)*		
		Sponsor Allocation to Managers	*Manager Allocation to Assets*	*Return*
Sponsor (Direct)				
Timing	A–P	Actual-Policy	Policy	Passive
Policy	P	Policy	Policy	Passive
Total Sponsor (Direct)	A			
Sponsor & Manager				
Timing	T–A	Actual	Actual-Policy	Passive
Selectivity	S–T	Actual	Actual	Actual-Passive
Total Sponsor & Manager	S –A			
Manager				
Timing	t–P	Policy	Actual-Policy	Passive
Selectivity	s–t	Policy	Actual	Actual-Passive
Total Manager	s–P			

Derivative Measures

Sponsor (Indirect) (equals Sponsor & Manager minus Manager)

Timing	(T-A) - (t-P)
Selectivity	(S-T) - (s-t)
Total	(S-s) + (P-A)

Sponsor (Total)

Sponsor (Direct)	A
Sponsor (Indirect)	(S-s) + (P-A)
	S-s + P

Continued

Derivative Measures   (Continued)

Total Timing

Sponsor (Direct)	A	-P
Sponsor (Indirect)	(T-A) - (t-P)	
Manager		t-P
T		-P

Total Selectivity

Sponsor (Indirect)	(S-T) - (s-t)
Manager	s-t
S-T	

Sponsor Components

Timing	T	-t
Selectivity	(S-T) - (s-t)	
Policy		P
Total	S	-s+P

Total Attribution

Total Timing	T-P	
Total Selectivity	S-T	
Policy	P	
Total	S	= actual retrun

or

Sponsor	S-s+P
Manager	s-P
Total	S

Although these relationships may seem complex, they provide a rich resource for those wishing to calculate performance attribution, as well as a variety of consistency checks. For example, the fact that the attribution components sum to the actual total return assures that the measurements are consistent with "the whole equaling the sum of its parts." Additionally, the sponsor and manager attribution measures are consistent with logic. The sponsor attribution measure of "S-s+P" says that the sponsor "owns" the investment policy (P) plus any performance differential resulting from non-neutral weightings of the managers (S-s). This makes sense because it captures what is directly under the sponsor's control. Similarly, the manager measure of "s-P" also makes sense since it attributes only the managers' discretionary deviations from policy to the managers.

The author believes that the above measurements are being presented for the first time, and are therefore unique. Accordingly, unique ways for evaluating these attribution measurements seem appropriate, as discussed in the next section.

EVALUATING THE MEASUREMENTS

The attribution measurements produce numbers which need to be interpreted. In the jargon of the statistician, the decision-maker must determine if the result is "significant" before he operates on the basis of that information. This section presents some ways to evaluate the following five key attribution measures:

Attribution Measures to Evaluate

Sponsor: Policy
            Timing
            Selectivity

Manager: Timing
            Selectivity

The framework for evaluating these measures is the one used in classical statistics, where the decision maker estimates the probability that the observed result is due merely to chance, rather than to skill or the absence of skill. This framework can be applied to all of the measures except policy. To evaluate the policy effect, the sponsor needs to review his risk tolerances and diversification opportunities; policy can only be evaluated with regard to its appropriateness in light of the emerging needs of the sponsor's plan. The other measures are evaluated relative to the available opportunities. For example, the sponsor-timing measure, "T-t," is evaluated by developing the probability distribution of possible (T-t)s. This is straightforward, since the only variable in play here is the allocation among the managers. Accordingly, an opportunity range is developed that reflects the permissible ranges of allocations among the managers. For example, if there were two managers with permissible allocations of 30-70% in each, the evaluation distribution would encompass the performance outcomes from all possible allocations conforming to these guidelines (e.g., (30,70), (40,60), (50,50), etc.). For simplicity, all such allocations can be assumed to have an equal likelihood, or one could devise more complex allocation probabilities. The evaluation of sponsor timing is then accomplished by determining the ranking of the actual measurement relative to this opportunity set. Sponsor selectivity is also based on manager over/underweightings, and is evaluated against a similar opportunity set. Similarly, manager timing ("t-P") is evaluated by developing the opportunity set of possible asset class commitments within the managers' guidelines. This is best achieved by evaluating each manager individually.

Evaluating manager selectivity is more complex. Here the opportunity set is the collection of portfolios that could be formed from the managers' universe of acceptable securities. To simplify evaluation, it is better to perform attribution at the manager level, thus evaluating each manager's execution of his style. The technology for creating these opportunity sets has been developed and is called Customized Performance Standards (CPS).[2] This technology constructs a distribution of portfolios that could have conceivably been held by the manager.

CPS begins with the money manager's description of his essence, or style. This description can be supplied at the security level or at the portfolio level. At the security level, the manager identifies the universe of stocks that could be held in his portfolio and the typical (or information-neutral) commitment to each stock. This is totally analogous to the identification of a single normal portfolio. At the portfolio level, the manager identifies the typical characteristics of his portfolio with regard to such fundamentals as dividend yield, capitalization, price/book, and so on. Of course, the manager can describe his style at both the security and the portfolio level. In addition, the manager describes the rules that he uses to construct portfolios, such as number of names, minimum and maximum positions, and so forth. The sponsor verifies that these descriptions and rules are consistent with his best interests or modifies them to coincide with his interests.

CPS uses this information to emulate the manager's decision set. A random sample of portfolios is drawn from the manager's stock universe, using his construction rules. Performance results are calculated across this opportunity set, and the manager's ranking is determined. This ranking is a pure indication of whether value was added, since it is the probability that a similar result could have been produced at random. The median of the opportunity set distribution represents a heuristic normal portfolio; it is the expected result that would fall out from following the manager's rules.

Multiple Time Periods

The attribution measures described here are straightforward to apply when a single decision is made at the beginning of the measurement period. Unfortunately, the world is not that nicely behaved, which means that the measures should be calculated for time periods between decisions. The decisions are sponsor allocations to managers and manager transactions. In other words, the benchmarks should be returns that are linked from decision point to decision point.

This is not a practical approach. A more reasonable approach would be to treat the process as if decisions were made quarterly. This simplifies the calculations, and conforms to the practice of evaluating performance quarterly. Each of the benchmarks would, accordingly, reset quarterly, and benchmarks for multiple quarters would be calculated by linking the quarterly benchmarks.

In this way, the benchmarks are calculated like any other time-weighted return. It should be noted, though, that cumulative attribution measures will not be derivable from quarterly attribution measures. This is because the attribution measures are differences between benchmarks, which, in turn, are geometric sums (linked rates). As such, you can't add or multiply the attribution measures across time periods to obtain a cumulative measure. However, a good approximation will usually be obtained by simply adding attribution measures across quarters.

Since all of this is new, and fairly complex, some examples may be helpful. These are provided in the next section.

SOME EXAMPLES

We begin with a summary of the investment policies of a sample plan shown in Exhibit 1. These policies set forth allocation guidelines to both managers and assets. The plan employs nine managers—five U.S. stock managers, a bond manager, a foreign-stock manager, a real estate manager, and a short-term fixed-income manager. The five U.S. stock managers are structured as an S&P 500 core with four complementary active managers. Each manager has a target allocation to his specialty, with a range around this target; the balance of each manager's portfolio is held in short-term instruments. Sponsor allocations to each manager are governed by a target allocation, with a range around the target. Asset allocation guidelines, shown in the bottom half of Exhibit 1, are overlaid on manager commitments and sponsor allocations to control risk and provide good diversification. These various guidelines have been constructed as a result of a comprehensive asset/liability analysis combined with a formal manager structure study.[3] The target allocations in Exhibit 1 are used to calculate the policy benchmark. The ranges are used to construct opportunity sets for evaluating the attribution measures.

EXHIBIT 1: INVESTMENT POLICIES

Manager Allocation Guidelines

Manager Name	Style	Manager Commitment			Sponsor Allocation		
		Target	Min	Max	Target	Min	Max
S&P	S&P Index	95	90	100	16	10	22
Lg, A	Large, Agressive	95	90	100	13	8	18
Sm, A	Small, Agressive	95	85	100	8	5	11
Sm, D	Small, Defensive	90	70	100	9	6	12
Lg, D	Large, Defensive	90	70	100	3	0	6
Bond	Bond Index	90	60	100	37	27	47
Forn	Foreign Stock	95	90	100	4	0	7
R.Es	Real Estate	90	60	100	6	0	9
$	Short Term	100	100	100	4	0	20

Asset Allocation Guidelines

	Target	Min	Max
Stocks	49	39	59
Bonds	37	27	47
Foreign	4	0	10
Real Estate	6	0	10
Short Term	4	0	40
Equity (Stocks & Foreign & Real Estate)	59	49	69

To perform attribution analysis, we need the performance and allocation history of the plan, as shown in Exhibit 2. The two columns labeled "Allocation" show the sponsor allocation to the "Manager" in the first column and the manager's allocation to his "Asset" specialty in the second. The two columns labelled "Passive Return" show the benchmark returns for the "Asset" specialty in the first column and for short-term instrument, or "T-Bills" in the second. The last column shows actual returns for each manager's total portfolio.

Exhibits 1 and 2 contain all that is needed to perform attribution analysis. Exhibit 3 provides attribution results for the fourth quarter of 1988. Exhibit 3 gives a summary of the key attribution analysis. As can be seen, the policy return of 2.33% is the dominant factor for the quarter; policy usually is the dominant factor, characteristically explaining about 90% of performance results. For this quarter, the second most important factor was

EXHIBIT 2: MANAGER ALLOCATION & PERFORMANCE HISTORY

| Manager | Style | Q | Allocation | | Passive Return | | Actual Return |
			Manager	Asset	Asset	T-Bills	
S&P	S&P Index						
	88	4	25.0	93.0	3.10	2.0	3.1
	89	1	24.0	100.0	7.03	2.2	7.2
		2	22.0	100.0	8.81	2.5	8.4
Lg, A	Large, Aggressive						
	88	4	13.0	100.0	2.8	2.0	4.5
	89	1	13.0	96.0	7.0	2.2	7.3
		2	14.0	98.0	8.9	2.5	5.8
Sm, A	Small, Aggressive						
	88	4	10.0	95.0	1.00	2.0	1.1
	89	1	10.0	98.0	6.86	2.2	8.0
		2	11.0	98.0	8.95	2.5	9.3
Sm, D	Small, Defensive						
	88	4	10.0	75.0	2.1	2.0	2.5
	89	1	11.0	73.0	7.8	2.2	7.0
		2	11.0	90.0	8.5	2.5	9.4
Lg, D	Large, Defensive						
	88	4	1.0	30.0	3.0	2.0	3.2
	89	1	3.0	56.0	6.5	2.2	7.9
		2	3.0	71.0	8.3	2.5	3.6
Bond	Bond Index						
	88	4	38.0	99.0	.75	2.0	.9
	89	1	38.0	99.0	1.13	2.2	1.3
		2	37.0	93.0	7.97	2.5	8.1
Forn	Foreign Stock						
	88	4	1.0	100.0	15.65	2.0	11.4
	89	1	1.0	100.0	.27	2.2	5.0
		2	1.0	100.0	−6.18	2.5	.7
R.Est.	Real Estate						
	88	4	0.0	100.0	2.07	2.0	0.0
	89	1	0.0	100.0	1.32	2.2	0.0
		2	0.0	100.0	2.25	2.5	0.0
$	$ Equivalent						
	88	4	2.0	100.0	2.0	2.0	2.7
	89	1	0.0	100.0	2.2	2.2	2.4
		2	1.0	100.0	2.5	2.5	3.1
Totl	Total Fund						
	88	4	100.0	55.0			2.2
	89	1	100.0	57.0			5.0
		2	100.0	59.0			7.7

sponsor timing, which subtracted .36% from performance. The next most important factor was manager selectivity, which added .21% to performance. The remaining two attribution measures—sponsor selectivity and manager timing—were neutral for the quarter. Overall, deviations from policy subtracted .13% from performance so that the actual return of 2.2% lags the policy return of 2.33%.

Exhibit 4 shows the benchmark performance used to calculate the attribution measures. The reader may verify that each attribution measure is derived from differences between benchmarks as described in the preceding.

Further detail is provided in Exhibit 5, which decomposes the attribution measures into their manager components. Exhibit 5a details the sponsor timing measure, which is calculated by multiplying the deviation of sponsor allocation away from policy by each manager's benchmark, or passive, return; the manager's benchmark return is calculated using the manager's actual commitment to his specialty, but substitutes his passive return for his actual specialty return. As demonstrated, the weightings of two managers had a material impact on performance. Underweighting the foreign manager subtracted .47% from performance, while overweighting of the S&P index added .27%. Overall sponsor timing of -.36% is near median, ranking 48th percentile, relative to the opportunity set permitted by the guidelines. In other words, sponsor timing is about what would be expected for the quarter. The negative median in the opportunity distribution is due to a short-term range of 0-20%.

Exhibit 5b completes the details of sponsor attribution by showing sponsor selectivity. This is manager selectivity, weighted by sponsor over/underweighting. Here we see a positive contribution from underweighting the foreign stock manager, because this manager underperformed his benchmark. Underweighting the foreign stock manager added .13% to sponsor selectivity; since this same underweighting subtracted .47% from sponsor timing, the net effect of underweighting foreign is a -.34% loss. Total sponsor selectivity is 0.05%, which is near expectation, ranking 55th percentile against the sponsor opportunity set.

Switching to manager attribution, Exhibit 5c details manager timing, which is the difference between two benchmark returns, weighted by the sponsor's target, or policy, allocation. The two benchmark returns are the passive returns that would have been earned with (1) the manager's actual commitment to his specialty and (2) his target commitment. As can be seen, the large defensive manager had poor timing, with 30% in stocks versus a 90% target; this caused a .6%, which ranks 100th percentile against this manager's opportunity set. By contrast, the foreign stock manager showed positive timing with a 100% commitment versus a 95% target, adding .68%, which ranks 5th percentile. The final column in the exhibit weights each manager's timing by his targeted sponsor allocation. The bond manager's timing subtracted .04% from performance through the joint effect of a -.11% timing loss coupled with a 37% target allocation. The total effect of manager timing was a modest -.03%.

Exhibit 5d completes the details with a breakdown of manager selectivity, which weights individual manager selectivity by the sponsor's policy, or target, allocation. Each manager's selectivity is his actual return minus the passive return that would have been earned using his actual commitment. For the fourth quarter of 1988, the foreign-stock manager shows poor selectivity of -4.2% as his actual return of 11.4% fell short of his 15.6% benchmark; this ranks 78th percentile relative to his opportunity set. Offsetting this negative result was positive selection by the large, aggressive manager of 1.7%, ranking 31st percentile against his opportunity set. Overall manager selectivity of .21% is material.

Exhibits 6 through 11 provide the same breakdowns for the first and second quarters of 1989.

Exhibits 12 qand 13 summarize Exhibits 5-11 by showing cumulative attribution for the full three quarters, from the fourth quarter of 1988 through the second quarter of 1989. The policy effect of 13.7% is the major performance component. The next most important component is sponsor timing of 1.4%. This good timing effect is the result of underweighting foreign stocks and real estate, while overweighting the S&P 500 index fund. In the actual case, these under/overweightings resulted from a delay in policy implementation, rather than an attempt by the sponsor to time these markets. A sponsor selectivity effect of -.49% partially offsets the good 1.4% timing measure. The managers also added .97% to performance as a result of a 1.02% selectivity effect offset by a -.05% timing effect.

To see how the managers and the sponsor have performed through time, Exhibits 13a and 13b give the quarter-by-quarter attribution history. Exhibit 13a shows the history of the timing measure, with the rates shown first, and then the rankings. The sponsor has distinguished himself in timing, particularly in the first and second quarters of 1989, adding .65% and 1.01% and ranking 2nd percentile and 6th percentile, respectively. On the manager front, both the large, defensive and the small, defensive managers exhibit significantly negative timing effects as both of these managers held significant cash positions during a rising market.

EXHIBIT 3: ATTRIBUTION SUMMARY FOR THE FOURTH QUARTER OF 1988

	Sponsor	*Manager*	*Total*
Policy	2.33		2.33
Timing	− .36	− .03	− .39
Selectivity	.05	.21	.26
	2.02	.18	2.20

EXHIBIT 4: BENCHMARKS FOR FOURTH QUARTER OF 1988

Sponsor
  Policy (P)   2.33
  Allocation (A)   1.99

Sponsor & Manager
  Tactical (T)   1.94
  Strategic (S)   2.20

Manager
  Tactical (t)   2.30
  Strategic (s)   2.51

EXHIBIT 5: BREAKDOWN OF ATTRIBUTION

5a: *Sponsor Timing*
Sponsor Allocation

Manager	Actual (A)	Policy (B)	Mgr. Cmt. (C)	Passive Return (D)	(A–B) D
S&P	25.0	16.0	93.0	3.02	.27
Lg, A	13.0	13.0	100.0	2.80	.00
Sm, A	10.0	8.0	95.0	1.05	.02
Sm, D	10.0	9.0	75.0	2.07	.02
Lg, D	1.0	3.0	30.0	2.30	−.05
Bond	38.0	37.0	99.0	0.76	.01
Forn	1.0	4.0	100.0	15.65	−.47
R. Est.	0.0	6.0	90.0	2.06	−.12
$	2.0	4.0	100.0	2.00	−.04
					−.36
				Rank	48

Opportunity	5	25	50	75	95
	.85	.17	− .41	− .59	− .73

5b: *Sponsor Selectivity*
Sponsor Allocation

Manager	Actual (A)	Policy (B)	Mgr. Cmt. (C)	Passive Return (D)	Active Return (d)	(A-B) × (d-D)
S&P	25.0	16.0	93.0	3.02	3.10	.01
Lg, A	13.0	13.0	100.0	2.80	4.50	.00
Sm, A	10.0	8.0	95.0	1.05	1.10	.00
Sm, D	10.0	9.0	75.0	2.07	2.50	.00
Lg, D	1.0	3.0	30.0	2.30	3.20	−.02
Bond	38.0	37.0	99.0	0.76	0.90	.00
Forn	1.0	4.0	100.0	15.65	11.40	.13
R.Est.	0.0	6.0	90.0	2.06	2.06	.00
$	2.0	4.0	100.0	2.00	2.70	−.01
activity						−.06
						.05
					Rank	55

Opportunity	5	25	50	75	95
	.29	.20	− .09	− .08	− .31

5c: Manager Timing

Manager	Spn. Alo Pol (B)	Mgr. Cmt. Actual	Mgr. Cmt. Policy	Passive Return w/ Mgr. Cmt. Actual (D)	Passive Return w/ Mgr. Cmt. Policy (E)	Manager Timing (D-E) Rate	Rank	5	50	95	B(D-E)
S&P	16.0	93.0	95.0	3.02	3.04	-.02	68	.05	0.0	-.05	.00
Lg, A	13.0	100.0	95.0	2.80	2.76	.04	5	.04	0.0	-.04	.01
Sm, A	8.0	95.0	95.0	1.05	1.05	.00	50	.10	0.0	-.05	.00
Sm, D	9.0	75.0	90.0	2.07	2.09	-.02	84	.01	0.0	-.02	.00
Lg, D	3.0	30.0	90.0	2.30	2.90	-.60	100	.10	0.0	-.20	-.02
Bond	37.0	99.0	90.0	0.76	0.88	-.11	91	.37	0.0	-.13	-.04
Form	4.0	100.0	95.0	15.65	14.97	.68	5	.68	0.0	-.68	.03
R.Est.	6.0	90.0	90.0	2.06	2.06	.00	50	.01	0.0	-.02	.00
$	4.0	100.0	100.0	2.00	2.00	.00	50	.00	0.0	.00	.00
											-.03

5d: Manager Selectivity

Manager	Spn. Alo. Pol. (B)	Act. Mgr. Cmt.	Returns w/ Actl. Cmt. Actual (d)	Returns w/ Actl. Cmt. Passive (D)	Selectivity (d-D) Rate	Rank	5	50	95	B(d-D)
S&P	16.0	93.0	3.1	3.0	0.1	43	0.5	0.0	-0.5	.01
Lg, A	13.0	100.0	4.5	2.8	1.7	31	4.0	0.0	-3.2	.22
Sm, A	8.0	95.0	1.1	1.0	0.1	49	4.5	0.0	-4.1	.00
Sm, D	9.0	75.0	2.5	2.1	0.4	43	2.9	0.0	-2.5	.04
Lg, D	3.0	30.0	3.2	2.3	0.9	14	1.1	0.0	-1.1	.03
Bond	37.0	99.0	0.9	0.8	0.1	36	0.4	0.0	-0.3	.05
Form	4.0	100.0	11.4	15.6	-4.2	78	7.1	0.0	-6.9	-.17
R.Est.	6.0	90.0	2.1	2.1	0.0	50	3.6	0.0	-3.8	.00
$	4.0	100.0	2.7	2.0	0.7	29	1.5	0.0	-0.9	.03
										.21

EXHIBIT 6:   ATTRIBUTION SUMMARY FOR THE FIRST QUARTER OF 1989

	Sponsor	*Manager*	*Total*
Policy	3.97		3.97
Timing	.65	−.11	.54
Selectivity	−.12	.60	.48
	4.51	.49	5.00

EXHIBIT 7:   BENCHMARKS FOR FIRST QUARTER OF 1989

Sponsor
  Policy (P)   3.97
  Allocation (A)   4.62

Sponsor & Manager
  Tactical (T)   4.52
  Strategic (S)   5.00

Manager
  Tactical (t)   3.86
  Strategic (s)   4.46

EXHIBIT 8:   BREAKDOWN OF ATTRIBUTION MEASURES

8a: *Sponsor Timing*
Sponsor Allocation

Manager	Actual (A)	Policy (B)	Mgr. Cmt. (C)	Passive Return (D)	(A–B) D
S&P	24.0	16.0	100.0	7.03	.56
Lg, A	13.0	13.0	96.0	6.81	.00
Sm, A	10.0	8.0	98.0	6.77	.14
Sm, D	11.0	9.0	73.0	6.29	.13
Lg, D	3.0	3.0	56.0	4.61	.00
Bond	38.0	37.0	99.0	1.14	.01
Forn	1.0	4.0	100.0	0.27	−.01
R. Est.	0.0	6.0	90.0	1.41	−.08
$	0.0	4.0	100.0	2.20	−.09
					+.65
				Rank	2

Opportunity	5	25	50	75	95
	.58	.28	.06	− .13	− .29

8b: *Sponsor Selectivity*
Sponsor Allocation

Manager	Actual (A)	Policy (B)	Mgr. Cmt. (C)	Passive Return (D)	Active Return (d)	(A-B) × (d-D)
S&P	24.0	16.0	100.0	7.03	7.20	.01
Lg, A	13.0	13.0	96.0	6.81	7.30	.00
Sm, A	10.0	8.0	98.0	6.77	8.00	.02
Sm, D	11.0	9.0	73.0	6.29	7.00	.01
Lg, D	3.0	3.0	56.0	4.61	7.90	.00
Bond	38.0	37.0	99.0	1.14	1.30	.00
Forn	1.0	4.0	100.0	0.27	5.00	−.14
R.Est.	0.0	6.0	90.0	1.41	1.41	.00
$	0.0	4.0	100.0	2.20	2.20	.00
activity						−.03
						−.12
					Rank	61

Opportunity	5	25	50	75	95
	.32	.10	− .06	− .19	− .30

8c: Manager Timing

Manager	Spn. Alo Pol. (B)	Mgr. Cmt.		Passive Return w/ Mgr. Cmt.		Rate	Rank	Manager Timing (D-E)			B(D-E)
		Actual	Policy	Actual (D)	Policy (E)			5	50	95	
S&P	16.0	100.0	95.0	7.03	6.79	.24	5	.24	0.0	-.24	.04
Lg, A	13.0	96.0	95.0	6.81	6.76	.05	41	.24	0.0	-.24	.01
Sm, A	8.0	98.0	95.0	6.77	6.63	.14	23	.23	0.0	-.47	.01
Sm, D	9.0	73.0	90.0	6.29	7.24	-.95	88	.56	0.0	-1.12	-.09
Lg, D	3.0	56.0	90.0	4.61	6.07	-1.46	100	.43	0.0	-.86	-.04
Bond	37.0	99.0	90.0	1.14	1.24	-.10	91	.32	0.0	-.11	-.04
Form	4.0	100.0	95.0	0.27	0.37	-.10	95	.10	0.0	-.10	.03
R.Est.	6.0	90.0	90.0	1.41	1.41	.00	50	.26	0.0	-.09	.00
$	4.0	100.0	100.0	2.20	2.20	.00	50	.00	0.0	.00	.00
											-.11

8d: Manager Selectivity

Manager	Spn. Alo. Pol. (B)	Act. Mgr. Cmt.	Returns w/ Actl. Cmt.		Rate	Rank	Selectivity (d-D)			B(d-D)
			Actual (d)	Passive (D)			5	50	95	
S&P	16.0	100.0	7.2	7.0	0.2	35	0.5	0.0	-0.5	.03
Lg, A	13.0	96.0	7.3	6.8	0.5	45	4.7	0.0	-3.8	.06
Sm, A	8.0	98.0	8.0	6.8	1.2	37	4.3	0.0	-3.9	.10
Sm, D	9.0	73.0	7.0	6.3	0.7	41	3.4	0.0	-2.5	.06
Lg, D	3.0	56.0	7.9	4.6	3.3	1	2.1	0.0	-1.7	.10
Bond	37.0	99.0	1.3	1.1	0.2	30	0.4	0.0	-0.4	.06
Form	4.0	100.0	5.0	0.3	4.7	20	7.0	0.0	-7.3	.19
R.Est.	6.0	90.0	1.4	1.4	0.0	50	3.6	0.0	-5.1	.00
$	4.0	100.0	2.2	2.2	0.0	50	1.5	0.0	-1.0	.03
										.60

EXHIBIT 9: ATTRIBUTION SUMMARY FOR SECOND QUARTER OF 1989

	Sponsor	*Manager*	*Total*
Policy	6.86		6.86
Timing	1.01	.10	1.11
Selectivity	−.39	.12	−.27
	7.48	.22	7.70

EXHIBIT 10: BENCHMARKS FOR SECOND QUARTER OF 1989

Sponsor
  Policy (P)   6.86
  Allocation (A)   7.83

Sponsor & Manager
  Tactical (T)   7.97
  Strategic (S)   7.70

Manager
  Tactical (t)   6.96
  Strategic (s)   7.08

EXHIBIT 11:   BREAKDOWN OF ATTRIBUTION MEASURES

11a: ***Sponsor Timing***

Sponsor Allocation

Manager	Actual (A)	Policy (B)	Mgr. Cmt. (C)	Passive Return (D)	(A–B) D
S&P	22.0	16.0	100.0	8.81	.53
Lg, A	14.0	13.0	98.0	8.77	.09
Sm, A	11.0	8.0	98.0	8.82	.26
Sm, D	11.0	9.0	90.0	7.90	.16
Lg, D	3.0	3.0	71.0	6.62	.00
Bond	37.0	37.0	93.0	7.59	.00
Forn	1.0	4.0	100.0	−6.18	.19
R. Est.	0.0	6.0	90.0	2.28	−.14
$	1.0	4.0	100.0	2.50	−.08
					1.01
				Rank	6

	Opportunity	5	25	50	75	95
		1.09	.65	.30	− .13	− .62

11b: ***Sponsor Selectivity***

Sponsor Allocation

Manager	Actual (A)	Policy (B)	Mgr. Cmt. (C)	Passive Return (D)	Active Return (d)	(A-B) × (d-D)
S&P	22.0	16.0	100.0	8.81	8.40	−.02
Lg, A	14.0	13.0	98.0	8.77	5.80	−.03
Sm, A	11.0	8.0	98.0	8.82	9.30	.01
Sm, D	11.0	9.0	90.0	7.90	9.40	.03
Lg, D	3.0	3.0	71.0	6.62	3.60	.00
Bond	37.0	37.0	93.0	7.59	8.10	.00
Forn	1.0	4.0	100.0	−6.18	0.70	−.21
R.Est.	0.0	6.0	90.0	2.28	2.28	.00
$	1.0	4.0	100.0	2.50	3.10	−.02
activity						−.16
						−.39
					Rank	88

	Opportunity	5	25	50	75	95
		.51	.18	− .07	− .27	− .49

11c: Manager Timing

Manager	Spn. Alo Pol. (B)	Mgr. Cmt. Actual	Mgr. Cmt. Policy	Passive Return w/ Mgr. Cmt. Actual (D)	Passive Return w/ Mgr. Cmt. Policy (E)	Manager Timing (D-E) Rate	Rank	5	50	95	B(D-E)
S&P	16.0	100.0	95.0	8.81	8.49	.32	5	.32	0.0	-.32	.05
Lg, A	13.0	98.0	95.0	8.77	8.58	.19	23	.32	0.0	-.32	.02
Sm, A	8.0	98.0	95.0	8.82	8.63	.19	23	.32	0.0	-.64	.02
Sm, D	9.0	90.0	90.0	7.90	7.90	.00	50	.60	0.0	-1.20	.00
Lg, D	3.0	71.0	90.0	6.62	7.72	-1.10	93	.58	0.0	-1.16	-.03
Bond	37.0	93.0	90.0	7.59	7.42	.16	37	.55	0.0	-1.64	.06
Forn	4.0	100.0	95.0	-6.18	-5.75	-.43	95	.43	0.0	-.43	-.02
R.Est.	6.0	90.0	90.0	2.28	2.28	.00	50	.07	0.0	-.03	.00
$	4.0	100.0	100.0	2.50	2.50	.00	50	.00	0.0	.00	.00
											.10

11d: Manager Selectivity

Manager	Spn. Alo. Pol. (B)	Act. Mgr. Cmt.	Returns w/ Actl. Cmt. Actual (d)	Returns w/ Actl. Cmt. Passive (D)	Selectivity (d-D) Rate	Rank	5	50	95	B(d-D)
S&P	16.0	100.0	8.4	8.8	-0.4	86	0.5	0.0	-0.5	-.07
Lg, A	13.0	98.0	5.8	8.8	-3.0	80	4.3	0.0	-4.5	.39
Sm, A	8.0	98.0	9.3	8.8	0.5	45	4.1	0.0	-4.0	.04
Sm, D	9.0	90.0	9.4	7.9	1.5	32	3.7	0.0	-3.5	.14
Lg, D	3.0	71.0	3.6	6.6	-3.0	100	2.1	0.0	-2.3	-.09
Bond	37.0	93.0	8.1	7.6	0.5	1	0.4	0.0	-0.3	.19
Forn	4.0	100.0	0.7	-6.2	6.9	8	7.4	0.0	-7.0	.28
R.Est.	6.0	90.0	2.3	2.3	0.0	50	3.6	0.0	-4.1	.00
$	4.0	100.0	3.1	2.5	0.6	32	1.5	0.0	-1.0	.02
										.12

EXHIBIT 12: ATTRIBUTION SUMMARY FOR 88/4 TO 89/2 (THREE QUARTERS)

	Sponsor	Manager	Total
Policy	13.70		13.70
Timing	1.40	–.05	1.34
Selectivity	–.49	1.02	.53
	14.60	.97	15.57

EXHIBIT 13: BENCHMARKS

Sponsor
| Policy (P) | 13.70 |
| Allocation (A) | 15.06 |

Sponsor & Manager
| Tactical (T) | 15.04 |
| Strategic (S) | 15.57 |

Manager
| Tactical (t) | 13.65 |
| Strategic (s) | 14.67 |

13a: Timing History

	S&P	Lg, A	Sm, A	Sm, D	Lg, D	Bond	Forn	R.Est.	$	Sponsor
884	.00	.01	.00	.00	-.02	-.04	.03	.00	.00	-.36
891	.04	.01	.01	-.09	-.04	-.04	.00	.00	.00	.65
892	.05	.02	.02	.00	-.03	.06	-.02	.00	.00	1.01
Total	.1	.0	.0	-.1	-.1	.0	.0	.0	.0	1.3
RANKS										
884	68	5	50	84	100	91	5	50	50	48
891	5	41	23	88	100	91	95	50	50	2
892	5	23	23	50	93	37	95	50	50	6

13b: Selectivity History

	S&P	Lg, A	Sm, A	Sm, D	Lg, D	Bond	Forn	R.Est.	$	Sponsor
884	.01	.01	.00	.00	-.02	-.04	.03	.00	.00	-.36
891	.03	.01	.01	-.09	-.04	-.04	.00	.00	.00	.65
892	-.07	.02	.02	.00	-.03	.06	-.02	.00	.00	1.01
Total	.0	.0	.0	-.1	-.1	.0	.0	.0	.0	1.3
RANKS										
884	43	31	49	43	14	36	78	50	29	55
891	35	45	37	41	1	30	20	50	50	61
892	86	80	45	32	100	1	8	50	32	88

Exhibit 13b repeats this historical record for selectivity. Here again the sponsor has distinguished himself with a -.5% cumulative effect. Offsetting this sponsor effect are good selectivity from the bond, foreign stock, and small, defensive managers.

These historical recaps are the tools that are needed to determine the strengths and weaknesses of the management team.

CONCLUSION

Plan sponsors strive to create the best investment programs they can. Part of this effort is directed to making program modifications as circumstances change. To make these modifications wisely, the plan sponsor needs to identify changes in the strengths of his management team, and to recognize that he is an integral part of this management team. Performance attribution to both sponsor and managers shows who owns what part of overall performance and who is adding or subtracting value. This is essential to successful program management.

NOTES

[1] Actually, there are 2^3, or eight, such combinations, but two possibilities are not needed.

[2] See Ronald J. Surz, "Customized Performance Standards," in Frank J. Fabozzi, editor, *The Institutional Investor Focus on Investment Management*, (Cambridge, MA: Ballinger Publishing 1989).

[3] See Chapter 10.

CHAPTER 13

Selecting an International Investment Manager

MARGARETT H. GORODESS
ASSOCIATE
BECKER, BURKE ASSOCIATES INCORPORATED

Over the last few years, more and more plan sponsors have made the decision to invest a portion of their plan assets in markets outside the United States. The two most common reasons for this decision are the low correlation of foreign markets with the U.S. markets and the potential for higher investment returns. In some cases the sponsor has carried out a detailed asset allocation study which determines that the addition of non-U.S. securities will increase the plan's expected return while maintaining the desired level of risk. In other cases, the sponsor is attracted by recent returns that have exceeded the returns of U.S. stocks and bonds. The importance of these factors to a specific fund sponsor is an individual matter that will directly impact the selection process.

The sponsor whose primary interest is diversification may be content with an index fund which will provide diversification at a relatively low cost. On the other hand, if performance is the primary objective, one may opt for active management whose goal is to beat a benchmark. Having said this, the decision is greatly complicated by the fact that in recent years international equity managers have significantly underperformed popular indices and have created a situation in which the indexing is expected, at least by some, to provide the highest returns. Whether the decision is motivated by diversification or performance, sponsors usually view the decision as a long-term commitment to improve the plan's risk/reward profile.

DEFINING THE MANAGER'S ROLE

Implementing the decision to invest outside the United States requires the sponsor to first determine the general scope of the manager's mandate. This would include the selection of a benchmark, a decision of whether or not to hedge currencies, the choice of active or passive management and, finally, selection of investment style. The next step is to evaluate the universe of potential managers and to select a specific firm to manage the assets. The final steps are to negotiate the contract with the manager, arrange for custody of the assets, and put in place a program for reporting and evaluation of the manager.

The pages that follow will detail the issues involved in the process of defining the manager's role, with emphasis on manager selection. The purpose of the chapter is to provide practical guidance for the sponsor, particularly one who is taking the first step toward international diversification.

Selecting the Benchmark

The selection of a benchmark has become a complex question, particularly in the area of non-U.S. equities. Until 1987, the only widely-used index was the Morgan Stanley Capital International World Index and its sub-index, the Europe Australia Far East Index (EAFE). As interest in international investing grew, competing benchmarks such as the Financial Times-Actuaries and Russell-Goldman were developed. Each attempted to provide a better proxy for the investable markets outside the U.S..

Some plan sponsors have been dissatisfied with existing indices which are weighted by market capitalization. During the 1980s, the rising prices of Japanese stocks have caused that market to grow from 40% to over 60% of the non-U.S. indices. The fact that a single market can dominate an index has created a demand for a new type of benchmark that reduces what some feel is an overrepresentation of Japan. The argument against capitalization-weighted indices is that the high prices of Japanese stocks exaggerates the importance of their stock market relative to those of other countries. A solution accepted by some has been to create a new index that weights individual market returns by each country's gross domestic product relative to the world economy. This reduces the Japanese component but creates other problems. For example, Germany has one of the largest economies in the world but a relatively small stock market. An index that increases the weighting of the German market can result in liquidity problems because there is not a direct relationship between the size of the underlying economy and the capitalization of the stock market. In other cases, plan sponsors have created custom benchmarks, specifying country commitments based on their own analysis of markets and comfort levels.

Benchmarks for non-U.S. bonds are going through a similar evolution. At first only a single index, the Salomon World Bond Index, was available. As investment in the asset class increased, the index was reexamined and other indices were developed in an attempt to more accurately represent the investable universe.

Hedged Versus Unhedged Benchmarks

Holding foreign securities exposes the U.S. investor to fluctuations in the value of the U.S. dollar. The impact of changes in exchange rates on returns has become a major topic of discussion. In the short term, currencies impact returns and increase volatility. On the other hand, it is argued that currency changes cancel each other out over a cycle and that the long-term expected return from the currency component is zero. By selecting an unhedged benchmark, the sponsor accepts both positive and negative currency impact on short-term returns. By selecting a hedged benchmark, the sponsor seeks lower volatility and anticipates returns that derive exclusively from the performance of the assets within their own markets.

In either case, the sponsor must decide whether he wishes the investment manager to manage currencies actively, deviating from the benchmark currency exposures. The two factors in the decision are the costs of hedging and the ability of the manager to add value with enough consistency to deliver returns that exceed the benchmark after expenses. If active currency hedging is desired, it may be done by the manager of the stock (bond) portfolio or by a separate currency specialist.

Active Versus Passive Management

In the early years of overseas investing by U.S. sponsors, virtually all managers used active country and security selection. The growth of passive management through international index funds parallels the earlier growth of domestic index funds. The decision on active versus passive management still depends, in large part, upon the sponsor's view of the possibilities of adding value through active management. During much of the 1980s, the median active manager of international equities has underperformed published indices. During this period, a key factor has been the managers' underweighting of Japan, which performed much better than their expectations. A second factor was the decline in the U.S. dollar. Most active managers use hedging defensively; that is, they seek to protect the dollar value of the underlying assets. Thus, they add value by hedging only when the dollar rises. They do not try to increase returns from currencies as the dollar falls. By contrast with previous years, active managers easily outperformed the standard benchmarks in 1989 as the dollar rose in value and the Japanese market underperformed.

As a compromise between fully active and fully passive management, many managers have developed products in which some portion of the process is passive and the rest active. Thus, we see active country allocation combined with passive security selection (indexing) within each individual market. Another variation is to hold country weightings in line with the index and to use active security selection within each country. Other permutations allow active decisions on countries and/or stocks, but use specific constraints designed to control the degree to which performance may deviate from index returns.

Global/International/Regional Portfolios

The plan sponsor must also determine whether his manager's mandate will be to invest globally (in all markets including the U.S.), internationally (excluding the U.S.), or regionally (in specific parts of the world such as Europe, Pacific Basin, etc.). The key here is the sponsor's desire to control allocation among markets. In fixed-income, global management has been well accepted. For equities, however, most U.S. sponsors have selected the international mandate, assuring that a specific allocation be maintained in non-U.S. equities. More recently, some plan sponsors have taken the route of hiring regional specialists, each of whom invests only in a specified number of markets. The plan sponsor takes responsibility for the regional weightings by controlling the amount of assets allocated to each manager. Obviously, this last method places the greatest burden on the plan sponsor.

SELECTING THE MANAGER

Finding Managers

Once the role of the international manager has been defined and benchmarks chosen, the sponsor can begin the process of selecting the appropriate manager. Although most larger plans are regularly contacted by firms marketing their international expertise, all sponsors should make an active effort to include the largest possible number of firms in their initial screening in order to ensure that their choices are not limited to those managers with the most aggressive marketing programs.

There are several sources of information on managers. These sources vary in cost and in the degree to which they will actively assist the plan sponsor. The most accessible and least expensive sources are professional or industry publications, which regularly feature directories of international managers. The information in these directories may be limited to addresses and contact names, but may also include a brief mention of investment approach, assets managed or other data. The plan sponsor would then need to gather and evaluate detailed information from each firm in order to evaluate its qualifications.

More detailed information may be found in data bases of managers sold by various consulting firms. The information may be provided either in hard copy or in a computerized form. In either case, the data base should be evaluated in terms of the number of managers included and the amount of information provided on each firm. It is also important to assess the vendor's role in determining the universe of eligible managers and in ensuring the accuracy of the information as well as its timeliness. The sponsor could do a preliminary screening on the basis of this information and would then need to solicit more detailed information directly from the managers in order to evaluate them.

Finally, the sponsor may elect to hire a consultant with a proprietary data base. The consulting firm should be evaluated in terms of its experience in manager selection, the breadth and depth of the data base and its freedom from conflicts of interest. The consultant should play an active role in assuring the accuracy of the manager information and should have first-hand knowledge of the firm, including personal visits to the managers. The consultant works with the sponsor to establish selection criteria, handles the preliminary screening of firms based on these criteria and selects the most qualified organizations. The consultant then prepares profiles of the candidates and reviews each organization with the sponsor. After the sponsor selects the firms to be interviewed, the consultant schedules presentations and assists in the interview process. After the sponsor has chosen the manager, the consultant should also assist in contract negotiations, in arrangements for custody of the assets and in the funding process.

Types of Investment Management Organizations

The number of firms offering international investing services to U.S. plansponsors has grown steadily in the last decade and now includes a broad diversity of organizations. Many international managers are affiliated with large multi-product organizations, particularly U.S. banks, U.K. merchant banks and Japanese securities firms. Some are joint ventures in which, typically, the U.S. organization provides marketing services while the foreign partners handle the actual investment management. In recent years, the number of independent investment counselors has increased, both in the U.S. and abroad. These newer managers are often boutiques that specialize in international investing.

The strengths and weaknesses of each type of organization are the same as those observed among domestic managers. In evaluating any firm, one should consider the depth and stability of personnel, breadth of resources, consistency of investment philosophy and process, and ability to retain clients. The amount of assets under management should be sufficient to indicate financial stability but not so large as to dilute investment results or the ability to service clients. The strength and stability of the organization as well as the consistency of its approach will be the key factors in its ability to provide superior investment products in the future. Past investment performance should also be evaluated, both relative to the benchmark and to the firm's stated investment style.

In addition, one should consider the organization's ability to communicate with U.S. plan-sponsors and to provide timely reporting. Previous experience in managing U.S. funds can provide some evidence that the manager is handling this aspect of the relationship successfully. The sponsor can gather additional information by contacting current clients and meeting as many members of the organization as possible.

Management Styles

For some years, the U.S. sponsor has viewed his domestic managers in terms of investment style. This approach has carried over into the international area and has caused manager styles to become more clearly differentiated. Like domestic managers, international managers exhibit a number of investment styles. It is important to understand the style and its consequences in selecting a manager or in structuring a multi-manager program.

One of the major problems in selecting an international manager has been to find a way to consistently define the differences and similarities among managers in order to make valid comparisons and effective decisions. The large number of variables and the scarcity of documentation are significant problems. Still, it is possible to make a meaningful analysis of the firms under consideration working with the available tools.

It is useful to think in terms of a matrix (shown in Exhibit 1) in order to analyze international equity style. Moving from left to right on the horizontal axis, one starts from a strong emphasis on valuation measures and goes to a strong emphasis on earnings growth. On the vertical axis, concentration on large companies is at the top and emphasis on small companies is on the bottom. Analyzing a manager's investment style and placing him within this matrix will help to clarify the differences among firms and will assist in constructing a multi-manager program. This process will lead to broad classifications similar to those used to describe domestic managers, such as "Large Cap-Growth", "Large-Cap Value", etc.

A second matrix (shown in Exhibit 2) can be added to further differentiate managers. In this case, the horizontal axis will go from strong emphasis on fundamental analysis of both countries and stocks to strong emphasis on quantitative analysis. On the vertical axis, broad diversification is placed at the top and concentrated portfolios at the bottom. Thus one can further characterize each of the style categories in the matrix in Exhibit 1 in terms of investment process and diversification.

EXHIBIT 1

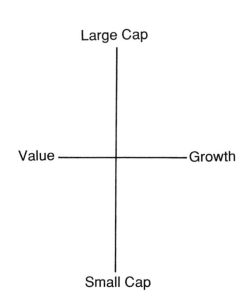

EXHIBIT 2

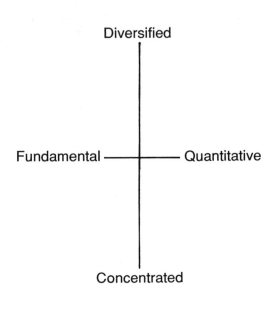

These four terms can, for example, characterize a manager as value-oriented manager, emphasizing large capitalization stocks, using a quantitative methodology to construct moderately diversified portfolios. This manager can then be compared to others with a similar approach.

The same type of analysis can be used to describe fixed-income managers. A matrix for locating bond-manager styles would have an emphasis on fundamental economic data on the left hand side of the horizontal axis and an emphasis on technical market analysis on the right hand side (see Exhibit 3). The vertical axis would go from a high degree of diversification (representation in most major markets) at the top to a high degree of concentration (holdings in very few markets) at the bottom. This would serve to characterize styles such as "Fundamental-Diversified" or "Technical-Concentrated." Another matrix (shown in Exhibit 4) focuses on duration and quality, although these characteristics are not as useful in differentiating among non-U.S. bond managers.

Now that progress has been made in analyzing the type of manager under consideration, this information can be used to formulate the questions necessary to evaluate the firm. For example, if a manager uses a fundamental approach, questions on his sources of research and their ade-

EXHIBIT 3

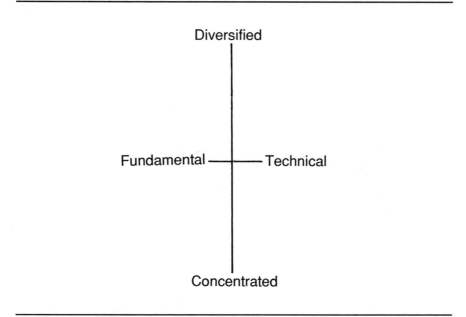

EXHIBIT 4

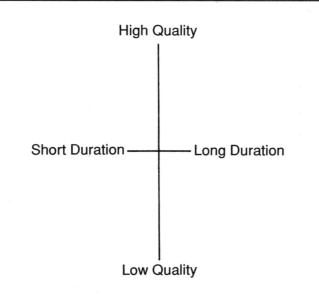

quacy to cover his universe of stocks are appropriate. If the manager's approach is highly quantitative, one would want to evaluate his computer expertise and data bases. Clearly the organization and its structure must be appropriate for its investment style.

Investment Process

The question of investment process was mentioned briefly in the discussion of ways to differentiate investment styles. One can safely generalize that most of the firms who were the early arrivals in the U.S. pension fund market employed a top-down investment process. Their decisions began with country weightings based on macroeconomic analysis and proceeded through sector analysis and stock selection. As the process unfolded, responsibility for decisions moved from a committee of senior professionals to regional specialists and security analysts.

More recently, firms employing a bottom-up process, which begins with stock selection, are becoming more numerous. For such managers, country weightings are the result of an accumulation of attractive stocks within each market. Managers using this approach frequently are found to emphasize quantitative analysis rather than fundamental country and stock research.

Evaluation of Investment Personnel

As with any domestic investment organization, the experience of the investment professionals and the stability and continuity of personnel within the organization are crucial for future success. It is important to become familiar with the investment staff and to evaluate their experience. One should be aware that pension fund management has not historically been an area of emphasis within large firms outside the U.S.. Thus the roles of security analyst and portfolio manager may be stepping stones to a career in a more prestigious position within the firm. This may be a reason for the relatively young age and short investment experience of personnel in these positions at some firms. It is, therefore, important to know if the senior professionals have their experience within the investment management area.

Retention of key personnel has been a problem at many major organizations in recent years. This is certainly due, at least in part, to the desire of many firms to establish themselves in the market for international management. In recent years, there has been substantial personnel turnover in the international area, sometimes involving entire investment teams. Thus, it is crucial to determine whether the current investment group is the one that is responsible for the historical performance record.

Looking toward the future, one must evaluate the steps that the firm has taken to ensure retention of its key personnel. The most obvious means are through competitive compensation levels, employment contracts and a stimulating working environment. Ownership interest in the firm is another incentive for professionals to remain together. One should also inquire about a firm's financial strength and its ability to maintain the quality of its operations. This is particularly true of a new firm, which may have to weather a prolonged period before it achieves profitability.

Evaluating Investment Performance

Investment performance is one of the most difficult areas to assess in the process of selecting a manager. Although past performance may not reliably predict future performance, a strong historical record inevitably carries a great deal of weight. This is true in selecting a domestic manager and is even more so in the international area. It is essential that the performance record be accurate and representative of the firm. Understanding a manager's historic performance is one of the tools for assessing his skill. This assessment problem is often compounded in the international arena by the small amount of data available and the lack of adequate analysis. Very few managers can provide a long track record in managing international funds for U.S. sponsors and it is difficult to analyze the sources of their investment performance.

Plan sponsors (and consultants) must require the same standards of performance reporting from international managers that they require from domestic managers. This means that the sources of performance numbers should be composites of accounts with similar objectives and should include all terminated accounts for the period they were under the management in question. Audited commingled funds or mutual fund records may also be accepted if they are the vehicle to be used for investment.

The performance of a single account (unless it is the only one under management) should not be accepted. Simulated performance should be viewed as an interesting work of fiction. It may provide some insight into the workings of the investment style, but cannot be taken as the equivalent of actual performance, even when presumably adjusted for trading costs and other factors.

Evaluating performance is often difficult. As mentioned earlier, in recent years most equity managers have underperformed their benchmarks.

Many organizations do not have a U.S. track record going back far enough to show how they performed in different investment environments. Peer group comparisons can be useful and most firms can show their results in comparison to a peer group of managers. The difficulty is that comparative backgrounds are small in number, particularly as one goes back in time, and they do not usually provide data for subgroups such as funds of similar style. The situation is improving as more and more plan sponsors hire international managers and data bases become broader.

One of the most useful ways of evaluating performance relates investment returns to the level of risk taken by the manager. This is commonly done by measuring the variability of returns (risk) and comparing it to the annualized returns achieved over the period. The risk/reward relationship can be shown on a scatter diagram, as in Exhibit 5.

EXHIBIT 5

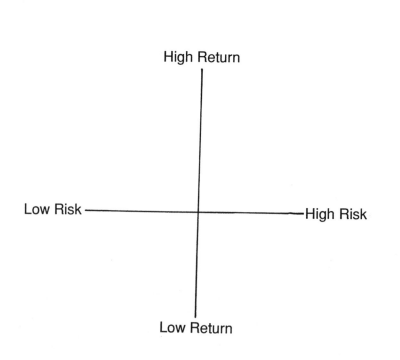

Performance attribution analysis is another important tool in understanding a manager's strengths and weaknesses. Each manager under serious consideration should be asked to provide an analysis of his performance. This would show the impact of his country weighting decisions, stock selection and currency management. The actual performance should then be compared to his stated philosophy. A firm that describes itself as emphasizing country selection should, over time, show the largest value added from those decisions. Similarly, a bottom-up stock picker should be able to demonstrate superior performance by his stocks compared to others in each individual market. The same is true for active currency management.

Choice of Investment Vehicles

International investing is available on an individual account basis and through commingled funds or mutual funds. The choice will depend on the amount to be placed, the need for customized investment, and the associated costs.

Sponsors investing less than $10 million will find some managers unwilling to manage their accounts separately. If the manager is willing to take smaller amounts, the sponsor should be sure that the manager will be able to implement his approach effectively in terms of diversification and the costs of execution.

Funds with restrictions, such as South Africa divestment, will find few pooled vehicles available. Special guidelines or custom benchmarks will obviously require separate management.

Mutual funds may sometimes be an acceptable vehicle, particularly for non-ERISA funds. The disadvantages of mutual funds designed for the retail market are in fees and performance. Mutual fund fees may include sales charges ("loads"), back-end loads (12(b)1 fees) and high expenses relative to institutional fund costs. Mutual fund performance can be adversely impacted by large cash flows in and out of the funds.

Commingled funds or employee benefit trusts are often available and may offer a cost advantage over separate account management. A number of organizations offer management and custody for substantially less than one would pay on a separate account basis.

Costs of Investing Internationally

The explicit costs of international investment, management and custody fees are high in comparison to domestic portfolios. This is true for both active and passive funds. However, both management and custody costs have been decreasing as the volume of U.S. investment abroad has increased.

Managers' fees for separate accounts are based on asset size with a decreasing scale for larger accounts. Most fee schedules of active managers start at a level of between 0.75% and 1.00% per annum. In some cases the fee is negotiable, particularly for larger accounts.

Custody fees typically include fees based on both asset value and transactions. Total custody costs are generally estimated to average 0.25% per annum, although this may vary significantly depending on the custodian and the turnover level of the manager. Like the management fee, custodian's fees are sometimes negotiable.

CONCLUSION

The selection of an international investment manager is a challenge for the plan sponsor. Finding the appropriate manager is crucial to the overall success of the international investment program. The structured decision process described here is meant to guide the sponsor through the determination of the manager's role, selection of the manager, and implementation of the program. Using the same principles that apply to successful selection of a domestic manager, the sponsor can deal with the complex field of international investing and effectively implement his decision to invest abroad.

CHAPTER 14

Fixing the Accounting Standards for Pension and Health Care Benefits: Advice for FASB

Keith P. Ambachtsheer
Publisher
The Ambachtsheer Letter

After years of discussion, debate, and sometimes heated argument, the Financial Accounting Standards Board (FASB) issued Statement 87 in the fall of 1986. Statement 87 details how companies must now report in their financial statements on the cost and financial status of defined benefit pension plans they sponsor. With the issuance of FASB 87, employment-based pension plans in the United States were immediately lifted to a higher level of visibility both within corporate America and outside it.

A story in *The Wall Street Journal* of January 18, 1988 gives an indication of FASB 87's notoriety. It opened: "It has to be one of the most feared and misunderstood accounting rules of all times . . . it may affect the way more than a trillion dollars is invested . . . and the lives of millions of people. . . ."

Now that FASB 87 has been around for a few years, it is appropriate to have another look at this feared and misunderstood accounting rule. In this chapter we explain why, despite the best efforts and intentions by the board, FASB 87 suffers from a number of structural and perceptual flaws. We suggest remedies and also offer some thoughts on the proposed accounting standards for nonpension postretirement benefits (mainly health care) just issued.

THE ECONOMICS OF DEFINED BENEFIT PLANS

FASB isn't issuing employee benefits-related accounting standards because it has nothing better to do. The accrued pensions and health care obligations of corporate America are over $1 trillion; single employer-defined benefit pension plan assets are $750 billion. The existence of assets and liabilities of this magnitude is highly material to the finances of corporations. They simply can not be ignored or just relegated to a few obscure notes in the financial statements.

The fundamental reason for this materiality is that corporate practice, union negotiations, legislation, regulation, and court precedents have, over the years, transformed what were once pure corporate gratuities into legally enforceable payment obligations. As a result, corporations now have more debt outstanding to their current and former employees than they do to either their bankers or their bondholders. Further, both tax law inducements and the Employee Retirement Income Security Act of 1974 (ERISA) require the funding of pension obligations. The existence of the resulting assets and the income these assets produce must be properly accounted for too.

In fact, defined benefit plans have become captive pension debt-servicing financial institutions. Many of them have assets and liabilities rivaling those of the corporation's mainline businesses. We will use this "captive financial institution" paradigm to examine how well FASB 87's rules and requirements reflect the realities of the going-concern financial impact of pensions for corporate America today.

FASB STATEMENT 87 IN REVIEW

We will not reproduce FASB 87 here. Its key features may be summarized as follows:

- The pension benefits that have accrued to current and former employees, based on today's salaries and discounted at today's interest rates, must be calculated and will be termed the *accumulated benefit obligation*, or *ABO*. Any pension asset shortfall in relation to the ABO must be recorded as a main balance sheet liability.

- The *projected benefit obligation*, or *PBO*, restates the ABO to take account of the fact that, unless the benefits earned are truly fixed-dollar benefits, the accrued obligation should be calculated not based on today's salaries, but on projected final salaries. Any promised *cost-of-living adjustments* or *COLAS* should also be reflected in the PBO.

- The increase in the PBO in any given year due to the benefits earned in that year is the *service cost* for that year.

- The *pension expense* includes interest on the PBO, less the expected return on plan assets. This difference is termed *net interest cost*.

- *Amortization costs* result from (a) an initial balance sheet *transition* surplus, or deficit, that is amortized over the future service life of active plan members, (b) *prior service costs* resulting from plan amendments are similarly amortized, and (c) *actuarial gains or losses* arise due to differences between actual plan experience and projected plan experience. The impact of these gains or losses on *pension expense* can be smoothed through a number of permissible techniques.

- Total *pension expense* in a given year is the sum of the *service cost*, the *net interest expense*, and the *amortization costs* for that year. Service costs will always be positive. In theory, the other two components can be either positive or negative. Generally, *net interest expense* will be either zero or negative. *Amortization costs* can be positive or negative, depending on the values of its three components.

- Plan *experience assumptions* should reflect "best estimates." Specifically, the *discount rate* to determine *service cost*, PBO and interest thereon should be a market-based long-term interest rate at which the liabilities could be settled. The *expected plan assets return* should represent management's best estimate, given the chosen asset mix policy. The *salary growth* projection should reflect productivity and inflation growth consistent with the *discount rate* and *expected plan assets return*.

FOUR SPECIFIC CONCERNS WITH FASB 87

We have four specific concerns with FASB 87:

1. The ABO concept is irrelevant in a going-concern context. Irrelevant information has no place in financial statements.

2. The settlement rate focus for the PBO discount rate also suggests a termination rather than going-concern focus. What matters in

valuing the liabilities of an ongoing pension plan is not a settlement rate, but the spread between the long-term return on the
default-free portfolio which comes closest to immunizing going-
concern pension liabilities, and long-term wage inflation (and
likely price inflation as well).

3. The *net interest cost* concept effectively permits the anticipation
   of risk-related investment profits within the captive pension
   debt-servicing financial institution before they are earned. This is
   inconsistent with generally accepted accounting practices, which
   have financial institutions reporting investment profits only after
   they have in fact been made, or, at least, could be made based on
   realistic values of the institution's assets and liabilities.

4. The *pension expense* concept mixes the apple of the cost of deferred compensation and the orange of the profitability of the
   captive pension debt-servicing financial institution. Financial
   statements are confusing enough without mixing apples and or-
   anges.

Fortunately, there are potential solutions in each of these four FASB
87 problem areas; these are discussed in the sections that follow.

THE ABO MUST GO!

There are two problems with the ABO concept. Because the ABO behaves
like a long bond, it may pull the asset mix policies of ongoing pensions
plans too far towards long bonds. Also, the ABO may lead to a serious
underassessment of actual accrued pension liabilities.

For example, suppose the best estimate of the going-concern (and
hence highly inflation-sensitive) projected benefit obligation in a pension
plan is $1.6 billion. How helpful is it to know that if the accrued pension
obligations could be settled at current long-term interest rates, $1 billion
would be needed and that obligation could be hedged with $1 billion worth
of long bonds? (Recent congressional actions related to the disposition of
plan surplus upon termination effectively eliminate any possibility of such
a transaction taking place anyway.)

If the plan sponsor has no intention to settle with plan participants
(and couldn't at $1 billion anyway), the ABO clearly has no operational
content. Is it not stating the obvious to say that pension plan accounting
rules that (a) lead to a potentially inappropriate investment policy and that
(b) potentially under- assess the true extent of accumulated pension entitle-

ments are inimical to the achievement of the long-term goals of those plans? Hence we say: "the ABO must go!"

"SETTLEMENT" OR "CONTINUATION" INTEREST RATE?

FASB 87 talks about using a "settlement rate" to value pension obligations. It seems to us that ongoing liabilities should be valued not at settlement rates, but at continuation rates. This is an important issue, and not just for pension accounting. The right answer to the discount rate question has a lot to say about measuring both the true cost of deferred compensation and the true value of accrued pension liabilities, as well as about identifying the key return benchmark for setting pension fund investment goals.

We let the authors of *The Financial Reality of Pension Funding Under ERISA* articulate a fundamental principle when setting the pension liability discount rate: ". . . the rate at which future pension obligations are discounted back to the present is critical. The appropriate rate is the riskless interest rate. The present value which results with this rate is the market value of the assets on which beneficiaries must have claim if they are not to be subjected to investment risk . . ."[1]

To put the matter in a costing perspective, if there is a very high degree of certainty that the pension debt will in fact be paid to plan participants as promised, the pension debt discount rate should reflect a very low probability of default. In fact, defined benefit plans are required by regulation to be well-funded and are generally sponsored by going-concern, large private and public sector entities. It follows then that, in fact, pension debt discount rates (both from funding and costing perspectives) should generally be a risk-free interest rate, or one not far from it.

But Which Risk-Free Interest Rate? . . . The Maturity Structure Factor

Unfortunately, risk of default is not the only factor that needs to be considered in determining the risk-free investment policy against a given pool of pension liabilities. There is also the *timing* of when the liabilities fall due. Fortunately, the timing element causes no major practical difficulty. Default-free debt trades regularly across a broad maturity structure, from 91-day Treasury bills to 20(+) year, zero-coupon bonds.

Generally, yield curves are upward sloping. This implies that, generally, the longer the duration of pension debt, the higher the liability discount rate that can be justified. As a practical matter, the bulk of the liabilities in the typical pension plan will not fall due within the next few years. Thus, it is the *long end* of the yield curve that will provide the right discount rate.

But Which Risk-Free Interest Rate? . . . The Inflation-Sensitivity Factor

Unfortunately, the default risk and term structure (i.e., payment timing) factors are not the only ones that distinguish one pool of pension liabilities from another. There is a further major element: the inflation-sensitivity of the pension liabilities pool. However, we can get some idea about how to adjust liability discount rates for this inflation-sensitivity factor. While we have little pricing experience with long term, inflation-indexed bonds in North American capital markets, such instruments have traded for almost 10 years now in the U.K.

Generally, the nominal yields on regular government bonds in the U.K. have been higher than the nominal yields (implied by adding the running inflation rate to the quoted real interest rate) in inflation-indexed bonds. That "spread" (which we will call the inflation risk premium) appears to be in the 50-100 basis points range. A positive inflation risk premium implies that generally, the less inflation-sensitive pension debt is, the higher the liability discount rate is that can be justified.

Conversely, the more inflation-sensitive pension debt is, the lower the liability discount rate should be. U.K. data suggests possibly 50 basis points should be subtracted from regular, current-coupon, government long-bond yields to arrive at the "right" nominal discount rate for fully inflation-indexed, long pension debt.

Three More Pieces in the "Right" Discount Rate Puzzle

The default risk, maturity risk, and inflation risk pieces of nominal long bond yields link these yields to the T-bill rate. The T-bill rate in turn may be broken down into three more sensible (but unfortunately not directly observable) pieces: the real interest rate, the expected inflation rate, and a "monetary policy effect." This latter yield component can be positive, negative, or zero, and it quantifies the impact on the Treasury yield curve of the current tightness or ease of monetary policy.

Exhibit 1 shows how these pieces might fit together today.

EXHIBIT 1

Rate Component	Estimated Current Level
Real Interest Rate	2.50%
+	
Expected Inflation Rate	4.50%
=	
Normal T-Bill Rate	7.00%
+/−	
Monetary Policy Effect	1.50%
=	
Current T-Bill Rate	8.50%
Normal T-Bill Rate	7.00%
+	
Maturity Premium	0.75%
+	
Inflation Risk Premium	0.50%
+	
Default Risk Premium	0.00%
=	
Current Long Treasury Rate	8.25%

So What is the "Right" Liability Discount Rate?

How do we get from this interest rate structure assessment to the "right" liability discount rate? The base liability discount rate is the sum of the real interest rate, expected inflation rate, and the maturity premium components. This base rate can be justifiably increased to the degree that the pension liabilities are less than 100% inflation-sensitive by adding the appropriate piece of the inflation risk premium.

Thus, the base liability discount rate in the example is 2.50% + 4.50% + 0.75% = 7.75%. This 7.75% could rise to 8.25% for pension liabilities with absolutely zero sensitivity to either wage inflation preretirement or to price inflation post-retirement. The typical plan is probably about 75% inflation sensitive, suggesting a pension liability discount rate between 7.9%-8.0% as typically appropriate today.

You Can't Have One Without the Other

But for inflation-sensitive liabilities, picking the "right" discount rate is not enough. Only "right" discount rate/wage inflation rate/price inflation combinations matter. A 4.5% price inflation expectation assessment was one of our discount rate building blocks. This came from a judgement that the current 4.5% running inflation rate has about an equal chance of rising or falling on a longer-term basis.

And what about wage inflation? It has had trouble just matching price inflation in recent years, but has outpaced price inflation by 2% per year in a much longer-term historical context. What about the future? We see a gradual return to a positive wage-price gap as labor demand catches up with supply, but probably not back to a 2% gap for quite some time.

Putting these "best estimate" judgements together, we see an 8%/6%/4.5% discount rate/wage inflation rate/price inflation rate combination as, if not "right," certainly the most highly defensible "best estimates" for most final-average earnings plans with either formal or informal post-retirement inflation protection today. The 4.5% price inflation expectation would only be used in the actual cost and liability calculations if postretirement benefits were fully indexed. For 50% of CPI COLA updates for example, a 2.25% update expectation would be used. Also implied in these calculations is a 3.5% long-term real interest rate.

Note that our discount rate/inflation deliberations above were dominated not by "settlement" thinking, but by long-term continuation thinking. Also, our focus was not on just a settlement rate, but on a continuation rate/wage inflation rate/price inflation rate combination. While we don't claim our 8%/6%/4.5% "continuation combination" is exactly right, we do claim the process is right.

The Pension Assets Return Goal

What does this pension liability discount rate discussion tell us about the investment policy for pension assets? Most importantly, it tells us to first identify the risk-free investment policy against a specific set of pension liabilities, and to determine what long-term return it is reasonable to expect from that policy.

For going-concern plans, where both preretirement benefit accruals and postretirement benefit payments are inflation-related (whether explicitly or implicitly), such an investment policy would ideally consist of a series of default-free, inflation-indexed bonds stretching out over the liability maturity spectrum. In the U.K., such a portfolio would have a prospective real return of 3.6% today.

Such a portfolio cannot be constructed with U.S. Treasury bonds. However, short Treasury bonds are probably a reasonable proxy, capturing a good part of the maturity premium, while at the same time embodying little inflation risk and, therefore, little inflation risk premium. Short Treasury bonds are yielding 8.25%. Removing the 450 basis points for inflation expectations, leaves 3.75%. Thus we confirm our previous calculation, putting the long-term real interest rate in the U.S. in the 3.5% - 3.8% range. So, if pension assets are to earn a positive "spread", they must earn more than the return on short Treasury bonds. This "earning a spread" idea is central to the discussion that follows.

NET INTEREST COST AND THE PENSION PLAN "SPREAD"

Specifically, in the pension expense calculation, FASB permits plan sponsors to book the "spread" they anticipate whether it is earned or not. In other words, the excess return on pension assets (i.e., its expected return over the discount rate on the PBO) doesn't first have to be earned before it is booked. It can be booked (in the sense of reducing pension expense) before the fact. This is equivalent to permitting the S&L industry to book profits on risky investments before it earns them. Is this FASB policy too?

We can best illustrate by example. Let's pick up again on the pension plan with the $1 billion ABO and the $1.6 billion PBO. Assume plan assets are also $1.6 billion. Say the $1.6 billion PBO was calculated with an 8% interest rate assumption and 6% and 4.5% for wage and price escalation, respectively. The issuance of new pension debt (i.e., service cost) is also done on an 8%/6%/4.5% basis. But, the way the accounting is done, a belief that pension assets will earn a 2% risk premium over the 8% discount rate (i.e., will earn 10% rather than 8%) reduces total pension expense below service cost, possibly by 30%-40%.

Why? Because booking the assumed 2% risk premium earnings on pension assets creates a $32 million credit in the pension expense calculation. As a result, FASB not only permits the booking of investment profits before they are earned, but also promotes the view that deferred compensation (such as pensions) is cheap. Surveys show that about two-thirds of plan sponsors are taking advantage of FASB's invitation to book pension investment profits before they are earned. That is, they are assuming expected pension assets returns in excess of their liability discount rate. We are with the one-third who have not taken advantage of FASB's invitation and are setting their expected pension assets return equal to the liability discount rate.

Below we propose the separation of reporting the expense of deferred compensation (i.e., service cost) and the profitability of pension debt-servicing operations. With such clear separation, no one would be misled to believe that investment profits (before they are earned or even after) reduce the cost of deferred compensation. New pension debt would be properly costed on an 8%/6%/4.5% basis. It would be transferred to the pension debt-servicing subsidiary on that basis. If the assets of the subsidiary subsequently earned a 10% rate of return, an investment-related gain in the subsidiary would arise and would be accounted for as such.

THE PENSION DEBT-SERVICING FINANCIAL INSTITUTION PARADIGM

There are two separate and distinct things going on when an employer sponsors a straight defined-benefit pension plan. First, the plan sponsor issues pension debt to employees as part of its total compensation scheme. Second, the plan sponsor pays a financial institution (either an outside insurer, or, more likely in the case of large employers, its own pension plan) to service that debt.

Thus, two separate and distinct things need to be accounted for. First, the cost of issuing pension debt (i.e., the apple) should be taken into account. Second, where the employer sponsors its own defined benefit plan, the financial affairs of that pension debt-servicing institution (i.e., the orange) should be accounted for separately. Pension accounting rules consistent with this "apple and orange" reality would produce the following two main business profit and loss line items on a regular basis:

1. Deferred compensation expense (i.e., the best estimate of the pension debt issued by the plan sponsor during the accounting period)
2. Contribution to earnings of pension debt-servicing operations (i.e., the underwriting and investment profits/losses of the pension plan subsidiary during the accounting period)

Two Reasons for Keeping the "Apple" and the "Orange" Apart

Why is it important to keep deferred compensation expense and contribution to earnings of pension debt-servicing operations as two separate items on the main business profit and loss statement? First, without a clean measure of deferred compensation to add to current compensation, the employer cannot determine its total compensation costs. The second reason is that the employer decision to manage its own defined benefit pension plan is akin to deciding to run a captive financial subsidiary. The profitability (or "cost effectiveness") of that decision should also be measured as cleanly as possible. We illustrate these points by example.

For example, suppose an employer paid out $1 billion in current compensation last year and issued $100 million of pension debt (i.e., its deferred compensation expense). Suppose further the pension plan subsidiary had $10 million in underwriting losses, but made $60 million on the spread between the return on pension assets and the discount rate used to cost pension debt.

FASB 87 would have this employer report current compensation of $1 billion, a pension expense based on the $100 million of service cost, the amortization components of the $10 million underwriting loss and the $60 million gain on investments. Clearly, such a pension expense item has no economic content. The economics are that there was a $1.1 billion total compensation expense last year (i.e., $1 billion current and $100 million deferred), and there was a $50 million profit on pension debt-servicing operations, which is to be appropriately amortized. Now that is useful information!

The Pension Expense Calculation Must Also Go!

Just like the ABO, the pension expense calculation should also be removed. This is not as dramatic a recommendation as it might, at first blush, seem. Why? Because all the calculation components of pension expense stay. But these components should lead to two end products rather than one as demonstrated below.

The current FASB 87 pension expense calculation has three components: service cost, net interest cost, and amortization costs. To briefly review:

- The service cost component estimates the value of future benefits earned during the current year using a market-determined interest rate and consistent salary growth and inflation assumptions.

- The net interest cost component is the interest on outstanding PBO pension debt (using the same discount rate as used above in the service cost calculation) less the expected return on plan assets (which we have argued above should also be set to the same discount rate value).

- The amortization costs component amortizes over appropriate periods the (a) plan surplus/deficit existing on the date of transition to the new accounting rules, (b) prior service costs incurred after the transition date, (c) investment-related gains or losses incurred after the transition date and (d) underwriting-related gains or losses incurred after the transition date.

In Exhibit 2, the column on the left depicts how these three components are currently combined to calculate pension expense. The column on the right uses the same basic components to calculate deferred compensation expense and pension debt-servicing subsidiary profit contribution separately. The two calculations approach of Exhibit 2 separates the impact on the plan sponsor's bottom line of two distinctly different economic activities: (a) 'paying' deferred compensation and (b) bearing investment and underwriting risk in the pension subsidiary. And that is as it should be. The single pension expense calculation is superfluous and should be done away with.

EXHIBIT 2

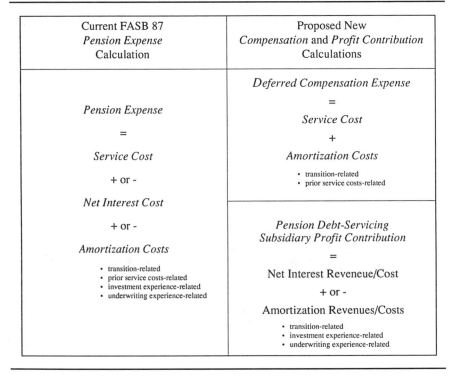

Current FASB 87 *Pension Expense* Calculation	Proposed New *Compensation* and *Profit Contribution* Calculations
Pension Expense = *Service Cost* + or - *Net Interest Cost* + or - *Amortization Costs* • transition-related • prior service costs-related • investment experience-related • underwriting experience-related	*Deferred Compensation Expense* = *Service Cost* + *Amortization Costs* • transition-related • prior service costs-related
	Pension Debt-Servicing Subsidiary Profit Contribution = Net Interest Reveneue/Cost + or - Amortization Revenues/Costs • transition-related • investment experience-related • underwriting experience-related

THE PROPOSED ACCOUNTING STANDARDS FOR RETIREE MEDICAL BENEFITS

For those conversant with the pension accounting rules, there were no surprises when FASB recently issued its long-awaited exposure draft on accounting for postretirement benefits other than pensions. All the usual suspects come into play: plan design including its integration with Medicare, workforce and retiree group characteristics, retirement age, and "best estimate" assumptions about quit rates, mortality rates, first-year plan-cost per retiree, per capita plan-cost growth rate, and the investment discount rate. The principle that all employment expenses be recorded during active service is also carried over.

Two important things about the FASB exposure draft are (1) that it is just that: a draft subject to further revision, and (2) that the final set of rules will not likely become operative for a few years yet. The first few rounds of calculations with the proposed rules could well generate some scary numbers for many employers. We believe that these "let's try it out" exercises will be instructive both to FASB and to these employers. FASB will learn more about how to create a final set of rules that is both practical and informative. Employers will learn more about how to control their exposure to both the health care debt already incurred and the debt to be incurred. Both are constructive consequences.

What the Numbers Might Look Like

Two reputable organizations have recently made estimates of outstanding retiree health care obligations for the U.S. corporate sector. Standard actuarial methods and reasonable assumption sets in line with FASB requirements were used. The U.S. Government General Accounting Office came up with an estimate of $221 billion. The original estimate by the Employee Benefits Research Institute (EBRI) came out marginally higher at $247 billion. However, EBRI was able to adjust its numbers for the recent legislation expanding federal Medicare benefits. The impact of this legislation is to reduce the $247 billion estimate to $169 billion, a 30% drop.

Taking the current equity market value of larger capitalization U.S. corporations (i.e., where the health care liabilities are) to be $2 trillion, the $169 billion outstanding retiree health-care debt estimate represents 8% of corporate equity outstanding. Still a significant number, but clearly not in the same ball park as the $1 trillion number reported in the September 12, 1988 issue of *Business Week*, which would represent 50% of large capitalization corporate net worth.

PENSIONS VERSUS NONPENSIONS BENEFITS: DIFFERENCES AND SIMILARITIES

While there is an ABO in the new exposure draft, it is in fact the PBO-equivalent in FASB 87. That is, the ABO calculation for nonpension postretirement benefits must reflect a health-care cost projection, as well as pay projections if they impact on the value of postretirement life insurance. This surely buttresses our argument that the old pensions (ABO) must go!

The major difference between pensions and nonpensions from a financial perspective is the approach to funding. Both tax laws and ERISA promote and require the funding of pension obligations. There are currently no such measures related to nonpension obligations. The result is that there are virtually no assets backing nonpension postretirement obligations. Thus, for now at least, the debt-servicing financial institution paradigm is not valid for nonpension obligations.

Nevertheless, FASB is again proposing that where there are nonpension postretirement assets, they again can be given an expected return on plan assets. This again opens the door for reducing postretirement benefit expenses with the expected spread between plan assets and the relevant risk-free liability discount rate. That practice is as inappropriate here as it is with pension expenses. Again, we would expect investment profits to be booked based on realizations (actual or potential), not just expectations.

FASB also proposes the same liability discount rate approach as with pensions. This may be the most serious flaw of all. Using an effectively risk free discount rate for pension liabilities is appropriate because these liabilities are secured by pension assets. But typically there are no postretirement health care assets backing health care liabilities. This means these liabilities are unsecured. Thus they should be calculated using a discount rate appropriate for the unsecured debt of the issuer. Generally this rate will be higher than the discount rate FASB is proposing. Consequently, the FASB proposal will lead to material overstatement of postretirement health care liabilities unless FASB is willing to change its mind on this point.

FASB 87's FAULTS SHOULD BE FIXED QUICKLY

Postretirement obligations by corporations to former and current employees have been growing materially in both quantity and quality, especially during the last 20 years. FASB's initiatives to have these realities properly reflected in corporate financial statements is to be commended. The principles behind the design of FASB 87 and the new nonpensions exposure draft are to be commended. Furthermore, much of the conversion of the principles into specific rules and requirements is unobjectionable.

However, there are a number of areas where the specific rules and requirements currently detract from the understanding of, and deter appropriate economic behavior in relation to, defined-benefit pension plans sponsored by U.S. corporations. We encourage FASB to review Statement 87 as soon as possible, and address its shortcomings. We also encourage FASB to consider our observations in the context of the new exposure draft on accounting for postretirement benefits other than pensions. Such an investment of time would have great payoffs in increased understanding of how defined-benefit pension and health care plans really work. That, in turn, would improve legislation and regulation, as well as corporate policy decisions on compensation and on employee benefits funding and investments.

NOTES

[1] Jack Treynor, Patrick Regan and William Priest, *The Financial Reality of Pension Funding Under ERISA* (Homewood, IL: Dow Jones-Irwin, 1976).

CHAPTER 15

Blurring Lines Between Public and Private Pension Funds

NICK MENCHER
CONSULTANT
BARRA

The differences between public and private pension funds have led to the perception that different rules, marketing approaches, and philosophies apply to these funds. This chapter argues that the distinction has in recent years become less clear.

At the same time, however, the different populations served by public and private funds impose a separate set of priorities and forces on fund management. The differing natures of these populations will modify the ways in which private and public funds move closer. This situation is primarily expressed in political and social influences, and officer salary differences between the two types of funds.

As public funds increasingly offer investment professionals valuable training and experience, which may become less available in the private sector, increased movement of professionals between the two types of funds can be expected. As professionals move back and forth between public and private funds, the interchange will accelerate the blurring of differences between the two worlds.

This blurring will result in the following:

- Large publics will meet and then pass private funds in the use of alternative investment vehicles.
- Political and social pressures on public funds will increase while the phenomenon of outside interference in fund management will spread to the private sector.
- Functional distinctions between public and private funds in the marketing of investment products and services will fade.

We also examine a few of the causes of the differentiation of publics from privates, particularly asset allocation strategies, to show how these factors are changing. We conclude by pointing out that an increasingly homogeneous pension fund industry may be a tremendous opportunity for investment professionals and pension funds themselves. A brief look at the ethical forces in fund management completes the chapter.

ASSET ALLOCATION

Asset allocation trends have major import for the investment management community, both on the buy and on the sell side. For those in the industry, changes in asset allocation patterns spell either gloom or jubilation—for example, the tremendous increase in the ranks of real estate managers and consultants following the increase in real estate asset allocation.

An examination of the data shows that asset allocation differences in public and private funds are narrowing. Exhibits 1 and 2 show asset allocation figures for corporate and public funds for the last ten years in bond and stock allocation, respectively.

While these figures are rough, and the public fund numbers may be slightly skewed towards conservative allocation,[1] it is clear there is a narrowing of the gap between public and private funds in bond allocation—from a difference of 30% in 1979 to a difference of 14% in 1988. Also, stock holdings have moved closer (though perhaps not as strongly as in the fixed-income area) with the gap narrowing from 27% in 1979 to 13% in 1988.

The increasing trend for public and private fund officers to think alike, at least in terms of overall asset allocation, is apparent when the present and future uses of asset classes are examined. Exhibit 3 shows 1988 usage and 1989 demand for a selected group of assets expressed as the percentage of funds that are using and plan to use these alternative asset classes.

It is clear from Exhibits 1, 2 and 3 that while asset allocation *amounts* may vary between public and private pension funds, the *popularity* of alternative assets within these two types of funds was close in 1988 and closer in 1989. From this we can assume that the *requirements*, in terms of skill for managing these assets in-house and managing outside managers, are roughly the same for both types of funds. It is also interesting to note that while the differences are small, the public fund demand for 1989, in terms of international stocks, international bonds, equity real estate and venture capital, is greater than the demand shown by corporate funds.

EXHIBIT 1: PUBLIC FUND AND CORPORATE FUND BOND ALLOCATION

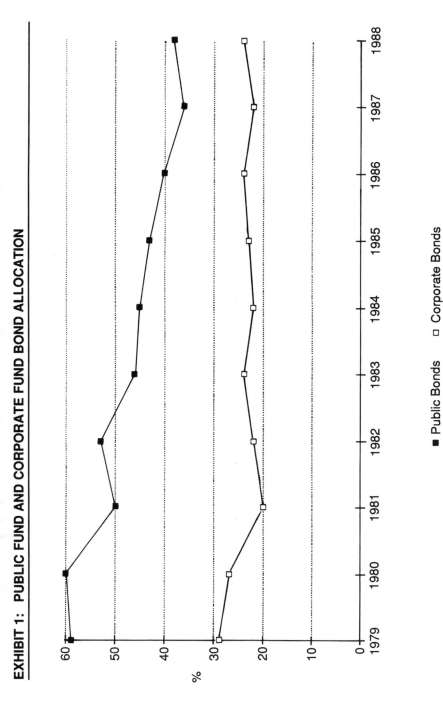

■ Public Bonds   □ Corporate Bonds

Source: The Money Market Directory of Pension Funds and Their Investment Managers.

EXHIBIT 2: PUBLIC FUND AND CORPORATE FUND STOCK ALLOCATION

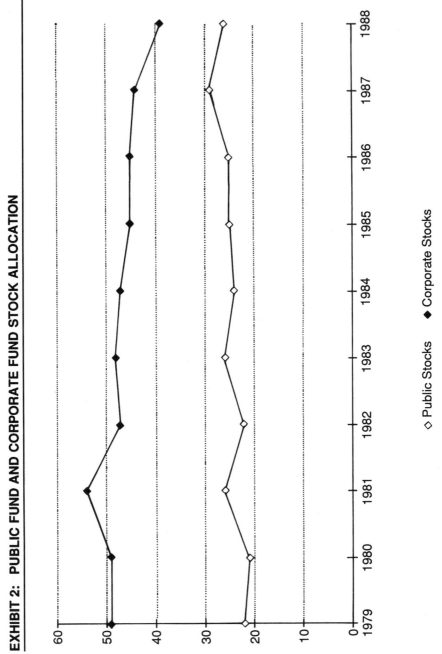

◇ Public Stocks   ◆ Corporate Stocks

Source: *The Money Market Directory of Pension Funds and Their Investment Managers.*

EXHIBIT 3:   DEMAND FOR ALTERNATIVE INVESTMENTS

Investment	Corporate Funds			Public Funds		
	1988[*]	1989[**]	Total Demand	1988[*]	1989[**]	Total Demand
Intl. Stocks	35%	9%	44%	25%	12%	37%
Junk Bonds	7	2	9	9	0	9
Intl. Bonds	33	2	35	21	7	28
Venture Cptl.	19	3	21	17	6	23
LBO Funds	6	2	8	7	1	8
Portfolio Ins.	4	2	6	3	1	4

[*] Used in.
[**] Planned to start using in.

Source: Greenwich Associates 1989 report, "Institutional Investment Management: Grace Under Pressure," p. 40.

A quick glimpse at the usage percentages for more traditional assets in Exhibit 4 shows a similar situation.

EXHIBIT 4:   DEMAND FOR OTHER INVESTMENTS

Investment	Corporate Funds			Public Funds		
	1988[*]	1989[**]	Total Demand	1988*	1989[**]	Total Demand
Growth Stocks	74%	4%	77%	76%	2%	78%
Passive Stocks	34	6	40	33	4	38
Passive Bonds	21	3	24	21	3	24

[*] Used in.
[**] Planned to start using in.

Source: Greenwich Associates 1989 report, "Institutional Investment Management: Grace Under Pressure," p. 40.

PUBLIC FUNDS TAKE THE LEAD?

The apparent slowdown of corporate fund use of alternative investments shown in Exhibit 3 reflects the increased percentage of fully-funded corporate plans.[2] It is interesting to note that corporate funds may be becoming more conservative than their public counterparts in asset allocation and selection, and that public funds, because of their funding needs, are branching out into more alternative investments. Readers of the trade press are bombarded by stories of public funds expanding their use of alternative assets as more and more state governments loosen investment restrictions. This trend indicates how the two types of funds are moving closer, and, as we will discuss later, presents an opportunity for pension professionals.

As increasing numbers of corporate funds reach or pass fully-funded status and shift to more conservative investment methods, public funds may take the lead in innovation. The moves by the Los Angeles County Employees' Retirement Association to investigate investments in financially troubled savings and loans[3] is an example of this shift.

Another example of the growing sophistication of public funds is the number of funds managing assets in-house.

In-House Management

Private and public funds have traditionally viewed the in-house/outside management issue in different terms. But a variety of factors are narrowing this difference, and we may soon see in-house management functioning to similar degrees in the private and public sectors.

Essentially, publics have moved from managing almost all their assets in-house, to a more balanced approach—with some assets managed in-house and some by outside managers. At the same time, private funds have moved more funds into in-house management.

Traditionally, public funds managed most or all of their assets internally because of state laws and limited investment availability. But in the last several years, many funds have moved assets to outside managers following the lifting of investment constraints, the increasing difficulty of maintaining in-house staffs, and the need to diversify fund assets. This flow of funds to outside managers was substantial in the early '80s, but has slowed in recent years.

Reasons for the decreased use of outside management, by both public and private funds, include: the generally poor performance of active managers and the rise in passive management, the cost of outside managers, and the increased availability of computer programs that assist in-house management.

Another trend accompanying the use of in-house management in the public sector is the realization by sponsors that salaries and bonuses must be increased to attract top talent. This is particularly important given the difficulty in managing some of the assets that are coming back in-house. Some funds have already increased incentives to levels closer to the private sector and others are planning to do so.[4] Later in this chapter, we discuss how certain opportunities in the public sector may outweigh those in the private arena and attract talented professionals to public funds.

But while public fund officers continue to use alternative assets and strategies, including in-house management, which require expertise, compensation has yet to catch up with their job descriptions.

WORKING CONDITIONS

While public and private funds have become more alike in terms of asset allocation and the in-house management issue, they maintain some traditional differences. One is salary level; public funds have traditionally paid officers far less than their corporate counterparts.

The average public fund officer's salary for 1988 was $55,000, whereas it was $97,300 for corporate fund officers. The compensation picture remains bleak at all levels—corporate officers received raises of 7% in '88 while their public counterparts received 4%, and bonuses for the 60% of eligible corporate staffers totalled $17,700 versus only $3,400 for the 6% of public fund staffers eligible. It is interesting to note that union funds paid considerably more than public funds in compensation ($84,000) and bonus ($8,600).[5]

Although unions require less in terms of expertise because of their more conservative investment strategies, they nonetheless pay more than publics. Why is it that public fund sponsors, who, as Greenwich Associates' Rodger Smith points out, "are responsible for considerably greater assets, on average, than their counterparts elsewhere," are so poorly paid in comparison with their colleagues?

The salary disparity would be understandable if there were wide differences in the types of employees who work for public and private funds. But research indicates that the differences that do exist indicate that public fund officers should in fact be paid *more* than their corporate colleagues.

First, the similarities. According to an Institutional Investor survey,[6] 62% of private and 50% of public fund officers are between the ages of 31 and 45, 81% of corporate and 70% of public fund officers have formal investment/finance training, and 56% of both types of officers worked in areas unconnected to pensions and investments before starting with funds. Additionally, 28% of both types of officers have had their titles upgraded over the past five years, and 60% of private and 55% of public fund officers say there is now more contact with senior officials than before, with 76% of corporate and 65% of public fund officers saying their bosses "ascribe more importance" to their jobs than they did five years earlier.

The differences between officers in the study indicate that public fund workers, contrary to the stereotype, approach their careers with more ambition, stability, and devotion, and have greater responsibility than those in the private sector.

When asked if the officer was a chartered financial analyst or studying to be one, nearly twice as many public officers said they were (11%) than corporate officers (6%). Examining the duties of the different types of officers, we find that 58% of public officers versus 26% of private officers manage assets in-house. And when asked what other types of responsibilities were involved in their jobs, both types of officers had similar responses, with one major exception—26% of corporate officers listed "investor relations" as part of their responsibilities, an area on which public fund officers spent no time.

Other differences are interesting—more than twice as many public fund officers as private officers plan to remain in their current job for more than ten years (25% versus 10%), and 68% of public officers plan to make pensions their career, whereas 38% of corporate officers plan to do so.

From these statistics, an interesting picture emerges: both types of officers are roughly of the same age and professional and academic backgrounds, and both see the responsibilities of their jobs commanding more and more attention. At the same time, public fund officers spend more of their time managing more money and are more committed, both to their current position and to the career of pensions in general. This worker portrait contrasts with their corporate colleagues, who more often appear to view their current positions as stepping stones.

When asked if they thought their positions were considered "dead ends" at work, 55% of public fund officers answered 'yes,' versus 26% of corporate officers. There is clearly some resentment among public fund officers, and salary is certainly one of the irritants. Some relief for the salary blues may come from performance-based fee arrangements for in-house public fund managers, but more needs to be done on the legislative level.

Many factors, including the inability of public funds to pay competitive salaries and the increased responsibility accompanying the blurring of the differences between public and private funds, suggest a new view of the position of public fund officer. Later in this chapter, we argue that the job of public fund officer may offer opportunities for investment professionals that are superior to those of the private sector. These opportunities will provide inducements for new professionals to enter the field and increase the exchange of staff between corporate and public funds. At the same time, a view of public pension work as "service" oriented may help keep some of these professionals in the public domain.

THE POLITICS OF PENSIONS

The publics also differ from private funds in the degree to which publics are vulnerable to political interference by governmental regulatory bodies and special interest groups. On the surface this difference is major, but we contend the lines are actually blurred and that certain aspects of the politics of pensions will spread to the administration of private funds.

We have said that the loosening of state regulations encourages the use of alternative assets by public funds. While state governments have tolerated the shift to types of investments legislators know little about, they have also focused on areas they are fully versed in—political and social agendas.

One example of the political aspects of fund management is the current feud between New York and Connecticut. When the governor of New York taxed commuters who work in New York but live in Connecticut, two members of the Connecticut state senate retaliated by proposing a law requiring the State of Connecticut Trust Funds to divest of all holdings in New York-based corporations.[7]

In Illinois, a state representative called for a ban on public fund investments in leveraged buy-out funds because of his feeling that they cause job losses and hardships. The move has drawn strong reaction from the chairman of the state's Board of Investment who opposes any legislation calling for modification of the "prudent man" rule—including divestiture of South African-related stocks. These legislative efforts, says the chairman, could lead to a return to the era when state legislatures provided lists of acceptable investments and would necessitate legal protection for trustees accused of violating the "prudent man" rule.[8]

While it is doubtful state legislatures will return to the days of specifying individual instruments, we do think they will increase socially inspired prohibitions against some classes of investments at the same time that they allow funds more leeway in other asset classes. For example, fund officers may find themselves free to invest in global securities so long as they are not in South Africa or in companies manufacturing nuclear weapons.

The increase in government involvement in the political aspects of fund management is typified by the laws of some 20 states asking funds to invest a specified percentage of assets in their home state. These laws create a touchy situation for sponsors pulled one way by fiduciary responsibility and the other by political considerations. One sponsor went so far as to call the set-asides a "giant slush fund" creating "a netherworld for interested parties.

These examples point to a trend in the pension community. While private funds seem to be retrenching, public funds are moving into the new world of alternative asset classes. These moves have brought the spotlight of public, regulatory and legislative attention to bear on public fund policy. The legislative scrutiny may not be to the good. We wonder whether state legislatures are truly ready to make decisions for public funds.

One practitioner who doesn't think politics and fund management mix is Stephen R. Myers, state investment officer for the South Dakota Investment Council. In a speech to the Institute for International Research, Myers said ". . . due to a strong bottom line private sector dominated board of directors and an enlightened, no nonsense legislature, we have been able to avoid the glitz of politics in South Dakota. One of the mainstays of successful investing is non-political investing."

Why has "political investing" soared? One reason is the perception that public funds are "state money," subject to the state government involvement we saw in the New York/Connecticut feud. This view is also apparent in actions like the recent New York City government's request that the assumed rate of return on city funds be increased to 8.25% from 8.00% to save the city around $137 million in pension contributions and to help reduce the $1 billion city budget gap.[10]

Public fund officers are clearly open to pressure from a variety of sources. It has been commonly perceived that private funds are less vulnerable to pressure and work only under the requirements of the Employee Retirement Income Security Act (ERISA). But this distinction is also becoming less clear. One striking example of the increase in outside pressure on the private sector is proposed legislation in Congress to require employee representation on boards of trustees that administer defined benefit plans. Some commentators feel this representation would result in extremely conservative investment goals, terminated funds and deadlocked boards.[11] Employee representation would also encourage the inclusion of social and political agendas in private fund management.

Sponsors Become Activists

The relation of shareholder activism to fund management is an example of social pressure on sponsors that is increasing in both the public and private spheres. Sponsor reaction to corporate activities has changed. Formerly, if a sponsor felt uneasy about investing in certain types of companies, so-called "sin" corporates or South African-linked firms, the simple choice was not to buy the company. But the ground rules are being changed by a combination of the increase in passive management and the perception, by some, that investor activism is a sponsor's responsibility.

The increased use of passive management has led to an unforeseen consequence—the spread of investor activism—and raises the possibility that this activism may carry over into the private pension community. James George, investment manager for the Oregon Public Employees' Retirement System, links activism to passive management as follows:

"[Investor activism] by the large funds is essentially an outgrowth of passive management and politically inspired sponsors. When funds are passively managed, they own a company because they have to own it."[12] George also stresses the potential for investor activism to be used by officials to turn the spotlight on their own political views and thus advance their careers—an approach still particular to public funds.

The link to equity positions is also made by James Martin of the College Retirement Equities Fund (CREF), ". . . we have huge core holdings that are permanent in character. Therefore, the old Wall Street rule, if you don't like them, sell them, doesn't really apply. We need to make sure management is accountable and companies follow a democratic process." Others point out that large plans may be prevented from selling some holdings because of the price impact of such a move.[13] There is a clear incompatibility between the elements of fiduciary responsibility to fund performance and the urge to sell assets from companies with questionable ethical practices and/or influences.

Social considerations in fund management may become even more sensitive in the future, when we expect to see an increase in laws like the recent California requirement that 15% of assets should be run by minority firms. Laws such as the California statute, which impose socially charged considerations on sponsors, create problems. For example, how can minority managers with no track record be properly analyzed in terms of the fiduciary requirement, recently spelled out for the union fund sphere in the *Whitfield* vs. *Cohen* case, that sponsors examine both a manager's track record and reputation in the industry? Similar concerns apply to private funds covered by ERISA.

One form of social pressure—investor activism—may begin to spread to the private sector. Corporate funds may be influenced by social and political pressure due to the use of passive management, a use which may increase as funds make less use of active management,[14] and as more funds become fully- or over-funded.

And there is no reason to believe that corporate funds will not react to the social and political views of their beneficiaries—particularly if workers are included on the board of trustees. After all, the soapbox some claim public fund officers are using for both a spotlight and a say in corporate America was supplied by the public, and there are as many John Q. Publics participating in private plans as on the public side.

A possible hint of things to come is contained in a recent request by the Labor Department's assistant secretary for pension and welfare benefits, David M. Walker. While revenues recovered from private plans for fiduciary violations rose from $42 million in '85 to $106 million in '87, Walker says labor is unable to effectively monitor the private sector. Therefore, he asks workers and retirees to help out by monitoring pension plan abuses.[15] That such a campaign may be quite vigorous doesn't seem too farfetched when we consider the financial sophistication of many of the baby boomers now entering middle age.

When these members begin flexing their muscles, private funds may come under some of the same pressures as public funds. And, because some argue that investor activism is, in some uses, merely the exercise of rights to uphold share values, fiduciary responsibility may be stretched to include the corporate exercise of investor activism. The potential for division in the corporate community from an environment where corporate sponsors exercise shareholder rights towards companies which may strongly resist, and the possibility for some type of 'revenge' among corporations divided by the exercise of these rights, makes for interesting imaginary scenarios.

What effect will a narrowing of the distinctions between public and private funds have on members of the investment community—particularly consultants and investment managers?

CONSEQUENCES FOR CONSULTANTS

The changes brought about by the narrowing of differences between public and private funds also effect the consultant community. The increasing sophistication of sponsors in both realms has led to a greater examination of the role consultants play and the value of the services they provide.

Evidence of this trend in the public sector, which traditionally makes greater use of consultants than the private arena, is seen in a study done by Asset International on public fund use of international investments. "The level of satisfaction with consultants varies more widely, and contrary to common wisdom an appreciable number of (public) fund managers avoid using consultants altogether," the study found.[16]

As more manager searches and asset allocation work are performed in-house, the demand for consultant services is shifting towards information, data collection and other quantitative services. This shift, clearly, is an ominous one for consultants whose primary line of work is in manager searches.[17]

There is another side to this trend—as more consultants enter the "boutique" revolution, thus becoming information providers, their ability to supply full service to those funds still requesting it will be hampered. Exhibit 5 shows that the smallest funds are those most likely to be in the market for sponsor services.

EXHIBIT 5: PENSION CONSULTANT USE

	Use Now	*Do not Use*	*Expect to Start*
Corporate Funds			
Over $1 billion	46%	52%	2%
$501–1,000 million	59	41	3
$251–500 million	48	52	5
$101–250 million	52	48	5
$ 50–100 million	47	53	5
Under $50 million	42	57	6
Public Funds			
Over $1 billion	73%	26%	1%
$251–1,000 million	71	29	2
$101–250 million	65	35	4
$ 50–100 million	70	30	0
Under $50 million	37	61	12

Source: Greenwich Associates 1989 report, "Institutional Investment Management: Grace Under Pressure," p. 62.

The problem with this scenario is that while smaller funds are in the market for consultants, consultants may not be in the market for smaller funds because the fees from working with larger funds are greater. The trend towards fewer "full service" consultants, as a result of the increasing sophistication of larger funds, means there may not be a consulting industry ready for the needs of smaller funds.

CONSEQUENCES FOR INVESTMENT MANAGERS

The split in marketing efforts by suppliers to public and private funds will ease as we see increasingly similar levels of sophistication, more similar asset allocation strategies, and increased personnel moves between these two areas. We may see marketing chores divided by fund size rather than fund type.

Certainly, marketing executives at management firms who still believe that public funds are the natural market for conservative fixed-income instruments will be surprised to learn that this style of asset allocation is on the downswing. For example, the California Public Employees' Retirement System recently allocated a mix of 35% for domestic fixed-income, 35% for domestic equities, and 16% for international assets.[18] A marketing representative who feels public fund sponsors are less sophisticated, still fixated on fixed-income, and less willing to make use of alternative investments than private fund sponsors is doomed to failure. If we agree that smaller public funds frequently follow the lead of their larger colleagues,[19] recent asset allocation figures show that small and large public funds are natural customers for management services. And, while the public fund decision process can take much longer than private fund decision-making, the size of the public fund market means extra effort is not wasted in selling products to public fund officers.

But marketing executives seeking public fund clients need to spend more time preparing their pitches if they wish to do business in this area. In a study of public and private fund managers, 58% of those polled faulted money managers for not doing their homework, and 26% said managers "don't understand how funds like mine work in terms of the decision-making process and in what we can and cannot invest."[20]

Given the factors regarding public funds that are discussed in this chapter—the increasing use of alternative asset classes, their continuing financing needs, and the size of the market—it should be clear that sales in this area are not the province of lower level salespeople whereas private funds are reserved for top salespeople.

Supplying products and services to public funds is an area where marketing people can improve. Another important question is how public funds can continue to be supplied with the most crucial component—capable officers. The increased demands for cutting edge investment management in the public sphere create, at the same time that they complicate, opportunities for talented professionals.

A NEW APPROACH TO PUBLIC FUND MANAGEMENT

How can public funds be provided with the personnel required to carry out the crucial role of managing funds? Certainly higher salaries is a key to attract and keep professionals. But those holding their breath for the narrowing of salaries between private and public funds will turn blue before the disparity shrinks appreciably.

Perhaps there are more fruitful approaches than salary inducements to secure able staffers of public funds. If we agree that there is as much action, and perhaps more, in terms of managing money in-house and of overseeing outside managers, in public funds than there is in private funds, then perhaps those entering the business might see public funds as the natural source for experience. If we see the underfunded, alternative asset-hungry public funds as the modern day finance "MASH units" in comparison with the geriatric homes of corporate fully-funded plans, the attraction of the public sector for those seeking experience is clear. And, according to one former public fund sponsor, "Most people don't appreciate just how much fun it is to work in the public sector."

Public funds, the sponsor continued, frequently offer employees more responsibility than the private sector and, because public boards are usually less financially experienced than private boards, less Monday-morning quarterbacking.

Aspiring finance professionals might look for work at funds like the District of Columbia Retirement Board, where unfunded liabilities to the tune of $1.6 billion have led to asset allocations in real estate, international equities and considerations of venture capital, LBOs and private placements.[21]

Of course, many of these professionals will eventually leave for the corporate side's higher salaries. But some may remain in public fund management to experience the increasing opportunities for the interesting work it offers.[22] In any case, the increase in movement from the public sphere to the private sector, an exodus currently underway, will narrow the differences between both types of funds.

Public funds may also develop an ethic of service which, while not a significant factor in the investment world, might persuade some investment professionals to work for less money in order to help pension beneficiaries in the public sector. While it cannot be assumed that an ethic of service to employees like postmen and sanitation workers is more effective in attracting managers and inspiring job loyalty than the same ethic at a private fund whose beneficiaries are mostly middle and upper management, there are indications—based on the profile of pension officers—that the service appeal could be an effective one.

Many public fund managers already feel that with social security paying minimal benefits, their pension fund has a tremendous effect on the retirement standard of living of its members. As one large public fund sponsor put it, "We make the difference between not having a pot to pee in after they retire and being able to visit the grandkids once a year." With many private funds more concerned with their effect on corporate balance sheets and their role as anti-takeover elements, the ethic of service, what one sponsor called "retirement dignity," may already be more evident in the public fund area than in the private sector. It is in the best interest of public funds, and society in general, to build on this ethic. Some evidence of this trait emerges from a look at the types of people working in the public sector. As we noted above, public fund officers are nearly twice as likely as private fund officers to say they plan to make pensions their career.[23]

But here is an irony not lost on many in the public sector: although some would say the public fund professional's salary should be commensurate with the importance of his or her fund in the lives of its beneficiaries, salaries paid to those responsible for public funds continue to lag behind those in the corporate sector. Assuming the salary gap will continue, public funds and their beneficiaries may benefit by providing the 'battlefield' training necessary to attract top talent and, for those who stay on in the public sector, the satisfaction of working with a population whose income is also often at odds with their importance to society—groups like teachers, librarians and police officers.

CONCLUSION

This chapter has looked at some of the factors responsible for the blurring of differences between public and private pension funds. We find that:

- Asset allocation patterns and the extent of in-house management employed by public and private funds are becoming more similar.
- Public funds will increase their use of alternative assets, eventually passing private funds.
- Political and social pressures on sponsors in the public sector will also influence those in the private sector.
- A more homogeneous pension fund industry will change the roles of consultants and the marketing of investment management.

We have also discussed possible ways of encouraging professionals to work for public funds, and have advanced an ethic of service which may help keep some of them working in the public sector.

NOTES

[1] The public fund numbers are perhaps overly conservative because they include union fund asset allocation figures. Because union asset allocation is traditionally even more conservative than public fund allocation, this inclusion may boost the public fund exposure to bonds and limit their exposure to equities.

[2] Hewitt Associates quoted in the December 26, 1988, *Money Management Letter*; 86% of companies were fully-funded for accrued pension liabilities and 71% were fully-funded for projected benefit obligations.

[3] "Fund Eyes S&L Opportunities," *Pensions & Investment Age*, May 15, 1989, p. 1.

[4] "Second Thoughts About Outside Managers," *Institutional Investor*, July, 1987, pp. 137-142.

[5] Data Source: Greenwich Associates 1989 report, "Institutional Investment Management: Grace Under Pressure," page viii.

[6] "Pension Officers Put on More Muscle," *Institutional Investor*, August, 1988, pp. 73-75.

[7] "Battle Between the States Heats Up," *Pensions & Investment Age*, April 3, 1989, p. 2.

[8] "LBO Shutout?" *Pensions & Investment Age*, May 1, 1989, p. 61.

[9] "State Development Efforts Target Public Plan Assets, But Trustees, Beneficiaries Are Wary," *Money Management Letter*, May 29, 1989, p. 1.

[10] "NYC Proposes Assumption Hike," *Pensions & Investment Age*, May 15, 1989, p. 2.

[11] "Equality No Benefit Here," *Pensions & Investment Age*, August 7, 1989, p. 10.

[12] Money Management Letter Forum, *Money Management Letter*, May 29, 1989.

[13] Ibid.

[14] For a further description of this trend, see Nick Mencher, "Where Are the New Opportunities?" *Investment Management Review* (March/April, 1989), pp. 57-62.

[15] Executive Director's Report, *AARP News Bulletin*, May, 1989, p. 3.

[16] "AI Study Finds Public Surge into Global," *Asset International*, February 6, 1989, p 1.

[17] For a detailed consideration of these issues, see Arjun Divecha, "Changing Players and Roles in the Institutional Management Industry," *Investing* (Fall 1989), pp. 112-116.

[18] "California to Boost International," *Pensions & Investment Age*, June 12, 1989, p 2.

[19] Some analysts argue that smaller funds actually find it easier to invest in alternative assets because of their comparative low profile when navigating the legislative process to approve such investments.

[20] "Plan Sponsor Survey: Some Managers Should Do More Homework," *Money Management Letter*, May 29, 1989, p. 10.

[21] "MML Profile: District of Columbia Retirement Board's Adrian Anderson," *Money Management Letter*, July 10, 1989, p. 10.

[22] While movement from the private sector to the public side is rare, it does occur. For example, one officer moved from a $425 million private fund to a $35 billion public fund to have an opportunity to manage "a plan of a different scale" according to "NYC Drafts Schering-Plough's Cox; Eyes Real Estate," *Money Management Letter*, July 24, 1989.

[23] This is admittedly a bare-bones argument. To fully bolster this case, the populations served by public and private funds need to be studied demographically. Yet there is some research and intuitive basis for the view that public fund members have less auxiliary savings, make less money while working and, in general, have greater reliance on their pension than private sector employees. The "retirement dignity" of the majority of Americans who belong to no pension plan is another matter.

Index

A

Accounting standards for pension and health
 care benefits, 8, 261-275
Accumulated Benefit Obligation (ABO), 43-44
 balancing in pension fund risk, 47-51
 and FASB statement 87, 262-265
Active return, 162
Active risk, 147-149
Adverse market performance, and investment
 policy, 5, 20-21
Agency theory, 174
Aggregate active risk, 147
Aggregate managed portfolio, 129. *See also*
 Sponsors; view of risk
Aggregate normal, 129
Aggressiveness, manager's, 147
Allocations to U.S. stocks and bonds, 196-197
Alphabet fund, 173
Asset allocation
 dynamic strategies, 57-58
 insurance strategies, 82-84
 linked to manager allocation, 7, 183-196
 concept and approach, 184-187
 examples, 187-196
 managing, 57-86
 market determination, 6
 and pension fund risk, 5-6, 15-16

policy, 57, 63-71
software, 205
tactical asset allocation, 57, 71-82
Asset Allocation Tools, 205
Asset class targets, 110-111
Asset price variability, 48
Attribution analysis, 227-240
Attribution evaluation, 224-226
Attribution measurements, 220, 222-224

B

BARRA multiple-risk factor model, 120n, 150, 153
Basic Retirement Funds, 27-30
Benchmark portfolios, 6-7, 105-120
    asset class targets, 110-111
    concerns and issues, 116-117
    construction, 114-115, 120n
    emerging trends, 108-110
    fixed-income, 111-112, 115-116, 120n
    manager benchmarks, 112-114
    risk control, 112
Blanchard, Ken, 93
Bond manager risk and reward/diversification,
        191, 193
Bond manager style matrix/diversification,
        191-192
Bond market, and interest rate sensitivity, 116
Bottom-up manager selection, 7, 254
Business risk versus investment risk, 174-176

C

California Public Employees' Retirement System,
        292
Capital asset pricing model (CAPM), 141n
Cash reserves, excessive, 67, 69-71
CDA Investment Technologies, 205
College Retirement Equities Fund, 289
Completeness fund approach, 19, 26n, 119n
Consultant's role in normal portfolios, 133-134

Continuation rate, 265
Corporate and public funds compared, 8, 279-296
    asset allocation, 280-283
    consequence for consultants, 290-291
    consequences for investment managers, 291-292
    increased percentage of public funds, 283-285
    politics of pensions, 287-290
    working conditions, 285-286
Criticisms of fund management, 4
Customized Performance Standards (CPS), 225

D

Defined benefit plans, economics of, 262
Defined benefits vs. defined contribution, 40
District of Columbia Retirement Board, 293
Diversification and skill, managers', 185-196
Drucker, Myra, 61

E

Ellis, Charles, 11
Employee Benefits Research Institute, 273
Employee Retirement Income Security Act
    (ERISA), 4, 107, 262, 265, 274, 288, 289
Ennis, Richard, 91
Equities, 48
Equity benchmarks, 6-7
Equity manager style matrix, 187, 189, 191
Equity manager risk and return, 187, 190, 191

F

FASB 87, 14, 37
    and ABO, 43-44
    accounting standards for pension and health
      care benefits, 261-275
    covariance with bond interest, 47
    pension plan surplus, 34, 38-42, 48
Financial Accounting Standards Board State-

ment 87. *See* FASB 87
Fixed-income benchmarks, 115-116
Fixed-income managers, 252
Fixed-income targets, 111-112
Fulfillment fund, 132
Fund structure. *See* Normal portfolios

G

George, James, 289

I

Inflation-sensitivity factor, 266
Information ratios, 7
In Search of Excellence, 93
Institute of Chartered Financial Analysts,
     89-90
Insurance strategies, 82-84
Internal investment management, 89-101
   challenges in the 1990s, 90-92
   value chain organizational structure, 92-99
International benchmark, 8
International investment manager, selection of,
     245-258
   defining manager's role, 246-248
International normals, 139-140
Investment management organizations, inter-
     national, 249-250
Investment manager structure, 18-19
Investment objectives, 16, 28
Investment performance, and manager selection,
     255-257
Investment policy, 7, 13-26
   components, 13-20, 27
   defined, 12-13
   IPS role, 24
   plan sponsor as risk controller, 21-22
   reviews, 22-23
   as stabilizer, 20-21, 26n
   statement (IPS), 23-24

Investment policy statement (IPS), 23-24
Investment risk vs. business risk, 174-176
Investment vehicles, international, 257

J

Japan, 8

L

Legislation, and pension fund management,
     3-4. *See also* FASB 87 *and* OBRA
Liabilities, analyzing the characteristics of,
     42-44
Liability discount rate, 267
Long-term policy. *See* Investment policy *and*
     Policy asset mix
Los Angeles County Employees' Retirement
     Association, 284
Low risk strategies, 7

M

Management. *See* Pension fund management
Manager benchmarks, 112-114
Manager performance fees, 7, 167-179
   benefits and disadvantages, 169, 171-174
   business risk vs. investment risk, 174-176
   current schemes and new incentives, 168-169, 170
   impact of, 178
   unequal benefits, 177-178
Manager risk and reward/skill, 188
Manager style matrix/diversification, 186, 187
Martin, James, 289
Maverick risk, 59, 62
Minnesota State Board of Investment, 27, 177
Misfit portfolio, 129
Misfit return, 162
Misfit risk, 147
Money manager selection, top-down approach, 201-215

asset allocation results, 205-207
asset-liability equation, 202-203
investment policy and strategy, 203-205
investment style and approaches, 207
manager review and selection, 207, 208-214
monitoring, 214-215
plan benchmark, 208
Multi-asset class portfolio, 140
Myers, Stephen R., 288

N

Net interest cost and pension plan "spread," 269-270
Normal portfolios, 90, 100n, 123-142
consultant's role, 133-134
definition and use of, 124-126, 134, 135-136
international normals, 139-140
issues, 134, 137-139
managers, 131-132
sponsor's point of view, 126, 127-131

O

Omnibus Budget Reconciliation Act (OBRA), 34, 39-40

P

Passive management, 149-155
PBO, 44-47
balancing in pension fund risk, 47-51
FASB 87, 262-264
Pension Benefit Guaranty Corporation (PBGC), 34, 39
Pension debt-servicing financial institution
paradigm, 270-272
Pension fund management
aggressiveness, 147
asset allocation policy link, 7, 183-196
business risk of vs. investment risk of sponsor,
174-176
diversification and skill, 184-196

fees, 7, 109, 130, 167-179
investment management performance, evaluating.
   See Normal portfolios
investment manager structure, 18-19
mission, 13-14
and normal portfolios, 131-132
passive, 149-155
performance, role in, 219-240
public and private funds compared, 8
relationship with sponsors, 7
requirements for successful, 5
risk control, 21, 34-38. *See also* ABO *and* PBO
selection of managers, 7, 201-215
structuring using fundamentals, 183-196
tracking error, 147
See also International investment manager,
   selection of
Pension fund risk, 7, 21-22, 33-53
Pension fund sponsors
   and benchmark portfolios, 105-120
   international manager selection, 245-258
   investment risk vs. business risk of manager,
      174-176
   normal portfolios, using, 123-142
   performance evaluation, 19-20
   relationship with managers, 7
   responsibilities of, 3-4
   as risk controller, 7, 21-22
   risk tolerance, 15-16, 27, 58-63
   role in fund performance, 8, 219-240
   view of risk, 145-163
   See also Investment policy
Pension fund surplus, 34, 48. *See also* FASB 87
Pension plan "spread," 269-270
Pensions vs. nonpensions benefits, 274
Performance evaluations, 19-20, 29-30, 131, 142n,
   219-240
Performance fees, 130, 167-179
   benefits and disadvantages of, 169, 171-174
   business risk vs. investment risk, 174-176
   current schemes and incentives, 168-169
   impact of, 178
   unequal benefits, 177-178

Performance measurement, sponsors and managers, 19, 219-240
  benchmarks, 220-221
  examples, 226-240
  measurements, 222-226
Policy asset mix, 16, 17-18, 28-29, 63-71
Policy reviews, 22-23
Porter, Michael E., 93
Portfolio risk, sponsor's view, 145-163
Portfolio volatility, 58-60, 62. *See also* Risk tolerance
Private and public pension funds compared, 279-296
  asset allocation, 280-283
  consequences for consultants, 290-291
  consequences for investment managers, 291-292
  increased percentage of public funds, 283-285
  politics of pensions, 287-290
  working conditions, 285-286
Projected Benefit Obligation (PBO), 44-47
  balancing in pension fund risk, 47-51
  FASB 87, 262-263
"Prudent man" rule, 287
Public and private funds compared, 8, 279-296
  asset allocation, 280-283
  consequences for consultants, 290-291
  consequences for investment managers, 291-292
  increased percentage of public funds, 283-285
  management of public funds, 292-294
  politics of pensions, 287-290
  working conditions, 285-286
Pyramid organizational model, 92-93

R

Real estate manager risk and reward/skill, 191, 195, 196
Real estate manager style matrix/diversification, 191, 194, 196
Rebalancing vs. drifting mix, 68, 70
Redefinition, 134
Retiree medical benefits, proposed accounting standards, 273

Risk, sponsor's view of, 145-163
Risk control, and benchmark portfolios, 112
Risk controller, 21-22
Risk premium and market performance, 74
Risk tolerance, 15-16, 27, 33-53
    and return prospects, asset allocation response,
        76
    rule for not exceeding, 58-63
Rockefeller Foundation, and performance fees, 176-177
Rosenberg Institutional Equity Management (RIEM), 98-99

S

Settlement rate, 265
Sharpe, William, 77, 82
"Slow rabbit," 138-139
Smith, Rodger, 285
South African business ties, 18, 257, 287, 288
Sponsors
    proposed role as long-term planners, 5
    responsibilities of, 3-4
    success of, 4, 5
    view of risk, 145-163
    See also Pension fund sponsors
State of Connecticut Trust Funds, 287
Statement of investment policy, 23-24
Successful pension fund management, requirements
        for, 5
Surplus, 34

T

Tactical asset allocation, 57, 71-82
Target portfolio, 126, 129, 146
Target return, 162
Ten-year returns of large pension plans, 65-67
Top-down approach to manager selection, 7, 201-215
Total return strategy. *See* Tactical asset allocation
Tracking error, manager's, 147, 149-150, 153, 155
Trust Universe Comparison Service, 214

U-V

United Kingdom, and inflation-indexed bonds, 266, 268
U.S. Government General Accounting Office, 273
Value chain organizational structure, 92-99
  benefits, 97-99
  components, 94, 96

W-X

Walker, David M., 290
Weighted asset list, 125. *See also* Normal portfolios
Weighted indices, 8, 18
Whitfield vs. *Cohen*, 289
Xerox pension fund, 61

About the Publisher

PROBUS PUBLISHING COMPANY

Probus Publishing Company fills the informational needs of today's business professional by publishing authoritative, quality books on timely and relevant topics, including:

- Investing
- Futures/Options Trading
- Banking
- Finance
- Marketing and Sales
- Manufacturing and Project Management
- Personal Finance, Real Estate, Insurance and Estate Planning
- Entrepreneurship
- Management

Probus books are available at quantity discounts when purchased for business, educational or sales promotional use. For more information, please call the Director, Corporate/Institutional Sales at 1-800-PROBUS-1, or write:

Director, Corporate/Institutional Sales
Probus Publishing Company
1925 N. Clybourn Avenue
Chicago, Illinois 60614
FAX (312) 868-6250